SPIRAL GUIDES

Travel With Someone You Trust®

PRAGUE

Contents

Written by Jack Altman
Where to... sections by Ky Krauthamer
Verified and updated by Heather Maher
American editor Tracy Larson

Edited, designed and produced by AA Publishing.
© Automobile Association Developments Limited 2002, 2007
Maps © Automobile Association Developments Limited 2002, 2007

Published in the United States by AAA Publishing
1000 AAA Drive, Heathrow, Florida 32746-5063
Published in the United Kingdom by AA Publishing.

ISBN-13: 978-1-59508-183-4
ISBN-10: 1-59508-183-6

Cover design and binding style by permission of AA Publishing
Colour separation by Leo Reprographics
Printed and bound in China by Leo Paper Products

10 9 8 7 6 5 4 3 2 1

A02693

the magazine

Magic and Mystery

Every great city has its myth – part truth, part imagination. Prague's myth, fed by tales of astrology and alchemy, is one of eternal magic and mystery – a city as Gothic and baroque as its bridges and buildings. Go at night to Charles Bridge, the most magical and mystical place in town, and you will see the statues of ecstatic martyred saints and bishops ready to fly up over the eery skyline of cold, spear-like Gothic spires and sensual baroque domes.

The myth makes Czech realists very angry and the tourism touts on Old Town Square very happy.

Emerging from his cyber-café, a realist puts away his cellular phone, just for a moment, to tell you this magical stuff was spawned by the ravings of that benighted 16th-century Habsburg emperor, Rudolf II, seeking to ease his real and imagined ailments with an elixir of eternal youth and to refill his mismanaged treasury by turning lead into gold. Maybe, say those who buy the myth (or sell it), but the magic is spawned in such fertile ground. The city seems its natural habitat.

Rudolf, Man of Wisdom and Woo-Woo

The fellow who launched the crazy gold rush was no idiot. Just weird. At 24, as Emperor and King of Bohemia, Rudolf came here in 1576 from the Habsburg court of Madrid, speaking and writing Spanish, German, Italian and Latin. He also endeared himself to the people by learning Czech.

Page 5: Malá Strana at the end of Charles Bridge

Below: Charles Bridge at sunset, when saints and ghosts get ready to fly

All That Glitters

As if to give alchemy a helping hand, people here stick the "golden" label on everything they can, starting with the town itself, long known as Zlatá Praha (Golden Prague). One of Prague's most venerable pubs is U Zlatého tygra (Golden Tiger). It vies with the Golden Pear, Golden Anchor, Star, Fox, Mouse and Serpent.

As an ardent patron of the arts, he accumulated in Prague one of Europe's finest collections of paintings. (Plundered during the Thirty Years' War, almost all ended up in Stockholm, Dresden, Munich and Vienna.) But he also collected strange stuff, meticulously inventoried, like two nails from Noah's Ark, a magic gold-framed gallstone, and a clump of the earth from which Adam was fashioned.

Philosophy and science were Rudolf's other passions. He discussed humanism with Italy's Giordano Bruno, the cosmos with Tycho Brahe from Denmark and Johannes Kepler from Germany. As court astronomers, Brahe completed a comprehensive study of the solar system and his disciple Kepler calculated the planets' elliptical orbits around the sun – both with astounding accuracy considering the telescope was not yet invented.

However, Rudolf also paid Brahe and Kepler to moonlight as alchemists and astrologers. They shared his belief in the fabled "Philosopher's Stone" that might bring gold and longevity – and in the influence of the stars on man's destiny. Also in town at the time was English mathematician John Dee, who dabbled in alchemy and performed magic tricks at Prague Castle. He fell in with fellow countryman Edward Kelley, a scoundrel who wasted no time on a day-job in "serious" science. Together, they fleeced Rudolf and his courtiers until Dee was called home to read the stars for Elizabeth I, and Kelley, whose run-ins with the law had already cost him two ears and a leg, took poison rather than go back to jail.

The Golem

Another essential figure in Prague's magic aura is the golem. It wasn't enough for some followers of Rabbi Loew

Left: Johannes Kepler plotted the orbit of the stars and did a little alchemy on the side

– a 16th-century contemporary of Rudolf's – that he was the great sage of the city's Jewish community. Despite his lifelong rejection of such esoteric nonsense, they had to endow him with the mystic powers of a pious Frankenstein who infused human life into a statue of clay that was known as the golem. The word appears in the Bible (Psalms 139, verse 16), meaning "unshaped flesh" (in modern Hebrew "raw material"). Jewish mystics applied it to a creature whose

Mathematician John Dee wowed Prague courtiers with his magic tricks

legend dates back at least to the 12th century, when ritual gestures and Hebrew letters were combined to perform the miracle of bringing the statue to life. Rabbi Loew, said his followers, knew the combination. Writer Franz Klutschak, and later Gustav Meyrink, neither of them Jewish, depicted the golem as Loew's assistant at the Old-New Synagogue (▶ 121–123) in tales as Gothic as the house of worship's architecture. Neglected while Loew tends to his sick daughter, the golem runs amok until the rabbi performs an appropriate ritual to calm him down. In 1915, Expressionist director Paul Wegener made a popular silent film entitled *The Golem*. Today, Prague has Golem boots and Golem jeans.

Going for Baroque
Many of the city's baroque monuments have been associated with mystic powers in the Catholics' 17th- and 18th-century campaign to revitalise the faith. In St Vitus Cathedral (▶ 89–91), the tomb of St John of Nepomuk was long proclaimed to contain the medieval martyr's still pulsating tongue (▶ 32). Pilgrims still flock to the Loreta sanctuary's replica of the Virgin Mary's home (▶ 103). In the Church of Panna Marie Vítězná (▶ 101), thousands seek to have prayers answered and illnesses healed by the Infant Jesus of Prague (Pražské Jezulátko), whose statue is venerated here.

Walking with the Ghosts
Beliefs past and present resonate down the centuries, their aura rising up from the cobbles. This is a town for the solitary walker – the Surrealist poets' *Pražský chodec* (Prague walker) and *noční chodec* (nocturnal walker), communing with the ghosts in the Old Jewish Cemetery (▶ 118–120) or the saints on Charles Bridge (▶ 52–55). Join them.

Left: In the Church of Our Lady of Victory, Mary watches over worshippers venerating the wax-covered statue of her infant Son

With the title role in a 1920s movie, the golem is prepared to do his thing

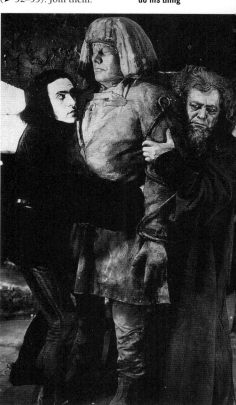

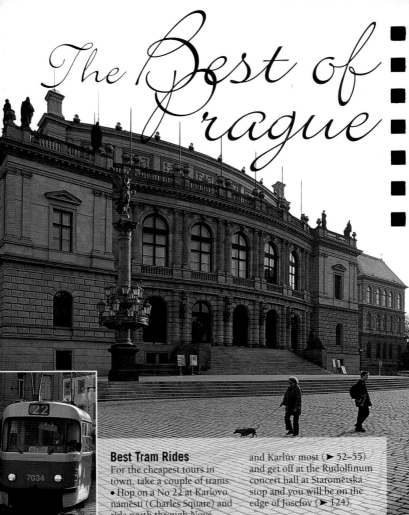

The Best of Prague

Best Tram Rides

For the cheapest tours in town, take a couple of trams.
• Hop on a No 22 at Karlovo náměstí (Charles Square) and ride north through Nové Město (New Town) to the Národní divadlo (National Theatre, ► 145–146). Cross the river to the foot of Petřín Hill (► 104), through Malá Strana and loop around Prague Castle's Královská zahrada (Royal Gardens, ► 93). Get off at Pohořelec for Strahov Monastery (► 97–98).
• For a close-up of the Vltava River and its bridges, pick up the No 17 at Palackého náměstí (Palacký Square) and ride north past Žofín Island and Karlův most (► 52–55) and get off at the Rudolfinum concert hall at Staroměstská stop and you will be on the edge of Josefov (► 124).

Best Boat Cruise

A relaxing way to see the city is from the river. Heated and air-conditioned cruises depart from the landing stage at the Čechův most (bridge), in front of the Hotel Intercontinental at the end of Pařížska street (EVD Passenger Shipping). One-hour cruise departs daily 11, 2, 3, 4; two-hour cruise with lunch and music daily 12–2; night cruise with dinner and music daily 7 pm; tel: 224 810 310, www.evd.cz.

Take the 22 from Charles Square to Prague Castle

Top: The Rudolfinum concert hall is reached by tram 17

Most Exciting Musical Experience

You can get in, for next to nothing, to a rehearsal of the Czech Philharmonic Orchestra at the Rudolfinum (➤ 124) and hear a resident or top guest conductor take one of the world's finest orchestras through its paces, usually culminating in a full performance of the main work. Tickets are available at the box office on náměstí Jana Palacha.

Most Enjoyable Places to Dance

In the entertainment complex built by President Václav Havel's grandfather in 1921, the Lucerna music bar has miraculously survived as the city centre's one major venue for live rock and jazz music. (Štepanská 61, tel: 224 217 108, Metro Můstek.)

Just steps from the Charles Bridge, on the Staré Město side of the river, Karlovy Kázně offers a variety of music from disco to drum and bass (tel: 222 220 502, www.karlovylazne.cz, tram 18, Metro Staroměstská).

Best Sports Event

The Czechs continue to produce Europe's top ice-hockey players, most ending up in North America's National Hockey League. In a beer-and-hot-dogs atmosphere, refreshingly hooligan-free, see HC Sparta Praha in Paegas Aréna, at Výstaviště exhibition grounds (Sat, Sep–Jun; tickets tel: 266 727 474, tram 5, 12, 17, Metro Nádraži Holešovice).

If You Only Have Time For One...

...**night at the opera**, visit the Stavovské (➤ 63).
...**baroque church**, make it St Nicholas Malá Strana (➤ 96).
...**synagogue**, make it the Staronová (➤ 121–123).

If You Go To Only Two...

...**pubs**, make them the U černého vola (Black Ox, ➤ 107) and the U Zlatého tygra (Golden Tiger, Husova 17, Staré Město).
...**gardens**, make them the Kolovratská in Malá Strana (➤ 84) and the *giardinetto* at the Belvedere (➤ 94).

Five Best Places For The Kids

• Petřín Hill Mirror Maze (➤ 104).
• Don Giovanni Marionette Opera, Palác Kinských, Staroměstské náměstí 12, Staré Město (tel: 224 216 365)
• Boat trip along the Vltava River from Na Františku Street (➤ 132).
• Hračky Jiří Trnka toy shop on Ostrovní 21 in Josefov (➤ 159).
• Prague Zoo, U Trojského zámku 3 (tel: 296 112 111).

Five Best Viewpoints

• Staré Město Bridge Tower (➤ 53).
• Metronome in Letna park (➤ 78).
• Strahov Monastery garden (➤ 97).
• Riverside café beside Smetana Museum (➤ 64).
• Top of Eiffel Tower on Petrin Hill (➤ 104).

Below: The first-floor gallery of the Staré Město Bridge Tower is an ideal viewpoint

Bottom: Looking down on the city from the heights of Letna park

Havel na Hrad ("Havel to the Castle") said the banners in November 1989. When he moved in to Prague's historic seat of power two months later, there was a radical changing of the guard, in every sense of the word – bright new uniforms and a new fanfare heralding a fresh new style of politics. After 50 heavy years of Communist rule, the Czechs had a leader with a sense of fun, a playful pixie of a man who was also a statesman of high moral purpose, who could be serious without necessarily being solemn.

Havel na Hrad

With Havel as their chosen leader, there was no turning back the crowds of 1989

Right: Václav Havel's supporters always associated him with jazz

Václav Havel had made an international name for himself in the 1960s as a playwright of absurdist satire. He won three "Obie" theatre awards in New York (for plays performed off-Broadway) – not even in Manhattan was he an establishment writer – but back home, the lucid denunciation of a morally bankrupt system propelled him into the presidency.

Silver Spoon

Despite a taste for T-shirts, blue jeans and beer at the pub, Havel was born in 1936 into one of Prague's wealthiest families, cultivated Czech patriots, staunchly anti-fascist, but anti-Communist too. Grandfather Václav built the Lucerna entertainment complex in 1921 – still going strong today (▶ 11).

Young Václav went for two years to an English-style boarding school at Poděbrady, but he was expelled in 1950,

Scooting Through the Corridors of Power
The trouble with living and working at Prague Castle is the corridors. They're too long. So, a decade before it became a worldwide craze, Václav Havel acquired a child's scooter to get around his presidential palace.

Havel to the Castle

principally because of his bourgeois background, just before the regime closed the school itself as "hostile to socialism", and he completed his secondary education at night school, with extra philosophy tuition from a professor friend of the family.

Absurd?

In the theatre, Havel started out as a stagehand, but after some collaborative efforts with the directors of the Balustrade Theatre (► 177), he established himself as resident playwright. If the absurdist plays of Ionesco

or Beckett shook the Balustrade audiences, Havel's work was an earthquake. The tragic farce of *The Garden Party*, *The Memorandum* and *The Increased Difficulty of Concentration* exposed the dehumanising effects of artificial bureaucratic nonsense in a totalitarian political system. With leaders so reluctantly abandoning their Stalinist ways, this was not absurd, it was everyday reality.

Dissidence and Jail

It wasn't only the "Prague Spring" that ended with Soviet tanks rolling through Wenceslas Square in August 1968 (► 143). Havel's international career as a playwright also ceased as he plunged into

"Living in Truth"

In 1978, Havel wrote what amounted to his political creed: *The Power of the Powerless*, a power which overcame ideology by simply "living in truth".

No regime, he said, could forever repress "the everyday, thankless and never-ending struggle of human beings to live more freely, truthfully and in quiet dignity".

a life of direct action against the regime. Writing now meant political and philosophical essays for the world's leading newspapers, and clandestine distribution at home. As one of 130 blacklisted writers, he was subjected to a dissident's classical routine of harassment, interrogation, beatings and jail. In January 1977 he was jailed for four months for the Charter 77 petition (243 signatories) that dared to accuse Czechoslovakia of breaching the Helsinki Human Rights agreements. More "subversive" writing and activism brought more jail sentences, the longest from 1979 to 1983.

Velvet Revolution

In 1989 he spent four more months in jail, after laying a wreath for victims of the Soviet invasion. By the end of the year, Havel was president. Though he had never shrunk from assuming leadership of the opposition, it wasn't planned. On Friday, 17 November, he was out in the countryside when 50,000 demonstrators gathered in Wenceslas Square. The Communist leadership collapsed, just as the Berlin Wall had fallen eight days before. Through the respect he had won for his unwavering courage and integrity, Havel had established himself in the popular mind as the country's natural leader, and parliament elected him as president on 29 December. One of his first acts was to go and tell the Communist-appointed "undercover" police that were left stationed outside his old apartment that they could go home now.

Above: Václav Havel, often serious, but still a man of the people

Below: Café Slavia, where Havel went to change the world

Havel's Hangouts

- **Zahradní dům**: the summer villa in the Royal Gardens (► 94)
- **Café Slavia**: where he met his first wife Olga (► 74)
- **Apartment House "2000"**, Rašínovo nábřeží 78: where he lived with Olga
- **Melantrich Building**: venue for the historic 1989 Dubček meeting, Václavské náměstí 36 (► 142)
- **Reduta**: the jazz club where he jammed with Bill Clinton (► 160)

THE JEWISH COMMUNITY

Prague and its Jews have always had a stormy relationship. It has been a story of pain, but also of joy. It has produced many brilliant personalities – scholars, imperial financiers, writers, musicians and industrialists – as well as unsung generations living in the ebb and flow of prosperity and persecution.

In a celebrated sermon in 1573, the great Rabbi Yehuda Loew ben Bezalel had a decidedly positive spin to offer on the recurring sequence of Prague's Jews being expelled and readmitted. He compared it to quarrels between fickle lovers who separate and reunite as the spirit moves them. Though it might be more realistic to speak of a marriage of convenience rather than love, the result has not been a bad one.

What is true is that, however Czech the Czechs now want Prague to be, the Jews are an inseparable part of the city's fabric – in the same way, Prague-born historian Peter Demetz says, as are the Germans and Italians.

Rabbi Loew, a pious sage respected by kings and paupers alike

In the Beginning

The first Jews here followed the first Bohemian dukes. Jewish merchants built their shops and houses in Malá Strana at the foot of Hradčany (Prague Castle, ► 82–85).

In a diary of 965, a traveller from Spain reports them selling tin, furs and slaves. They accompanied Vratislav II across the river when he moved to a new castle at Vyšehrad (► 149–151) and crossed back again when the court returned to Hradčany. In between times, they traded wheat, wool, cattle and horses for silks, jewels, gold, wine and Oriental spices. Business was good, life was good.

Trouble

The First Crusade (1095) put a stop to the good times. The contagion of the Christian knights' anti-Jewish pogroms spread to Prague. To escape the plunder, fire, forced baptism and killing, the Jews tried to leave town and the duke confiscated their property. In the 13th century, they moved to the area on the right bank that is now called Josefov. According to the needs of the royal treasury, monarchs alternately protected and plundered Jewish property and in the worst of the medieval pogroms, in 1389, mobs urged on by fanatical priests massacred over 3,000 Jewish men, women and children. In the next century, Hussite reformist street-battles against the Catholic establishment (► 18) habitually ended with

The Golden Age

After decades of humiliation – wearing a yellow patch to identify them as Jewish, aggressions and mass expulsions for all but the wealthiest – the last half of the 16th century ushered in an era of shining achievement for the Jewish population in Prague.

Following in the footsteps of his father, Maximilian II, Emperor Rudolf II forged close ties with the Jewish community. Practically all his cherished goldsmiths were Jewish, and two men stood out: Mordechai Maisel, financier to the emperor and mayor of the Jews, who personally paid to pave streets and build housing, a hospital, schools, synagogues and the Jewish Town Hall (► 126); and Rabbi Yehuda Loew, the community's outstanding spiritual leader, a scholar of unbending integrity who scorned the occultist mysticism and magic which later mythmakers associated with his name (► 8–9).

The Jewish Town Hall still stands as a monument to the community's heyday

Right: The Habsburg's humanist Emperor Joseph II was honoured for emancipating the Jews of his empire

a raid on the Jewish Quarter. The Hussites' fights for religious freedom had not overcome the centuries-old anti-Semitism of the people.

Czech, German or Jewish?

Emperor Joseph II's law of 1782 emancipating the Jews of his Habsburg Empire sowed the seeds of future conflict in Prague. For the sake of efficiency rather than ethnic or cultural reasons, it made German and not Czech the language of Jewish administrative and business life. Liberated from their ghetto (renamed Josefov in 1850 to honour the emancipator), Prague Jews identified with the prosperous, cultivated German community, going to German-language schools, university and theatre. After 1918, the ambiguity of Jewish status in Czechoslovakia became apparent in successive censuses which classed the Jews first as Germans and then as Czechs. But to the German SS troops occupying Prague in 1939 they were just Jews, 45,000 of them to be deported to the concentration camps.

Today, the remnants of the community, around 1,500 who identify themselves as Jewish, sustain a memory going back ten centuries.

Below: For 45,000 Prague Jews, a thousand years of history ended in the concentration camps

Defenestration

Prague's Lethal Windows of Opportunity

Being thrown or jumping out of a window has for centuries been a peculiarly Prague way of dying. Defenestration has launched riots and pogroms and it even sparked the Thirty Years' War.

Pikes and Lances

The prototype began on a Sunday morning in July 1419, following a sermon by fiery preacher Jan Želivský. Feeling was still running high four years after Reformist leader Jan Hus was burned at the stake as a heretic by a Church Council in Germany. Catholic priests had expropriated Hussite churches and "purified" them by scrubbing down altars "profaned" by disputed communion practices. Protesters were jailed and Želivský led his congregation to Nové Město's town hall to demand their release. Breaking into the council chamber, the Hussites seized the intractable mayor and a dozen aldermen and hurled them out of the window. Those not impaled on the crowd's pikes and lances were clubbed to death. The rebels then ransacked Catholic churches and rampaged through the Jewish Quarter, a common target for mob rage.

Plague and Plunder

The second defenestration took place in September 1483. In plague-ridden Prague, religious unrest was growing with rumours of a Catholic plot to execute Hussite leaders. Once again, Hussites marched into the New Town Hall and threw mayor and aldermen out of the window.

Onto the Dunghill

Defenestration earned its capital "D" on 23 May, 1618, a day of farce that ended in horror. Facing King Ferdinand's refusal to halt Catholic discrimination, radical Protestant preacher Václav Budova and Count Matthias

The Hussites

Inspired by the Reformist writings of English theologian John Wycliffe, Jan Hus (c1372–1415) and his Hussite followers fought the corruption and immorality prevalent among the establishment clergy. A major tenet of the Hussite creed was to give communion wine – as well as bread – to all believers, not just the clergy. Their leader's excommunication and execution made Hussitism the backbone of the Czech nationalist fight against the Catholic establishment of the Habsburg Empire.

Thurn, a hot-blooded soldier, plotted to kill the king's two governors in Prague Castle. They led a group of Protestant parliamentarians to the castle's Bohemian Chancellery (➤ 84) to confront Vilém Slavata and Jaroslav Martinic. Cutting short all efforts to talk, Thurn and his men grabbed the two governors – along with an unlucky secretary, Johannes Fabricius, who was in the wrong place at the wrong time – and threw them, in now time-honoured fashion, out of the window. For a change, the victims had a safe landing – on a dunghill, said Protestants; on the Virgin Mary's cloak, said Catholics. Less amusing were the raids on the Jewish Quarter and monasteries in which Franciscan monks were killed. Worse still, the violence escalated into a generalised Bohemian revolt and the Thirty Years' War (1618–48).

Top: The Defenestration of 1618 that lanched the Thirty Years' War

Above: The famous window in Prague Castle's Bohemian Chancellery

Pushed or Jumped?

More recently, three weeks after the Communists' coup d'état of February 1948, the foreign minister Jan Masaryk, the government's token bourgeois, fell from a window in Černínský palác (➤ 180). Did he jump or was he pushed? Was this popular son of President Tomáš Masaryk suicidally depressed by his country's plight or was he murdered as an obstacle to Communist power?

Opposite: An obelisk marks the spot where the king's governors landed

Left: Jan Masaryk already looks worried, a year before he fell out of the window

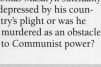

Where
Lou Reed
meets...

From the world première of Mozart's greatest opera to a president who was friends with rock stars like Frank Zappa and the Rolling Stones, Prague has always loved music. Everywhere you go there are fliers for classical concerts, chamber music, free-jazz or Dixieland jam sessions, rock and techno.

Figaro Here, Don Giovanni There

Not until the Czechs' nationalist movement got into top gear in the 19th century did their own great classical composers, Bedřich Smetana and Antonín Dvořák, make their mark on the European scene. Before them, Wolfgang Amadeus Mozart could have told them what terrific taste Prague had in things musical. In 1786, Vienna had given his *Marriage of Figaro* première at best a lukewarm reception. It closed after just nine performances. The Prague production later the same year got rave reviews. Wolfgang was brought to town for four weeks in January 1787 and found, as he wrote in a letter: "The talk here is about nothing but Figaro. Nothing is played, sung or whistled but Figaro." At a ball he attended, he observed with delight that the music had been pirated for quadrilles and waltzes. He conducted the opera himself and presented a new orchestral work, now known as the *Prague Symphony*.

Rock star Lou Reed's friendship with Václav Havel began when he interviewed the future Czech president for *Rolling Stone* magazine

Before he left, Mozart was commissioned to write the most ambitious of all his operas, *Don Giovanni*. He came back nine months later to complete it, invited by pianist František Dušek to work at his Villa Bertramka – now a Mozart shrine and museum (► 99). Typically, he completed the overture one day before its world première. On Monday 29 October, 1787, at what is now the Stavovské divadlo (Estates Theatre, ► 63), Wolfgang of course arrived late to take his seat at the clavier and conduct the orchestra. Reception by public and press was rapturous. Again, the Viennese reaction was much cooler, but, as Mozart told his friends: "*Meine Prager verstehen mich*" ("My Prague people understand me").

Four years later, just three days after his death and burial in an anonymous pauper's grave in Vienna, hundreds of his admirers in Prague attended a memorial service at the Church of St Nicholas Malá Strana, where he had himself played the organ (► 96). It seems appropriate that Miloš Forman shot his Oscar-winning film *Amadeus* not in Vienna but in the streets of Prague.

Bedřich Smetana and Antonín Dvořák

Music has always played a patriotic role in Czech life. Prague's two main opera houses make the point. *Národ sobě* (The Nation to Itself) is written in gold over the proscenium arch of the Národní divadlo (National Theatre, ► 145–146) while the façade of the Stavovské divadlo (Estates Theatre, ► 63) proclaims *Patriae et Musis* ("To Fatherland and the Muses").

Not that composer Bedřich Smetana (1824–84) needed any prompting. His most overtly patriotic opera *Libuše*,

Mozart played on this church organ in St Nicholas Malá Strana

The Stavovské divadlo (Estates Theatre) where *Don Giovanni* had its world première

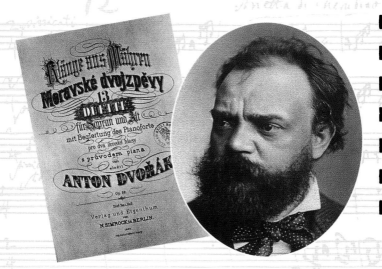

solemnly portraying the nation's legendary foundation by a mythic princess, premiered at the opening of the new Narodní divadlo (National Theatre) in 1881.

His best-known works, the romantic opera *Prodaná nevěsta* (*The Bartered Bride*) and symphonic poem *Má vlast* (*My Country*), are joyous paeans to the Czech landscape and country life.

Every year, *Má vlast* opens the city's international music and theatre festival, Prague Spring. Such was the national appeal of *The Bartered Bride* that it was staged by Prague's Jewish inmates at the Theresienstadt "showcase" concentration camp (► 170).

The gloriously melodic Antonín Dvořák (1841–1904) was the first Czech composer to gain an international reputation. Though less explicitly nationalist than Smetana's work, his music never lost its unmistakably fresh Czech quality.

Some people feel that his famous *New World Symphony*, which he wrote in 1893 while directing the Conservatory of Music in New York, may show gospel and other American influences, but Prague music-lovers point to its equally strong Bohemian folk themes.

Right: On Charles Bridge, John of Nepomuk enjoys a chorus of *When the Saints Come Marchin' In*

These are even more apparent in Dvořák's *Slavonic Dances* and his opera *Rusalka*.

Walking on the Wild Side

Not the least of President Václav Havel's early appeal to his free-spirited supporters was his taste for jazz and rock. In the leaden years of Communist rule, this music was part of the dissidents' culture. They liked in particular

Frank Zappa's often sophisticated blend of rock, rhythm and blues, and Stravinsky. In 1968, when the Prague Spring revolt was crushed by Soviet tanks, they heard his 1967 album, entitled *Absolutely Free*. And 23 years later, Zappa played at a concert in Prague Castle, celebrating the departure of Soviet forces. Other guests at the castle were Lou Reed and Mick Jagger, brought there by one of Václav Havel's top advisers, the Czech rock star Michael Kocáb.

By 1994, it seemed perfectly natural for Havel to offer fellow president Bill Clinton a saxophone as a state gift. They then went off to the Reduta Jazz Club on Národní Street (► 160), where Bill blew a few riffs of *My Funny Valentine* and Václav tried his hand at a bit of percussion.

The Masters' Museums
• **Wolfgang Amadeus Mozart** – Villa Bertramka, Mozartova 169, Smíchov, tel: 257 317 465; daily 9–6, Apr–Oct; 9:30–4, Nov–Mar
• **Bedřich Smetana** – Muzeum Bedřicha Smetany, Novotného lávka, Staré Město, tel: 222 220 082; Wed–Mon 10–5
• **Antonín Dvořák** – Vila Amerika, Ke Karlovu 20, Nové Město, tel: 224 918 013; Tue–Sun 10–5

The Best Beer in the World

The rich flavour and deep amber colour of Czech beer are, Czechs insist, unique, despite the many attempts to copy them.

The Top and Bottom of Czech Beer

For at least 1,000 years, Czech monks, nuns and ordinary folk have been fermenting malt, water and hops to produce their "liquid bread". Each brewery swears by the quality of its spring waters to complete the concoction. "Bottom-fermented" beer – with the brewer's yeast at the bottom of the liquid – produces a brew faster but also lighter (10°) than the strong "top-fermented" varieties (12°) preferred by traditionalists.

The Not So Velvet Revolution

Purists insist that one of the few things that was better under the Communists was beer, as it was still brewed in the old-fashioned way. Privatisation of the breweries (many are now owned by South African, British and German companies) improved efficiency but also produced a more homogenised, weaker and less velvety taste. It is still better than other beers, they say, but for the old full-bodied taste,

Drink the cool brew before its head disappears

you have to hunt down pubs that serve beer from smaller independent breweries.

Where and What to Drink

Here is a shortlist of beers and bars with an authentic atmosphere. The beer is served by the half-litre – if you want less, ask for *malé pivo* (0.3 litre).

• **Plzeň** (Pilsen) was a town, 80km (50 miles) southwest of Prague, long before it became known, like champagne, as a way of making one of the great beers. Its **Pilsner Urquell** (Plzeňský Prazdroj to the Czechs) was the first bottom-fermented beer. Sip it at the **Hostinec Na Kampě** (► 107).

• **Budvar**, perennially embroiled in lawsuits with American Budweiser for use of the German version of the name, is a mild brew from the town of České Budě-jovice. Try it in the old bar of Staré Město's medieval **U Medvídků** (► 73).

• **Velkopopovický kozel**, drunk in draughts as long as its name, is a popular light and tangy bitter served at the Hradčany **U Černého vola** (► 107).

• **Staropramen**, mild and hoppy, is a Prague-brewed beer served at the Malá Strana student pub **U Černého orla** (► 107).

• **U Fleků**, tourist trap that it is, is worth a try for its own dark, strong (13°) **Flek**, with its 500-year-old tradition.

• **Kacov** is one for the connoisseur, independently brewed, bitter and unfiltered, and served in Žižkov at **U Bergnerů**, Slezská 134.

Below: The Plžen breweries have made Czech beer world famous

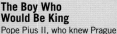

The Boy Who Would Be King

Pope Pius II, who knew Prague and Bohemia well, warned in 1453 that Hungarian-born King Ladislas, newly crowned at the age of 17, would never be accepted by the people "until he masters the Czech language and beer-drinking". He failed in both tasks and died four years later.

HITLER AND STALIN IN PRAGUE

Life could never be easy sitting in a corridor between Germany and the Soviet Union. The people of Prague got it coming and going – Hitler's troops in 1939 and Stalin's underlings in 1948.

Cold Supper in the Castle

The German occupation was swift. In the early evening of 15 March, 1939, less than six months after Britain's Neville Chamberlain had returned from Munich promising "Peace for our time...peace with honour", Adolf Hitler drove up to Prague Castle in his black Mercedes. Apart from the first units of German troops stationed on Old Town Square and a few German students cheering on Na příkopé Avenue, the streets were empty. There were no happy crowds to greet the Führer like those in Vienna exactly a year earlier, but no armed resistance, either – President Emil Hácha had ordered Czech troops to stay in their barracks. The castle gates were locked and there was no supper on hand for the visitors. Hitler had to send out for bread, ham and beer. Dismissing the Pilsner as too bitter, he settled for water while working on a final draft creating the Reich Protectorate of Bohemia and Moravia (Slovakia had just become an "independent" state). The next day, he read out the proclamation from a third-floor window, declaring:

"With this, Czechoslovakia has ceased to exist", and went back to Berlin.

The Price of Resistance

As so often in Prague's history, students made the first open attempts at resistance to German occupation. Demonstrations in October and November 1939 ended in nine executions, the deportation of 1,200 students to concentration camps and the closing of all institutions of higher education for the remainder of the war.

In 1941, Reinhard Heydrich, brilliant, icy, calculating "brain" of the German SS and vicious exponent of the carrot-and-stick, took over as Reichsprotektor. In quick succession, he ordered executions among the city's intelligentsia and sent thousands of Jews to the concentration camp north of Prague at Terezín (Theresienstadt, ➤ 170). At the same time, he raised factory workers' pay and food rations, offered them weekends at luxury hotels, and even invited some to dine with him in Prague Castle.

To stop Heydrich sapping the people's will to resist, Czechoslovak exiles had him assassinated by agents they had parachuted in from London. He was killed while driving from a northern suburb to his castle office in May 1942. Reprisals were terrible: thousands were executed in and around Prague, the villages of Lidice and Ležáky were wiped out, and mass deportations took place from Theresienstadt to Auschwitz.

The Perfect Stalinist

Unlike Hitler, Joseph Stalin never set foot in Prague. He didn't have to – he had Klement Gottwald. The post-war Czech Communist Party chief, prime minister and president until his death in 1953 was the perfect Stalinist. He learned the trade in Moscow, where he had gone in 1938 after the Munich Agreement. Stalin sent him back to Prague in 1945 to rebuild the Communist Party

Left: German troops march through the gates of Prague Castle

Bottom: Typical wooden beds in a dormitory at Theresienstadt concentration camp

Below: A menorah commemorates Jews who died at Theresienstadt and those who were deported to extermination camps

into a powerful electoral machine. Ignoring the Soviet–German pact of 1939, Gottwald had no trouble selling Stalin, the opponent of the Munich sell-out, as the country's liberator in 1945. Nationalising private property was popular then, as was Communist support for the expulsion of German-speaking Czechs – in total 2.5 million.

In the 1946 elections, the Party won 40 per cent in the Czech lands and 30 per cent in Slovakia, enough to make Gottwald prime minister in a coalition government. Gottwald felt strong enough to pledge himself to parliamentary democracy and even accept Marshall Plan aid from the US – until Stalin called him to Moscow and changed his mind. In February 1948, he out-manoeuvred his

Show Time

Never did the Czechs' natural talent for the theatre appear in more bizarre form than in the trial of Rudolf Slánský in November 1952. Like Stalin's Moscow in the 1930s, the Soviet Bloc capitals held show trials. These were staged not to condemn real criminals but to rid the Communist dictators of their most dangerous rivals on trumped-up charges of subversive activity identified with Stalin's designated enemies – Leon Trotsky and Yugoslavia's Josip Tito. Slánský had been Gottwald's highly capable No 2. Now he, along with 13 co-defendants, stood accused in the city's Pankrác prison of leading an "Anti-State Conspiratorial Centre". The trial lasted a week. Like any good show, it had a script, preprinted with copies for all participants, complete with the judges' questions and defendants' answers. A dress rehearsal had been filmed and taped for Gottwald's approval. The defendants were charged with being "Fascist-Trotskyist-Titoist-Zionists" – Gottwald shared Stalin's obsessional anti-Semitism and 11 of the accused, including Slánský, were Jewish. They duly recited their scripted "confessions", including assent to the anti-Semitic slurs. Ironically Slánský and his co-defendants had helped create the system which would now hang them.

Social Democratic rivals in parliament and forced President Edvard Beneš to accept a new government. They were all Communists except for Jan Masaryk, who three weeks later fell to his death from a window (► 19).

Such was the climate of conspiracy and paranoia around Gottwald that when he died on 14 March, 1953, few believed the official cause of pneumonia from a chill caught five days earlier at Stalin's funeral.

Klement Gottwald was Czechoslovakia's dictator and Stalin's puppet

For many people coming to Prague, Franz Kafka – along with Václav Havel, Dvořák and Good King Wenceslas – is one of Prague's most famous citizens. Many Czechs feel Kafka's status is unfair because of the gloomy image of Prague he evokes in his novels. "Kafkaesque", after all, is applied to anything with a darkly complex, bizarre and illogical quality.

The Kafka Kult
from Taboo to T-Shirts

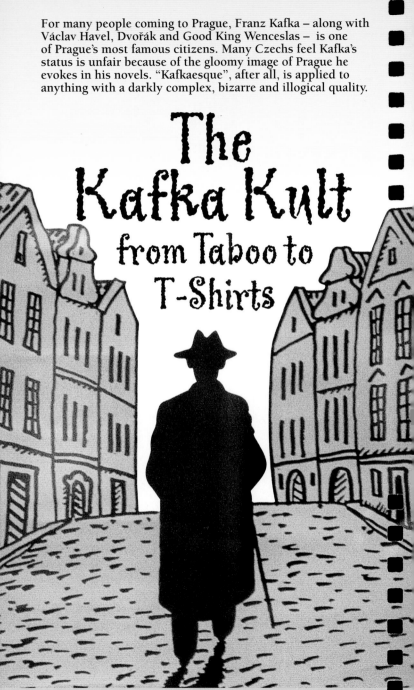

Many Czechs have not had a chance to read Kafka. He wrote in German and few of his works were translated into Czech or were available in bookshops until quite recently. He was a non-person in the Stalinist era and, after a brief flowering of interest in the Prague Spring of the 1960s, he was rejected again in the bleak "normalisation" years from 1968 to the Velvet Revolution of 1989.

The Kafka Industry

What would Franz do today if he were to return to Prague and see the souvenir vendors on Charles Bridge selling his effigy on T-shirts, coffee mugs, trays, calendars and postcards? He would most certainly laugh – contrary to the received view, he is reputed to have had a great sense of humour.

He might be touched to see his name on a square, náměstí

Franze Kafký, on the site of his birthplace (the house has gone) at the edge of Josefov (► 127). He might head for the café in the Hotel Evropa (► 142), where he held a public reading of his superb story *The Judgment* in 1912. And if he did go into the Kafka bookshop, it would probably be to find out how many of these T-shirted people were actually reading his books.

Kafka Facts
• Franz Kafka was born in 1883, when Prague was still at the heart of the Austro-Hungarian Empire.
• He cared little about politics, writing in his diary on 2 August, 1914: "Germany has declared war on Russia. Swimming in the afternoon."
• He died in 1924, the year Adolf Hitler wrote *Mein Kampf* and Stalin emerged to succeed Lenin.

Above: A bronze bust of Kafka mounted during the brief thaw of the 1968 "Prague Spring"

Below left: One of the city's shops bearing Kafka's name

Opposite: One of many Kafka images

What to Read
• *The Castle* is about the quest of the hero, K, to get to the Castle to take up his job as a land surveyor. For lovers of Kafka, there is something satisfying rather than frustrating in the fact that the book remains unfinished – the last chapter even stops in the middle of a sentence. The novel is about a quest, not an achievement, and it would have been banal, profoundly un-Kafkaesque, for K actually to get into the Castle.
• *The Trial* begins: "Someone must have made a false accusation against Josef K. because, without his having done anything wrong, he was arrested one morning." Thus starts one of the most harrowing nightmares in world literature.
• Kafka's short stories are for many people the finest things he wrote. *The Metamorphosis* is the most famous, about a man who wakes up one morning to discover he has turned into an insect. *The Judgment* tells of a son pressured by his father into committing suicide. *In a Penal Colony* describes with meticulous care a machine that executes each condemned man by writing his crime on his body.

Did You Know?

- **Dishonest merchants** used to be lowered over the side of Charles Bridge (▶ 52–55) in wicker baskets for a chastening dip in the Vltava River. There have since been proposals to revive the tradition for some of the bridge's fly-by-night jewellers offering gifts at very suspect prices.

- The skeleton of martyred Czech priest **John of Nepomuk** (▶ 9) was exhumed in 1719. Over 300 years after John had been tortured to death by Wenceslas IV, the royal surgeon extracted from the skull what he said was a tongue – still alive and pulsating. On the basis of this miracle, John was beatified. In 1961, the Vatican declared this not to have been the saint's tongue but a piece of rotten brain.

- More **beer** is drunk in the Czech Republic than anywhere else in the world – per capita, 160 litres (35 gallons) a year – and less than half of one per cent is imported.

- In the **summer of 1989** thousands of East Germans "on holiday" climbed into the Lobkovický palác (German Embassy) garden (▶ 102) and camped there while seeking West German citizenship. They left their rickety East German Trabant cars in surrounding streets, and the Czechoslovak government was obliged to lay on trains to take them into West Germany.

The growing flood of refugees led a few months later to the fall of the Berlin Wall. Today in the embassy garden stands David Černy's interesting modern sculpture, *Quo Vadis?*, a gold-painted Trabant raised on legs.

- **Good King Wenceslas** was actually only a duke. At the age of 22 he was murdered by his pagan brother Boleslav, who objected to his excessive zeal in spreading the Christian gospel. Whether he helped peasants gathering winter fuel has not been recorded.

- The **Velvet Revolution** (▶ 14) that put Václav Havel in power was named after his pal Lou Reed's rock group, The Velvet Underground.

Wenceslas was perhaps good, but he wasn't really a king

Finding Your Feet

First Two Hours

Arriving by Air

- Completely rebuilt since the 1990s, **Ruzyně Airport** (tel: 220 113 314) has all the amenities of any modern European airport – ATM cash dispensers, exchange facilities, car-rental and hotel-booking agencies.

Getting into Town

The airport is nearly 20km (12 miles) northwest of the city centre, and whether you choose taxi, express minibus or a combination of bus and underground train, expect between 30 and 50 minutes to get to your hotel.

- **Taxis** Reputable companies with English-speaking operators include AAA (tel: 140 14) and Profi Taxi (tel: 844 700 800). Beware the silver Mercedes taxis at the curbs, they have a reputation for overcharging. A ride into the centre should cost around 500Kč (€17). Insist that the driver run the meter, ask for a receipt at the start.
- **Čedaz** white mini-buses are parked outside the arrivals hall and operate 6 am–9 pm. Tickets from the Čedaz information desk in the arrivals hall cost 90 Kč. The bus will take a party of up to four directly to their hotel in Prague for a fixed price of 480Kč. Parties of 5–8 people cost 960Kč.
- **City buses and metro** As you exit the arrivals hall, walk straight across the parking lot to the second bus shelter (the first is for arrivals). Buy a 20Kč ticket (coins required) from the yellow ticket machine, board the 119 bus punch your ticket and keep it. The bus ends at Dejvická Metro station, transfer to the C-line (green) on the same ticket for the city centre.

Arriving by Train

- **Hlavní nádraží**, Wilsonova Boulevard, is Prague's main railway station for the overnight train from London – via Brussels and Cologne (information: tel: 221 111 122; www.cdrail.cz). International trains also arrive at **Nádraží Holešovice** – but watch out for unscrupulous taxi drivers.
- It has restaurants, food kiosks, ATM cash-dispensers, exchange facilities, a tourist information office and hotel-booking agency, plus a 24-hour left-luggage office. It is only a few minutes' walk from **Václavské náměstí** (Wenceslas Square). Its underground Metro station is on the C-line.

Arriving by Bus

- **Florenc**, Křižikova Boulevard, is the main bus station for international buses, on the east side of town.
- It has few amenities apart from a 24-hour left-luggage office, but the adjacent **Florenc B- and C-line Metro station** takes you quickly into the city centre.

Tourist Information Offices

- The **PIS** (Pražska informační služba – Prague Information Office, www.pis.cz) has information on attractions, opening times, a ticket agency and English-speaking personal guides, as well as free maps of the city centre and public transport routes. Listed below are the main offices:
- **Staroměstské radnice (Old Town Hall)**, Staroměstské náměstí 1, tel: 420 12 444; open Mon–Fri 9–6 or 7, Sat–Sun 9–5 or 6
- **Hlavní nádraži (Main Railway Station)**, Wilsonova, Entrance Hall, tel: 420 12 444; open Mon–Fri 9–7, Sat–Sun 9–4
- **Pražský hrad (Prague Castle)**, Information Centre, 3rd Courtyard, tel: 420 12 444; www.hrad.cz; open daily 9–5

Orienting Yourself

The Vltava River divides the city into two distinct areas. On the right bank, **Staroměstské náměstí** (Old Town Square) is the hub. On the left bank, commonly known as Mala Strana (literally "Little Side"), **Malostranské náměstí** (Mala Strana Square) is the centre of the action, leading up to Pražský hrad (Prague Castle).

The Major Neighbourhoods

■ **Staré Město** (Old Town) is the right bank's historic quarter, taking in the river bend immediately east of Karlův most (Charles Bridge). It is bounded by Národní Street, Na příkopě, náměstí Republiky and Revolucní.

■ **Josefov**, once the separate Jewish neighbourhood, is now the Old Town's northern section, running from Staroměstské náměstí (Old Town Square) to the Vltava River.

■ **Hradčany** is the left bank hilltop area immediately around Pražský hrad (Prague Castle).

■ **Malá Strana** runs along the left bank, below Prague Castle, taking in Kampe Island at the foot of Charles Bridge and surrounding the parkland and gardens of Petřín Hill.

■ **Nové Město** (New Town) lies on the right bank, east of Revolucni to Wilsonova, and south of Národní Street to Vnislavova.

■ **Vyšehrad** is the castle district south of Vnislavova.

■ **Vinohrády**, **Karlín** and **Žižkov** are residential neighbourhoods east of Wilsonova.

■ **Smíchov** is a working-class neighbourhood south of Malá Strana's Holečkova Street.

■ **Letná** and **Holešovice** are left-bank commercial and residential neighbourhoods east of Hradčany.

Getting Around

The best way to visit the sights in each of Prague's historic centres is on foot. For trips between and around neighbourhoods, use the excellent tram system, and the underground Metro, which is inexpensive, fast and reliable. There is an English-langugage website, www.dp-praha.cz, for detailed information on Dopravní podnik (Public Transport Company). Take taxis only when you really need door-to-door service.

Metro

The fast and clean, Russian-built system of three colour-coded underground lines cover the city's main areas, intersecting at stations in the centre (Museum, Můstek and Florenc – see map on inside back cover).

■ **Train times** are 5 am–midnight, with a train every two or three minutes during rush hour and four to ten minutes off-peak. The platform's digital clock tells how many minutes have passed since the last train.

■ The **A-line**, coded green, links the city centre and Malá Strana. Key stations are Muzeum, Václavské náměstí (Wenceslas Square), Staroměstská and Malostranská.

■ The **B-line**, coded yellow, runs between the northeast and southwest suburbs via Florenc, náměstí Republiky, Můstek and Národní třida.

- The **C-line**, coded red, runs from Holešovice through the city centre via Florenc, Muzeum and south to Vyšehrad Castle.
- **Useful signs** to look out for include *výstup* (exit) and *přestup* (transfer).

Trams

The network of electric trams, which is being progressively modernised, is the most enjoyable way of zipping around town, with the added bonus of being able to sightsee on the way.

- Tram **times** are 4:30 am–midnight, with trams running every six to eight minutes during peak hours, and every six to 15 minutes outside these hours. **Timetables** at tram stops show the departure time from that stop.
- There is a **night service** running midnight–4:30 am. Eight trams, numbered 51 to 58, cover the left- and right-bank neighbourhoods, and run about every 30 minutes. All pass through Lazarská in Prague's city centre.
- The best **sightseeing** trams are Nos 22 and 23, from Vinohrady through Nové Město across the river to Malá Strana and the Hradčany district.
- There is also a **nostalgia ride** in the old-fashioned No 91 tram running from Náměstí Republiky via major right- and left-bank sights to Výstaviste, 40 minutes each way, at a special rate of 20Kč for the return trip.

Buses

- Essentially a service for outlying **suburbs**, few buses come into the city centre. The one time you are likely to need a city bus is if you choose public transport coming in from the airport.
- **Times** are about 4:30 am–midnight, with **night buses** (Nos 501–512) running hourly from midnight to 5 am.

Tickets

- Tickets must be bought **before** boarding a tram, train or bus.
- You can **buy** tickets at Metro stations, travel agencies, news-stands (*traffika*), *tabac*, department stores and many hotels.
- **Single tickets** can be bought from automatic machines, but they offer a variety of types of ticket (all of which are explained on the machine) and may require a moment's study before you put your money in.
- On **trams** and **Metro**, punch the ticket to validate it, in electronic machines at the entrance to the Metro platforms or inside the tram.
- A **transfer ticket** (around 20Kč per adult, 10Kč per child) is valid on unlimited tram and Metro changes for 70 minutes from the time of punching.
- A **discounted ticket** (around 14Kč per adult, 7Kč per child) is valid for 20 minutes on the Metro for five stations and 1 tram.
- **Tourist tickets**, the simplest solution, provide unlimited travel on Metro, trams and buses for an extended period and are validated just once, when first used. Write your name and date of birth on the back of the ticket.

Prague Card

The Prague Card is a three-day **tourist pass**. One version allows entry to Prague Castle and the city's major museums and historic buildings (adults:590Kč; children/students 410Kč). Another version covers entry fees plus unlimited travel on the Metro, trams and buses (adults: 810Kč; children/students: 630Kč). Buy the cards at any Prague Information Service office (► 34) the main train station (► 34), the American Express office (Václavské náměstí 56), Čedok travel office (Na příkopě 18), or Muzeum Metro station.

These cost around 80Kč for 24 hours, 220Kč for 3 days, 280Kč for 7 days and 320Kč for 15 days.

- **Children** under six years and pet animals, which must be muzzled or in a carrying case, travel free.

Taxis
After a prolonged post-Communist period of rip-off tactics, the authorities have clamped down on rogue drivers.

- **Taximeters** must be running. It is quite acceptable to ask the driver: "*Zapněte taxametr, prosím*" ("Please start the meter").
- **Receipts** can be printed out from the taximeter on request: "*Prosím, dejte mi potvrzení*" ("Please give me a receipt").
- The **roof lamp** on official taxis should be yellow with TAXI in black capital letters. The registration number and taxi company name should be on the front doors.
- **Fares** are around 30Kč boarding fee, plus 22Kč per kilometre inside the city limits, and 4Kč per minute waiting charge. Outside the city limits, including the airport, a flat charge should be negotiated in advance. For these and other long trips, it is best to have your hotel order your taxi through a dispatching office which provides a set fare.

Reliable taxi companies offering a 24-hour service include:
AAA (tel: 222 333 222); **Halotaxi** (tel: 224 114 411); and **Radiotaxi** (tel: 272 731 848).

Driving
Your car is best saved for an excursion out of town. Driving within Prague can be horrendous for the uninitiated. Here are some of the rules.

- Drive on the **right**. **Headlights** are compulsory in winter.
- **Seat belts** front and rear are compulsory in and outside town.
- There is zero tolerance for **alcohol**.
- **Trams** have priority at all times. Stop immediately when the tram stops ahead of you.
- **Speed limits** are 50kph (31 mph) in town, 90kph (56 mph) on country roads (reduced to 30kph/19 mph preceding railway level-crossings) and 130kph (81 mph) on motorways.

Car rental
- You must have a valid **driving licence** from your country of residence.
- You must be **over 21**.
- **Payment** must be guaranteed by an international credit card.
- All **major international companies** are represented in Prague, but the local companies are much cheaper. You could try one of the following:
Dvořák Rent-a-Car, tel: 224 826 260; **AA Auto**, tel; 724 322 322; **CS Czechocar**, tel: 261 222 079; or **Vecar**, tel: 224 314 361.

Admission Charges
The cost of admission for museums and other attractions mentioned in this guide is indicated by the following symbols:
Inexpensive = under 60Kč
Moderate = 60–150Kč
Expensive = over 150Kč

Accommodation

Its austere socialist past now forever behind it, Prague ranks high among Europe's top destinations, and its hoteliers are eager to attract discriminating visitors. Overall, standards are rising faster than prices. This is still a city in constant flux, so come with a sense of adventure.

Types of Accommodation

Few cities can match Prague's historic **small hotels and pensions** for sheer aesthetic appeal. They offer historic charm and authenticity, usually occupying houses dating from the Middle Ages, 17th and 18th centuries and elaborate 19th-century wedding-cake houses.

An **unhosted apartment** can be an economical and very pleasant alternative to a hotel – many are located in attractive old neighbourhoods. They offer an apartment soley for the use of the person who has booked it, normally equipped with either a full kitchen or a cooker and fridge. Some are fully furnished with TV, radio and so on, and others are more like simple hotel rooms, except with cooking facilities.

The £££ establishments in this book almost always provide the standard luxury amenities and service. Facilities vary widely, but you can count on scrupulously clean premises. Except at the more expensive hotels, you should expect narrow beds without sprung mattresses.

Travellers with special requests or needs should be aware that nothing is guaranteed. If you have concerns over air-conditioning, lifts or wheelchair access, try to get them answered prior to arrival.

Where to Stay

Most visitors dream of staying in picturesque Staré Město (Old Town) or Malá Strana – but you need to book well in advance if you want to be guaranteed a room in either of these areas. There are far more rooms available in Nové Město (New Town), and the diverse inner suburbs like Vinohrady, Žižkov and Smíchov offer a wide choice of accommodation. A good network of public transport brings the city centre within relatively easy reach of most outlying districts.

Prices

Room rates generally drop 20–50 per cent during the low season. At many hotels, prices also drop slightly in mid-summer. Some smaller hotels give discounts for cash. Reservation assistants don't always divulge their secrets unasked – so don't be shy! Room rates generally include taxes and breakfast, except in some luxury hotels.

Booking

It is advisable to book your hotel in advance, as visiting Prague is becoming increasingly popular. Peak season runs from April to October, or longer at some hotels, with the peak of the peak in May, June and September. The competition is fierce during major holidays.

Booking Agencies

If you arrive in the city without a place to stay and need assistance with planning your visit, these are excellent places to try.

■ **DC Travel** is a long-established agency. Use their website or call to find a suitable apartment, hotel or pension in the city or country. They can also arrange airport transfers, sightseeing tours, cultural tickets, and out-of-

town excursions. Tel: 224 816 346. www.visitprague.cz
- **E-travel** is another experienced, full-service accommodation and booking agency. Tel: 224 990 990/7. www.travel.cz
- **PIS** (Pražska informačni služba – Prague Information Office, ➤ 34) is the city's official tourism and accomodation agency. Tel: 420 12 444; www.pis.cz

List of Places to Stay
Here is a selective list of some of the city's best lodgings, in alphabetical order. A handful of standard names in the hotel industry also have branches in Prague, among them Hilton, Marriott, Radisson and the Holiday Inn.

Prices
Price categories below are for the least expensive double room in high season, including VAT.
£ under 3,000Kč ££ 3,000–6,000Kč £££ over 6,000Kč

Betlem Club ££
From the cellar breakfast room up through a warren of stairs and Gothic galleries to rooms furnished mostly in 1970s style, with brass and mirrors, this is an authentic, old Prague house which has been transformed into a funky, affordable small hotel. Betlěmské náměstí (Bethlehem Square) oozes charm.

🕂 195 D3 ✉ Betlěmské náměstí 9, Staré Město ☎ 222 221 574; fax: 222 220 580; www.betelmclub.cz

Dům U Krále Jiřího ££
This affordable pension in the heart of the Old Town occupies a typically rambling Gothic house. Some rooms are furnished in mock-Gothic style, but with an eye for modern comfort, including satellite TV. There is one large, two-person apartment that's hardly more expensive than the 12 standard double rooms, and a larger apartment with a kitchen. An Irish pub, Czech beer hall and music club are in the courtyard.

🕂 195 D3 ✉ Liliová 10, Staré Město ☎ 221 466 100; fax: 221 466 166; www.kinggeorge.cz

Dům U Velké Boty £
This welcoming and well-run eight-room bed and breakfast is overseen by Charlotte, husband Jan, and sons Jakub and Tomáš. From the painted armoires to hand-carved sleigh

beds, all the furnishings in the large, bright bedrooms are lovingly-restored antiques. The hotel faces a quiet square in Malá Strana across from the German Embassy and is just a few steps from Nerudova street, which leads up to the castle. There are five double rooms and two suites, and a family suite with two connected rooms. Few modern amenities – the rooms lack televisions – but in such a perfect location, why stay inside?

🕂 194 A4 ✉ Vlašska 30, Malá Strana ☎ 257 532 088; www.bigboot.cz 🚇 Malostranská

Hotel Anna £
A member of the Small Charming Hotels group, the 22 rooms here are spacious with comfortable beds, elegant writing desks, large windows and pictures of the old city of Prague on the walls. There are wine bars and quiet pubs near by, and three blocks away, the old vineyards are now a gorgeous, wooded park.

🕂 201 F3 ✉ Budecská 17, Vinohrady ☎ 222 51 31 11; www.hotelanna.cz 🚇 Náměstí Míru

Hotel Cerny Slon ££
Tucked in the shadow of the spires of Tyn Church, off Staroměstské náměstí, this cosy hotel is in a 14th-century building on UNESCO's protected list. Everything has been

modernised inside, but the architecture has remained Gothic. The 16 rooms are decorated in a charming, simple style with antique furniture and lace curtains. Original ceiling beams and fresh flowers throughout make this hotel feel more like a home. There's a fine wine bar in the cellar, and a restaurant serving traditional Czech dishes with courtyard seating near the church.

🔲 195 E4 🖂 Týnská 1, Staré Město
☎ 222 321 521; www.hotelcernyslon.cz

Hotel U modrého Klíče (Blue Key) ££–£££

A medieval house converted in 1999 with stylish Italian furnishings, a sauna and whirlpool baths, and kitchenettes in most rooms, the Blue Key is an extremely comfortable and not overly expensive small hotel. Most of the rooms face into a courtyard rather than the busy street. Not all the rooms are accessible by lift (elevator), so check when you book if this is important to you.

🔲 194 C4 🖂 Letenská 14, Malá Strana
☎ 257 534 361; fax: 257 534 372

Hotel U Šuterů £

This simple and pleasing pension, on a small side street just off Václavské náměstí, is located above a great traditional Czech restaurant of the same name. The building dates back to the 14th century, and many rooms retain the original period architecture. There are ten bedrooms with private bathrooms, a mini-bar, direct-dial telephone and satellite TV. This convenient hotel is often full, so book early.

🔲 195 F2 🖂 Palackého 4, Nové Mesto
☎ 224 948 235; www.usuteru.cz
🚇 Můstek

Hotel Zlatá Hvězda £££

Perched on the top of Nerudova with a birds-eye view over Malá Strana, this is a former royal residence dating from 1372. The elegant rooms have gleaming parquet wood floors, antique beds, writing desks and dressers, and crystal chandeliers. Satellite TV a safe,

refrigerator and mini-bar are standard. There's an excellent restaurant with a magnificent deck overlooking the ascent to the castle.

🔲 194 A4 🖂 Nerudova 48, Malá Strana ☎ 257 533 833;
www.hotelgoldenstar.com
🚇 Malostranská

Domus Henrici £££

Tranquility and elegance define the atmosphere at this hotel located between Strahov Monastery and the the Loreto convent. Guests wake to church bells and even though it is in the heart of the city, birdsong drifts through the windows from nearby wooded Petřin Hill. The 8 elegant rooms have whitewashed walls, modern luxuries and hand-carved furniture. The exceptional personal service ranges from organising tickets to driving guests to dinner across the river and even sourcing fine local wines.

🔲 196 B1 🖂 Loretanská 11, Hradčany
☎ 220 511 369; www.domus-henrici.cz

Inter-Continental Praha £££

When a mover or a shaker comes to Prague, it's a good bet they'll stay in this swanky 1970s edifice just a few steps from the Staronová synagoga (Old-New Synagogue, ► 121). The spacious public areas have that on-the-go, "grand hotel", hum and the staff pride themselves on being able to accommodate visitors' every desire. Of the 364 rooms, the standard doubles are slightly on the small side, however, while the business-class rooms come equipped with faxes and data ports for your computer. The restaurant offers fine Continental cuisine.

🔲 195 E5 🖂 Náměstí Curieových 43/5 (at Pařížská), Staré Město ☎ 296 631 111; fax: 296 631 216;
www.ichotelsgroup.com

Maximilian £££

Efficient and luxurious, this Austrian-owned hotel sits unobtrusively on a quiet square near the Anešký klášter (St Agnes Convent, ► 128). All 72 rooms have fax machines and safes and come with spacious beds and bathrooms. But the best rooms are those facing the square. Guests who book at the last minute get a 10–20 per cent discount.

➕ 195 F5 ✉ Haštalská 14, Staré Město ☎ 225 303 111; fax: 225 303 110; www.maximilianhotel.com

Palace £££

An evergreen on any list of Prague's best places to stay, this century-old art nouveau-style hotel offers great comfort without being ostentatious. Most of the 124 rooms have king-size beds and all have Internet access through a keyboard linked to the TV. Two floors are reserved for non-smokers. The cool, quiet lobby makes a pleasant spot for a brief escape from Nové Město's liveliness. You can have a drink here with piano accompaniment in the afternoons and evenings. Children under 12 stay free in their parents' room. The restaurant is in "English-club style" with an expensive Continental and international menu.

➕ 195 F3 ✉ Panská 12, Nové Město ☎ 224 093 111; fax: 224 221 240; www.palacehotel.cz

Pension Březina £

This friendly 3-star hotel is in a great location, just five minutes from Wenceslas Square and close to a major tram and Metro stop, with restaurants, shops and a park near by. The 50 rooms are spotless and well-furnished with their own bathrooms, free internet, and air conditioning. There are four simply-furnished rooms for budget-minded travellers and a two-room apartment for families or groups.

➕ 201 E3 ✉ Legerova 41, Vinohrady ☎ 224 266 779; www.brezina.cz/brezina.htm

Pension Standard £

Two attic suites in this handsome pension overlook the Vltava River and Pražský hrad (Prague Castle, ► 82). The house is an attractive, seven-storey place in a long line of similarly attractive but highly eclectic houses fronting the river. Although the 11 double rooms miss out on the view, they are very reasonably priced and come with more amenities than you might expect, including air-conditioning and minibar. There is also a restaurant, which is rare for an establishment of this size, offering Czech cuisine.

➕ 195 D1 ✉ Rašínovo nábřeží 38, Nové Město ☎ 224 916 060; fax: 224 912 040; www.standard.cz

Savoy £££

An art nouveau-style, medium-sized establishment – one of Prague's contributions to the luxury hotel market. The Savoy, however, may be the most comfortable of them all. The 61 standard rooms are well equipped for business travellers with four telephones and PC ports, and the deluxe doubles are capacious. One floor is reserved for non-smokers. The Hradčany restaurant, with its massive sliding glass roof, makes a fine spot for summertime dining and serves Contintental cuisine.

➕ 196 B2 ✉ Keplerova 6, Hradčany ☎ 224 302 430; fax: 224 306 128; www.hotel-savoy.cz

Sax ££

Even with just 22 rooms, this efficient hotel qualifies as a sizeable place in its diminutive hillside neighbourhood below Pražský hrad (Prague Castle, ► 82). The cool, white-and-grey-toned atrium is lined with three floors of rooms. The low-key décor scheme continues with light pastel bedspreads and pale woodwork. Unashamedly urban, the Sax blows a different tune from many other Malá Strana hotels. There's no restaurant, but a breakfast room is available.

➕ 194 A4 ✉ Jánský vršek 3 (at Břetislavova), Malá Strana ☎ 257 531 268; fax: 257 534 101; www.sax.cz

U krále Karla ££

This small hotel (19 rooms) has a wonderful location at the top of

Nerudova Street (► 102), just below Prague Castle. It is exquisitely furnished throughout in the styles of most periods from Renaissance to neo-Gothic, from the charming breakfast room to the long, stained-glass skylight on the top floor. Parking is very limited. The restaurant serves standard Czech fare.

➕ 194 A4 ✉ Úvoz 4 (at Nerudova), Malá Strana ☎ 257 530 594; fax: 257 533 591; www.romantichotels.cz

Villa Voyta ££

Ensconced in a leafy suburb, this pretty art nouveau mansion provides 13 elegant rooms decorated in period style. The hotel is about a 20-minute taxi ride from the city centre. The eight equally comfortable rooms in the annex across the street can be linked to create suites of varying sizes. All rooms in the annex, and most in the villa, are air-conditioned. The better rooms also come with video players and stereo systems, a touch you won't find at most hotels charging higher rates. The villa has a reputable restaurant in art nouveau style, with (fairly expensive) French and Czech food.

➕ 201 off F1 ✉ K Novému dvoru 124/54, Lhotka, 14200 Prague 4 ☎ 261 711 307; fax: 244 471 248; www.villavoyta.cz

Food and Drink

Prague's genius loci *makes eating and drinking an unpredictable and memorable experience. Anything can happen – an exquisite mirrored dining room deep inside a decaying rococo palace; smoked eel by the Vltava River in summertime; a beer garden under blossoming linden trees.*

In the restaurants, cafés and pubs of Prague, the word is "change". New restaurants open (and close) at a dizzying rate. The variety of cuisine is ever increasing, as are quality and standard of service – but still at affordable prices, thanks to low overhead costs. Despite the addition of such specialities as Brazillian *churrasco* restaurants, Prague is not the place for a culinary round-the-world tour. Tested European dishes, game and freshwater fish are still the reliable choices. And don't forget the famous beer.

Czech Cuisine

Czechs like to say that their best cooks stay at home. If you're not lucky enough to be invited into a Czech home, however, you can still taste the local cuisine despite the plethora of other dining options.

- **Lunch** is customarily the main meal. A typical one might include *polévka* (soup), often an onion or garlic broth. *Kulajda* (dense, tangy potato and mushroom soup) is a South Bohemian speciality.
- For the **main course**, *vepřové* (pork) features strongly – everyone eagerly anticipates the annual pig slaughter and subsequent feast. At inexpensive restaurants pork dishes are generally more appetising than *hovězí* (beef). Meat courses are typically accompanied by *knedlíky* (fluffy bread dumplings) or *hranolky* (French fries). Fish is less popular, but as a traditional Bohemian food, especially in the autumn, it appears on menus even in humble establishments – try *pstruh* (pond-raised trout), *štika* (pike) or *úhoř* (eel).
- **Vegetables** are becoming more available as the city becomes more cosmopolitan. A standard Czech meal may include just some *zelí* (sauerkraut) or *obloha* (picked vegetables). *Šopsky s*alát (salad) is typically cucumber, tomato and red pepper with a slightly sweet vinegar dressing.

- Traditional **desserts** are *palačinky* (crepes), filled with chocolate syrup, fruit or ice-cream, and *ovocné knedlíky* (fruit dumplings), which are substantial enough to be served as a main course.
- **Beer** (*pivo*) is, of course, the main accompaniment. Lager beer was invented in the Bohemian town of Plzeň (Pilsen in German, thus Pilsner). You won't find the sheer variety of malt beverages that Munich, Brussels or Dublin can muster, but Prague can go head to foamy head with anyone on taste and beat them hands down on price.
- Czech **wine** is worth trying as well. Under communism, mechanised vini-culture devastated the old Moravian and Bohemian wine industry. But in recent years the country has begun producing excellent varietals. The best reds (*červené*) include Frankovka and Svatovavřinecké; whites (*bílé*) to try are Rýnský ryzlink (Riesling), Tramín Červený and Veltlínské zelené.

Restaurace, Hostinec or *Vinárna*?

Restaurant, pub or wine bar? The sign outside may not completely disclose what's inside.

- Many establishments use the word ***restaurace***, but resemble more a pub: the beer's draught, cold and thirst-quenching, while the food provides more of an accompaniment, although there may be an extensive menu.
- The ***hostinec*** is a pub or inn where some kind of hot food is served.
- The locals at the neighbourhood ***pivnice*** (beer hall) may look askance at strangers, but generally turn out to be friendly enough. If there are no free tables, ask to share: "*Je tu volno?*" ("Is this place free?").
- *Vinárna* is literally "a place for wine", and includes stand-up counters for a quick drink, dimly lit cellar wine bars and some of the city's finest restaurants.

New Brews

A city guide published in 1913 listed no fewer than 27 "grand cafés" in Prague. Three remain in business, reminders of a vanished Czech-German-Jewish cultural mélange that nurtured such café regulars as Bedřich Smetana, Franz Kafka and Albert Einstein. These are the Café Slavia (► 74), Café Louvre (► 158) and the café in Obecní dům (► 139). The culture, and the coffee houses, vanished in the wake of World War II and 40 years of communism. The situation grew so dire that in the early 1990s a good cup of coffee was as rare in the city as an authenticated sighting of native son Kafka, who died in 1924. Yet the city yearned for the return of literary cafés, musical cafés, all-night cafés – and the ten million tourists who descended each year on the newly accessible city just wanted a tolera-ble cappuccino. And so a new generation is reviving something of the hot-house atmosphere of those vanished cafés. Today everyone gathers at coffee houses to read the papers, talk shop and watch the world go by.

For a more mellow refreshment stop, the **tea room** (*čavojna*) may be just your cup. The wide-eyed tea zealots who run these places travel the world to find the most aromatic varieties and learn the secrets of proper brewing, whether in Japan, Nepal, Vietnam or Zimbabwe. What's more, most tea rooms are non-smoking zones.

A Survival Guide to Dining in Prague

- During peak season you should **reserve** whenever possible. Otherwise go at 11 am or 6 pm for an early lunch or dinner. Most inexpensive places, and many in the upper price brackets, stay open all day and nearly always have free places in late afternoon.
- **Casually presentable dress** suffices nearly everywhere, but you should ask about dress guidelines when making reservations at the chicest places.

- **Useful words** are *jídelní lístek* (menu), referring to a fixed-price meal for tourists, generally comprising roast pork and dumplings; *denní nabídka* (daily specials), served at less expensive restaurants; and *polévky* (soup); *jídla na objednávku* (main dishes cooked to order).
- **Service** has improved greatly. You can now count on prompt, efficient, knowledgeable and friendly service in most restaurants – but not necessarily all at once! As with everything else in Prague, you need patience to savour the experience to the full. Service is almost never included in the bill, except in the case of large groups. At the more expensive establishments, tip around 10–15 per cent. In pubs and inexpensive restaurants, give a small tip, usually by adding a few crowns to round up the total.
- Major **credit cards** are accepted at most of the restaurants listed in this guide (these should be indicated on the door). Many inexpensive restaurants, pubs and cafés only accept cash.
- **VAT** is always included in the bill.

Prices

The symbol for the restaurants listed in each chapter of this guide indicates what you can expect to pay for an average, complete dinner for one person, including drinks, tax and tip.

£ = under 350Kč **££** = 350–800Kč **£££** = over 800Kč

Bests...

...**Asian:** Orange Moon (➤ 71)
...**Bohemian:** Mlynec (➤ 71)
...**café:** Kavárna Slavia/Café Slavia (➤ 74)
...**coffee:** Ebel Coffee House (➤ 74)
...**historic interior:** Pálffy Palác (➤ 105)
...**Italian:** Don Giovanni (➤ 70)
...**pizza:** Pizzeria Rugantino (➤ 71)
...**riverside fish restaurant:** Rybářský klub (➤ 106)
...**hip scene:** Tretters (➤ 73)
...**tea room:** Dobrá Čajovna (➤ 158)
...**terrace:** Hergetova Cihelná (➤ 105)
...**view:** U Zlaté studně (➤ 107)

Shopping

As the re-establishment of a free market is so new to Prague, there are no specialised shopping districts. Shops of every kind are scattered across the historic core and often lurk in unexpected corners of this most unsystematic of cities.

Czech Specialities

- There are three main **traditional Czech** products: crystal and glass, porcelain and marionettes. It is hard to go wrong, as value for money is excellent. Simply styled glassware and porcelain can be quite inexpensive and very attractive. At the higher end of the market, brands such as Moser are world famous – but don't expect to find bargains.

- Other **popular buys** are garnet jewellery, crafts, shoes and leather goods, and locally made spirits – especially the herbal liqueur Becherovka.
- Prague is also a **bargain basement** for good deals on domestic products like women's fashions, classical CDs and musical instruments.
- Due to 50 years of isolation, the market in **antiques and fine art** has huge growth potential and canny shoppers can find good deals, but also items of dubious authenticity. Reputable dealers will provide the necessary customs documentation for genuine antiques and artworks.

Where to Shop

- In general **Nové Město** (New Town) offers the largest stores.
- **Staré Město** (Old Town) and **Josefov** (Old Jewish Quarter) have boutiques, souvenir stalls and lots of chic international fashion and accessory stores.
- In **Malá Strana** and around **Pražský hrad** (Prague Castle), it is best to let yourself wander among the tiny shops.

Markets

- You can't miss the crowded **Havelská street market** in Staré Město (Old Town), with crafts, toys and clothes alongside fruit and vegetables. It runs from dawn to sunset, every day.
- **Staroměstské náměstí** (Old Town Square) returns to its commercial roots at Easter and Christmas, when it fills with booths offering traditional crafts, grilled sausages and hot mulled wine.
- Throughout the city there are *tržnice,* little courtyard markets, selling fresh produce, inexpensive clothing, shoes, umbrellas, coats and bags.

Service

The typical downtown Prague shop has undergone a metamorphosis. Whereas a few years ago you'd have faced a long counter manned by humourless matrons who, if you could communicate with them at all, would grudgingly hand over the goods, the norm today is an open-plan shop with English-speaking staff. However, the path to better service is a bumpy one, so expect shop assistants to swing between sincere enthusiasm and studied neglect.

Opening Times

- Downtown shops and department stores often stay open until 7 or later on weekdays, and close a couple of hours earlier on Saturday and Sunday.
- Elsewhere most shops keep to traditional hours of 9–6 on weekdays and 9–1 on Saturday, closed on Sunday.

Entertainment

Beloved by opera fans and admirers of the rich Central European orchestral sound, Prague offers a surprisingly broad range of performing arts to cater for all tastes.

Information and Bookings

- You can buy **tickets** to all kinds of events at a huge number of ticket agencies, major hotels, the city tourist information office (PIS), and travel agents.
- Tickets to **major performances** are scarce on the day of the show, but it's worth stopping off at the box office if there's an opera or symphony you particularly want to catch. Opera tickets are easiest to come by in winter.

■ **Bohemia Ticket International**, Na příkopě 16, Nové Město; tel: 224 215
031; www.ticketsbti.cz, sells leftover Státní opera (State Opera House)
tickets at half price on the day of the perfomance.
■ For tickets for the **Prague Spring Festival**, contact www.festival.cz; visit the
PIS Prague Information Office (► 34) or **Ticketpro**, Rytířská 12 (tel: 296
333 333; www.ticketpro.cz).

Further Information

Check the Night and Day section of the English-language *Prague Post*
(www.praguepost.com), which is published on Wednesdays, and Prague TV
website (www.prague.tv) for weekly listings and reviews.

Opera and Classical Music

■ The city has three **opera houses** – Stavovské divadlo (Estates Theatre,
► 63), Národní divadlo (National Theatre, ► 145–146) and Státní opera
Praha (Prague State Opera, ► 152).
■ **Ticket prices** for opera are high by local standards, but affordable by
Western ones.
■ The **Czech Philharmonic** and **Prague Symphony** orchestras offer world-class
music performed in stunning surroundings. The Czech Philharmonic
plays in the Rudolfinum (► 124) and the Prague Symphony Orchestra in
Smetanova síú (Smetana Hall) in the Obecní dům (Municipal House). The
works of Mozart, Vivaldi and Bach are often included in their repertoires.

Theatre and Dance

Leaving aside the thriving Czech-language dramatic theatre, there's still
plenty to choose from.
■ **Blacklight theatre**, a local invention, entertains the crowds nightly at a
variety of venues with its blend of mime, clowning and lighting effects.
You can find out about tickets to these shows from Ticketpro; tel: 296
333 333; www.ticketpro.cz
■ **Non-verbal theatre and dance** play regularly to knowledgeable audiences.
Top-flight performers appear at Archa (► 160) and in festivals such as
Tanec Praha every June (see below).

Pop and Jazz

■ You can hear fine **jazz**, which has a long tradition of excellence in Prague,
at a variety of downtown clubs. Check with the *Prague Post* for what's on.
■ Check in the *Prague Post* for local **rock**, **blues** and **folk** concerts.
■ **World music** is also popular in the city. Check with PIS for what's on.

Festivals

There are a growing number of well-attended festivals. For more detailed
listings see the individual chapters.
■ The venerable **Prague Spring Music Festival** brings the best classical
performers to the city every year from 12 May to 3 June (www.festival.cz).
■ The **Prague Autumn Festival** does the same in September, albeit at a
slightly lower level (www.pragueautumn.cz).
■ June brings the **Prague Writers' Festival** where major English-language and
other writers give readings and hold discussions (www.pwf.cz).
■ In June there is **the United Islands of Prague world-music festival**
(www.unitedislands.cz) and the **Tanec Praha** celebration of **contemporary
dance** (www.tanecpraha.cz).
■ The top two **film festivals** are Apirl's FebioFest (www.febiofest.cz) and One
World international human rights documentary film festival
(www.jedensvet.cz).

Staré Město
(Old Town)

Getting Your Bearings

Staré Město (Old Town) is Prague's historic hub. This was the "Royal Route" kings took to their coronation because they knew it was here that they would draw the biggest crowds. Today ancient and modern mix well here, cyber-cafés buzzing and beeping in medieval vaulted cellars.

Staré Město sits in a bend of the Vltava River. It extends from the monumental Karlův most (Charles Bridge) via Staroměstské náměstí (Old Town Square), site of the majestic sv Mikuláš (St Nicholas) Church, and east to the end of Celetná Street.

KAPROVA

ZÁTECKÁ

MAISEL

PLATNÉŘSKÁ

sv František

KŘIŽOVNICKÁ

Mariánské náměstí **7**

Karlův most **1**

Klementinum **6**

Křižovnické náměstí **3**

KARLOVA

Vltava

SMETANOVO NÁBŘ

Muzeum Bedřicha Smetany **2**

4 Muzeum loutkářských kultur

HUSOVA

sv Jiljí

NÁPRSTKOVA

Betlémské kaple **5**

North of Celetná is the historic Týn Church and its courtyard, the Ungelt. Its southern section embraces a maze of cobblestoned lanes and alleyways that are so dense that trams have to go around, not across, the neighbourhood.

The subtle, magic essence of Prague is here, artfully blending the stark spikes of dark Gothic spires and the exuberant curves and colour of baroque palaces. In the shops on busy Karlova and Celetná, you will find both excruciating junk and exquisite crystal. On Husova Street, hearty pubs alternate with refined bistros. Listen to opera at the Stavovské divadlo (Estates Theatre) or rousing Dixieland on Staroměstské náměstí (Old Town Square). Or blissful silence in Ungelt.

★ Don't Miss

1 Karlův most (Charles Bridge) ➤ 52

9 Staroměstské náměstí (Old Town Square) ➤ 56

10 Týn Church & Ungelt ➤ 60

15 Stavovské divadlo (Estates Theatre) ➤ 63

At Your Leisure

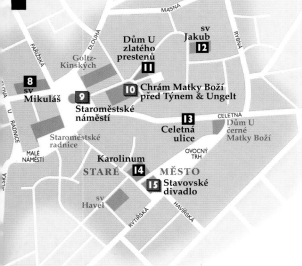

MASNÁ

DLOUHÁ

PAŘÍŽSKÁ

Goltz-
Kinských

**Dům U
zlatého
prestenů**
11

**sv
Jakub**
12

RYBNÁ

8
**sv
Mikuláš**

ALOVÁ

U RADNICE

9

**10 Chrám Matky Boží
před Týnem & Ungelt**

**Staroměstské
náměstí**

Staroměstské
radnice

MALÉ
NÁMĚSTÍ

ŽILSKÁ

13
**Celetná
ulice**

CELETNÁ

Dům U
černé
Matky Boží

OVOCNÝ
TRH

Karolinum

STARÉ **14** **MĚSTO**

**15 Stavovské
divadlo**

sv
Havel

RYTÍŘSKÁ

HAVÍŘSKÁ

0 ————— 200 metres

0 ————— 200 yards

Page 47: The
popular Karlův
most (Charles
Bridge)

Below: Looking
past the Old
Town Hall to
the spires of
Týn Church

From dawn to dusk, a stroll through five centuries.
Follow in the footsteps of kings and musicians.

Staré Město
(Old Town) in a Day

9:00 am

Make an early start to avoid the mob that will descend on
Karlův most (Charles Bridge, ➤ 52), Prague's most popular landmark.
Those 30 statues make this more than just another bridge (below, statue of
St Barbara, St Margaret and St Elizabeth). Save the climb up the Old Town
Gate Tower for another day, preferably at sunset, take in the river scene and
then head off east on Karlova Street alongside the **Klementinum** (➤ 65),
passing **Křižovnické náměstí** (➤ 64) *en route*.

10:00 am

Time for a coffee on **Staroměstské náměstí**
(Old Town Square, ➤ 56–59). Choose the café for
the view you want – of the town hall, the church,
the palaces or the **Jan Hus Monument** (➤ 58),
before strolling over for a closer look.
This would be a good time to pick
up information and maps at the
Old Town Hall tourist office. Look
around the **Church of sv Mikuláš**
(St Nicholas, ➤ 66–67) and
cross the square
to the pas-
sage between
the Stone
Bell House
and the Týn
School.

11:30 am

It's interesting to compare the **Týn Church**
(➤ 60–62) with St Nicholas. There is plenty
to see here, inside and out, before you
stroll around **Ungelt** (top right, ➤ 61) and
explore its craft shops and art galleries.
Browse at the Anagram English
Bookshop for its first-class
selection of Czech literature
in English translation.

Or visit the Prague City Museum at the **Dům U zlatého prestenů** (House of the Golden Ring, ➤ 67).

1:00 pm
Stay on Ungelt for a seafood lunch at Rybí trh restaurant (➤ 72).

2:30 pm
Try some window-shopping or serious bargain-hunting on **Celetná ulice** (➤ 68) with the **Museum of Czech Cubist Art** at No 34 (➤ 69).

4:00 pm
Back to Staroměstské náměstí (Old Town Square) to the second floor of the Grand Café Praha, a surprisingly charming place right opposite the **Astronomical Clock** (opposite, ➤ 57), for tea or coffee and to watch the world go by.

5:30 pm
Operas start early in Prague, so either shower and relax back at the hotel or go over to Ovocný trh for a pub snack at Na Ovocném trhu before the show (➤ 63).

7:00 pm
End the day in style with an opera at the **Stavovské divadlo** (Estates Theatre, below, ➤ 63), the best way to see this magnificent house.

O

Karlův most
(Charles Bridge)

The bridge and the famous statues on its parapets are the stuff the city's dreams are made of. Not all the statues are masterpieces but together they form a bewitching parade between the two historic halves of the city. By day, the thoroughfare is thronged with people strolling past stalls of souvenirs, art and near-art, to and from Prague Castle on the hill.

Up until the 19th century, this was Prague's only bridge across the Vltava River. Indeed, for 500 years it was known just as the Stone Bridge until 1870, when it was finally named after its original builder Charles IV, German emperor and king of Bohemia. Royal processions carried kings across to be crowned or buried in Pražský hrad (Prague Castle, ► 82–85). Knights galloped across in jousting tournaments. Merchants met here to do business. Criminals and "heretics" were hanged or decapitated here. German SS troops paraded in 1939, followed by Communist militia in the coup d'état of 1948. On a more upbeat note, jazz and rock musicians have succeeded the medieval minstrels to sing here for their supper. Karlův most's magic hour is midnight.

Blessed by its saints, the light of Charles Bridge is at its best in late afternoon

The Staré Město (Old Town) Bridge Tower was a mainstay of the city's medieval defences

In the Beginning

Winter floods of the fast-flowing Vltava River wrought havoc with the Charles Bridge's predecessors. The earliest recorded bridge, noted when the body of Bohemia's patron saint Václav (Wenceslas) was carried over in the 10th century to be buried at Prague Castle, was a flimsy wooden affair often swept away. A stone bridge, built by King Vladislav I in 1170 and named after his wife Judith, was also regularly breached by floods.

Charles IV, crowned Emperor in 1355, found the bridge in ruins and had architect Peter Parléř design a new one while working on St Vitus Cathedral (▶ 89–91). After his elaborate vaulting for the church's nave and choir, the master builder had little trouble with the 16 arches for the bridge. Built just to the south of the old one, the new bridge, 516m (1,640 feet) long and 10m (33 feet) wide, uses some of the old pier foundations, resulting in an S-curve from one bank to the other.

Staré Město (Old Town) Bridge Tower

With its chisel-blade roof and golden globes, corner turrets and battlemented gallery, this superb tower gate has a silhouette that is both formidable

Heads

The morning after an Austrian Catholic army had executed 27 Protestant leaders in 1621 during the Thirty Years' War, 12 of their severed heads were displayed on the Staré Město Bridge Tower. They stayed there for ten years until a Protestant army of Saxons seized the city long enough to take them down and give them a decent burial in Týn Church (▶ 60–62).

The Top Ten

Of the bridge's 31 statues and sculptures, the following deserve a longer look (numbers refer to their position on the plan below):

• **St Ivo (2)** by Matyás Bernard Braun shows the lawyers' patron saint with a blindfolded Justice.

• The **group of saints Barbara (4)** – patron of silver miners, with **Margaret** and **Elizabeth** – is a joint work of the great Brokoff family workshop.

• Jesuit missionary **Francis Xavier (10)**, with Chinese, Indian and Arab converts, is generally considered Ferdinand Maximilian Brokoff's masterpiece.

• Most famous of the sculptures, the bronze **John of Nepomuk (15)**, also by Brokoff, stands at the centre of the bridge from where the archbishop's corpse was thrown into the river 300 years before.

• **St Ludmila (16)**, grandmother of St Wenceslas, was Bohemia's first martyr, depicted here holding the veil that was to strangle her.

• **St Jude Thaddaeus (19)** by Jan Meyer shows the apostle with the cudgel of his martyrdom.

• The Augustinians had Jan Bedřich Kohl sculpt **St Augustine (22)** upholding the flaming heart of his order.

• **St Nicholas of Tolentino (23)** distributes bread to the poor.

• Quintessence of the baroque statues is Matyás Braun's Cistercian nun, **St Lutgard (25)**, about to act out her vision of kissing the wounds of Jesus.

• The university medical faculty commissioned Jan Mayer's **Cosmas and Damian (30)**, patron saints of physicians, twin brothers flanking Jesus.

The Statues and Sculptures

1 Madonna and St Bernard
2 St Ivo
3 Madonna, St Dominic and St Thomas Aquinas
4 St Barbara, St Margaret and St Elizabeth
5 Bronze Crucifixion
6 Pieta
7 St Anne with the Madonna and Child
8 St Joseph
9 St Cyril, St Methodius and three allegorical figures
10 St Francis Xavier
11 St John the Baptist
12 St Christopher
13 St Wenceslas, St Norbert and St Sigismund
14 St Francis Borgia
15 St John of Nepomuk (above)
16 St Ludmilla and St Wenceslas
17 St Anthony of Padua
18 St Francis in ecstasy
19 St Jude Thaddeus
20 St Vincent Ferrer and St Procopius
21 Bruncvik (Roland Column)
22 St Augustine
23 St Nicholas of Tolentino
24 St Cajetan
25 St Luitgard
26 St Philip Benitius
27 St Adalbert
28 St Vitus
29 St John of Matha, St Felix of Valois and Blessed Ivan
30 Jesus, St Cosmas and St Damian
31 St Wenceslas

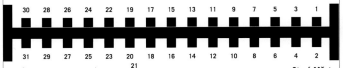

30 28 26 24 22 19 17 15 13 11 9 7 5 3 1

31 29 27 25 23 20 18 16 14 12 10 8 6 4 2
21

Malá Strana
Bridge Tower

Staré Město
Bridge Tower

KARLŮV MOST: INSIDE INFO

Top tip Go early morning or late afternoon to climb to the top of the **Staré Město (Old Town) Bridge Tower**, built at the end of the 14th century. The viewing gallery, on the first floor, provides a wonderful view of Prague Castle and Staré Město.

and elegant. Originally endowed with a portcullis lowered to ward off attackers, it served as a firewall against enemy assaults on Prague Castle or the city. Most notably in 1648, at the very end of the Thirty Years' War, the tower withstood the Swedes' artillery in their last assault on the city. On the tower's eastern façade over the Gothic arch, the statue of St Vitus is flanked by the enthroned figures of a tired-looking Charles IV on the left and his son Václav IV on the right. Beneath them is a row of ten Bohemian coats of arms. Standing in the upper windows are the patron saints Adalbert and Sigismund.

The Statues

The bridge had only a bronze crucifix until the Jesuits launched the series of sacred sculptures now gracing the parapets. The first statue, erected in 1683, was of St John of Nepomuk (Jan Nepomucký, ► 32), a Czech martyr promoted by the Church as a popular counterpart to the national hero – and Protestant – Jan Hus (► 18).

By 1714, inspired by the Bernini statues on Rome's Ponte Sant'Angelo, Czech baroque sculptors produced some 25 statues for the bridge. Respectable copies and six new statues were added in the 19th and 20th centuries. Some of the baroque originals, mostly in weather-beaten sandstone, can be seen in the dungeons of Vyšehrad Castle (► 149–151).

St Anne praying to the Madonna and Child

TAKING A BREAK

Less than two blocks from the bridge is the **Café Rincon** (Na Zabradli 1, Staré Mesto; daily noon–2 am; tel 222 222 173) with picture windows and outdoor seating providing a stunning view of the river and castle to go with salads, sandwiches, coffee and cakes.

➕ 193 D3 ✉ Staré Město, Praha 1 🏛 Staré Město Bridge Tower: 10–6 Mar; Jun–Sep 10–7; 10–10 Apr, May, Oct; 10–5 Nov–Feb 🎫 Bridge Tower: inexpensive 🚊 Tram 17,18

9

Staroměstské náměstí

(Old Town Square)

This colourful, bustling square is undoubtedly the centre not only of the Old Town (Staré Město) but of the whole city. Historically, it has been a magnet for all sections of the population. A town hall, merchants' mansions, princes' palaces and two majestic churches – St Nicholas (► 66) and Týn (► 60–62) – look down on the massive modern monument to the nation's reformist hero, Jan Hus.

The square began in the 11th century as the city's marketplace, both for local peasants and for merchants from all over Europe. It was known then just as Velké náměstí (Great Square) and acquired its current name only in 1895. Vestiges of the era's Romanesque houses can be seen in the vaulted basements of today's largely baroque mansions.

The centre of trade was the obvious place for the town hall, formed by knocking together adjacent houses. The square was the best address in town. The wealthiest citizens – import and export merchants, bankers and business representatives for the Kutná Hora silver mines (► 162–166) – built mansions. The royal family and nobles put up palaces here, which were much more comfortable than their damp and draughty castle.

Besides buying and selling at the market, people gathered here to throw rotten eggs at rascals clamped in the town hall

Crowds start to mass on Old Town Square

The Town Hall clock tells you more about the stars than the time of day

pillory, cheer champions in tournaments, kings at their corona-
tions, and executioners decapitating the monarchs' enemies.

Staroměstské radnice (Old Town Hall)

The present largely Gothic edifice on the west side of the
square represents a conglomeration of several houses acquired
over the centuries, starting with a house for the town scribe
in 1296. The belfry, 66m (216 feet) high, was built in 1364,
incorporating 17 years later the municipal chapel, with its distinctive oriel window.

Only a fragment remains from a
northern neo-Gothic wing bombarded
by the Germans in 1945. The main
entrance is through the south side's
15th-century portal. Civic weddings
and art exhibitions are held here, and
there are 20-minute guided tours of the
chapel and the council chamber where
Bohemian kings were elected, until the
arrival of the Habsburgs. The tower is
worth the climb (or use the lift) for the
rooftop view. (The tourist information
office is at the rear, ► 34.)

Astronomical Clock

Set against the belfry, the Town Hall's
top tourist attraction draws its crowds
when fanciful characters are set in
motion every hour, on the hour, 9–9.
The clock was built in 1410 not so
much to tell the precise time (of no
great interest in those less hurried
days) as to show the state of the uni-
verse, the position and movement
of the stars and planets – and their

Death in the Morning

Old Town Square's most spectacular
public execution took place on 21
June, 1621, at the height of the Thirty
Years' War (► 19). Eight months after
the Catholics' decisive victory at Bílá
Hora (White Mountain), Prague's
imperial governor had 27 Protestant
leaders condemned to death. At 5 am,
the castle's cannons boomed out over
the city to summon people to the
spectacle. With drums rolling and
trumpets blaring to drown out any last
words of protest, the executioner cut
off the heads, each with one blow, of
24 nobles and knights. For them,
decapitation was a "privilege" of rank.
Three commoners were hanged. Today,
this traumatic moment in Prague history is marked by 27 white crosses set
in the paving on the east side of the
town hall.

astrological impact on daily life. The hour's last chime starts a procession in the upper windows of the 12 Apostles, copies of 18th-century woodcarvings destroyed in 1945.

Flanking the 24-hour clock, the skeleton of Death tolls his bell and shows by an hourglass that time is up for his Turkish neighbour and the figures of Vanity and Usury opposite, all shaking their heads in disbelief. The windows shut, a cock crows and the show is over. Below the clock, the revolving calendar dial's 12 rustic scenes were painted in the 19th century by Josef Mánes.

Monument to Jan Hus

Revered more as a patriotic symbol than an artistic masterpiece, the ponderous monument facing Týn Church celebrates Jan Hus, the hero of Czech religious reformism (1370–1415). Sculptor Ladislav Šaloun completed it in 1915 for the 500th anniversary of Hus being burned at the stake, charged with heresy.

A conservative opponent of church corruption, Hus stands among his militant disciples, the humbled Protestants later forced to emigrate, and a mother and child symbolising national renewal. The Nazis covered it in swastikas, and in 1968, during the Soviet invasion, Prague students draped it in black cloth. On the monument's base are Hus's famous words: *Pravda vítězí* (Truth prevails).

The Square's Houses

The mansions, palaces and merchants' houses here are fine examples of the city's civic architecture, many with characteristic rib-vaulted arcades – their arched ceilings supported by stone ribs crossing at a diagonal – that prove a blessing in the rainy months.

On the west side of the square at right angles to the town hall, the **Dům U minuty** (The Minute House) is renowned for its splendid Renaissance *sgraffito* friezes of knights, princes and allegorical figures. It has served variously as the town pharmacy, home to Franz Kafka and municipal offices.

On the south side at No 20, **Dům U zlatého jednorožce** (House of the Golden Unicorn), once Smetana's music school, has an 18th-century façade, Gothic portal and vaulting, and a

The rococo Goltz-Kinský Palace adds a light touch to the east side of Staroměstské náměstí

13th-century Romanesque basement that at one time formed its ground floor.

Over on the east side, the grand, 18th-century rococo **Goltz-Kinský Palace** was designed by Kilián Ignác Dienzenhofer, who also built the Church of St Nicholas across the square (➤ 66–67). In the 19th century it housed the German Gymnasium (high school) and the haberdashery store of Franz Kafka's father Hermann.

Set back to the right of the palace, in fine stylistic counterpoint, is the four-square Gothic **Dům U kamenného zvonu** (House of the Stone Bell). A baroque façade was removed in 1970 to reveal its handsome 14th-century honey-coloured limestone and graceful mullioned windows. The goldsmith's mansion is now a modern art gallery.

TAKING A BREAK

There are plenty of open-air cafés in the square. Or, for lunch, take the narrow alley to the left of Týn Church, and go down the passageway on the left side of the courtyard to find U Budovce (Týnská 7, Staré Město), for homemade soups and sandwiches.

🔢 195 E4 ☎ Old Town Hall exhibitions 12 444; Dům U kamenného zvonu (Stone Bell) 224 828 244 🕐 Old Town Hall: Mon 11–6, Tue–Sun 9–6, Mar–Oct; Mon 11–5, Tue–Sun 9–5, Nov–Feb; Stone Bell: Tue–Sun 10–6 🚇 Staroměstská 🚌 17, 18 💰 Old Town Hall Tower: inexpensive; Stone Bell: moderate

STAROMĚSTSKÉ NÁMĚSTÍ: INSIDE INFO

Top tip Closed to traffic, the square is now a favourite spot for **people-watching** from the open-air cafés.

One to miss Avoid the square's mob scene for the noontime "show" at the Astronomical Clock.

🔟

Týn Church and Ungelt

With their dramatic clusters of spires, the two towers make the venerable Týn Church one of the Old Town's most striking landmarks. This historic focus of the Czech nation's struggle rises behind the graceful white Venetian-style gables of the former Týn School on the east side of Old Town Square.

The Treasures

After taking in the silhouette from across Old Town Square, take the narrow Týnská ulička between the House of the Stone Bell and the Týn School to get to the church – full name Chram Matky Boží před Týnem (Church of Our Lady Before the Týn).

A Danish flag graces the tomb of gold-nosed astronomer Tycho Brahe

Its north portal has a splendid Gothic pediment of *The Passion of Christ* (1390), sculpted by Peter Parléř. Inside, the slender nave's baroque ceiling was built after a fire in 1689, but the aisles' original Gothic vaulting has survived. Notice the fine 15th-century **stone pulpit** and, on the main altar, Karel Škréta's *Assumption of the Virgin Mary* (1649). Just right of the presbytery steps is the russet marble **tomb of Tycho Brahe** (1546–1601), renowned court astronomer to Rudolf II (► 7–8).

Opposite: There's a defiant air to the bustling spires of Týn Church, proud shrine of Czech nationalism

Ungelt

The courtyard behind the church is where German merchants met from the 12th to the 18th centuries to find lodgings, do business and pay customs duty (*Ungelt* in medieval German – which gave it its name). It has been tastefully refurbished. Warehouses and customs offices have been converted into shops, art galleries and studios, cafés, restaurants and an elegant hotel. Along the north side is the **Granovský palác** (1560), a handsome Renaissance mansion built over earlier Romanesque dwellings.

Strife-Torn Týn

The church has born witness to much of the blood and thunder of Prague's religious conflicts. The German merchants built a chapel here in the 1100s. As trade expanded, they began a bigger church in 1365. Work stopped during the insurrection that followed the burning of Jan Hus (► 18) – roof timber was diverted for gallows to hang Hussite rebels. Many German merchants prudently left town and the rebels' successors completed the church as a counterpart to the cathedral of St Vitus (► 89).

Tycho's Nose Job

Astro-alchemist Tycho Brahe was attracted to gold. He lost a bit of his nose in a duel and had a new part made up in gold and silver. When his tomb was opened in 1901 the costly appendage had gone.

The Hussites' champion, King Jiři z Poděbrad (George of Poděbrady), pointedly went to Mass at Týn Church after his coronation in 1458. The statue of this last Czech-born king of Bohemia was placed in the gable overlooking Old Town Square. In 1623, after the Catholic victory at Bílá Hora, Jesuit students tore down the statue and chalice, later replaced by the present effigy of the Virgin Mary, with the gold of the chalice melted down for her sceptre, crown and halo.

The Fateful Battle

For most Czechs, 8 November, 1620, is an infamous date second only to the day the Munich Agreement handed their country to Adolf Hitler, on 30 September, 1938. Early in the Thirty Years' War, the Catholic victory over the Protestants at Bílá Hora (White Mountain) sealed the fate of Czech nationalism for 300 years. On a hilltop on the western outskirts of modern Prague, Czech Protestant leaders gathered 21,000 mercenaries from Moravia, Germany, Austria and Hungary to fight the Habsburgs' Catholic army, commanded by Maximilian of Bavaria. The numerical superiority – 28,000 – of his German, Spanish and French soldiers (including philosopher René Descartes) was offset by their uphill fight. However, the Protestants' Hungarian troops fled at the first assault, little more than a probe, and the Czech force collapsed. Its leaders were unable to rouse the citizens of Prague to resist and Maximilian entered the city without firing a shot. The Czech Protestant aristocracy and intelligentsia were – often literally – decapitated, with 36,000 families and all non-Catholic clergy driven to emigrate. Bohemia was annexed to the Habsburg Empire until 1918.

TAKING A BREAK

Cross the courtyard to dine in the Gothic cellars of **Metamorphosis**. Or join other visitors at Ungelt's sports café in the northwest corner – for satellite sports and beer.

Above: The handsome Granovský palác overlooks Ungelt Square

✚ 195 E4/F4 ✉ Church: Staroměstské náměstí; Ungelt: Týnský dvůr
Ⓜ Staroměstská 🎫 Free

TÝN CHURCH AND UNGELT: INSIDE INFO

One to miss Beware of flyers advertising "free" entrance to the Ungelt Jazz Club on Týnská Street. Upstairs is free, but the jazz, in the basement, is not.

15

Stavovské divadlo
(Estates Theatre)

Historically Prague's most important theatre, offering Mozart some of his greatest operatic triumphs (➤ 20–23), the Stavovské divadlo has been restored to the neoclassical splendour of its 19th-century heyday.

The lofty façade presents a fittingly theatrical backdrop at the west end of Ovocný trh. The portico, with twin Corinthian columns, is thrust gently into the square by two gracefully curving wings. Crowning the columns is the inscription *Patriae et Musis* (To Fatherland and the Muses). The elegant blue-walled interior has five tiers of boxes in a U shape around the orchestra stalls.

"Where Is My Home?"
Theatre has always been vital to the Czech national identity, but, apart from Mozart's Italian operas, *The Marriage of Figaro* and *Don Giovanni*, and a couple of Czech plays, the repertoire was German, and remained so until 1920, when Czech nationalists drove out German directors to the cry of "The Stavovské for the nation!" After World War II, Communists reclaimed its Czech identity, naming it after Josef Kajetán Tyl, composer of the national anthem *Kde domov můj?* (*Where Is My Home?*). Today, the Stavovské is triumphantly cosmopolitan. Czechs take their opera seriously and dress accordingly. Evening dress is not a must but it's worth making an effort.

TAKING A BREAK
For a meal or drink before the show, try **Dům U Závoje** (Havelská 25, Staré Město) a wine bar/restaurant which offers excellent menus and wines.

➕ 195 F3 ✉ Ovocny trh 1 ☎ 224 901 448 ⏰ Performances 7 or 7:30 pm Ⓜ Můstek
💷 Moderate

At Your Leisure

Bedřich Smetana sits with his back to the Vltava River that features in his symphonic poem

2 Muzeum Bedřicha Smetany

The riverside Smetana Museum devoted to the most patriotic of Czech composers (► 21–22), Bedřich Smetana (1824–84), is housed in a remarkably ornate neo-Renaissance building. The small collection of memorabilia – his spectacles, furniture from his home, garnet necklaces he bought for his wife, his musical scores – provides only a modest peek into the great man's life. You'll get a better idea of

him from the occasional recitals of his chamber music that take place here.

➕ 195 D3 ✉ Novotného lávka ☎ 222 222 082; www.nm.cz 🕐 Wed–Mon 10–5 🚃 17, 18 💰 Inexpensive

3 Křižovnické náměstí

The "Knights of the Cross Square" is a forecourt to Charles Bridge, and people arrange to meet at the foot of the 19th-century **statue of Charles IV**, the king who built the bridge.

On the north side of the square, **Sv František** is the baroque church of the Czech knights, once gatekeepers to the bridge. Its imposing dome was modelled after that of St Peter's in Rome. See the interior's fine purple marble columns and the cupola's ceiling fresco of *The Last Judgment* by Václav Vavřinec.

Incorporated into the Klementinum on Karlova Street, the Jesuit **Church of sv Salvator** has an Italian-style Renaissance façade and an elaborate baroque interior.

➕ 195 D3 🚇 Staroměstská 🚃 17, 18

4 Muzeum loutkářských kultur (Puppet Museum)

Tucked away among Karlova Street's kitschy souvenir shops is this oasis of genuine folk art. Run by UNIMA (International Institute of Marionette Art), the museum displays, in Gothic-vaulted cellars, beautifully carved and costumed puppets mostly from the 19th and early 20th centuries, but inspired by a Czech tradition dating back to the Middle Ages. There are also puppets from Asia, Africa and other

European countries, with many on sale at the museum shop. All the displays are static, and unfortunately there aren't any puppet demonstrations. (For puppet shows ➤ 11, 76.) Their website, www.puppetart.com, is worth a look.

➕ 195 D3 ✉ Karlova 12 ☎ 222 220 928 ⊙ Museum: daily 12–8; shop: daily 10–7 Ⓜ Staroměstská 🚊 17, 18 💷 Inexpensive

🟦 Betlémské kaple

The Bethlehem Chapel is a 20th-century reconstruction of a major shrine to Czech national history, the chapel in which Jan Hus preached his Reformist brand of Christianity in the early 1400s (➤ 18). Built 1391–4 and totally destroyed in the 18th century, the chapel, with its distinctive roof of twin wooden gables, was resurrected in 1950 in a post-war campaign to restore Czech self-esteem. Every detail of the structure has been meticulously

The Priest and the Whore

Prague is famous for its ghosts and Celetná Street has two. Coming out of one of the street's many covered passages, a lady of the night bumped into a priest and thought she would try her luck with him. The outraged priest hit her on the head with his cross, and she fell dead at his feet. Horrified at what he had done, he died of a stroke. The lady can still be seen pursuing her holy killer, most frequently after the pubs close.

reproduced from the original, displayed inside as part of a permanent exhibit of the revered chapel's history.

➕ 195 E3 ✉ Betlémské náměstí ⊙ Tue–Sun 10–6:30, Apr–Oct; Tue–Sun 10–5:30, Nov–Mar Ⓜ Národni třída 🚊 6, 9, 18, 22 💷 Inexpensive

🟦 Klementinum

Over 30 houses, three churches, ten courtyards and several gardens were demolished to make way for the sprawling complex of the former Jesuit college. Extending east from Křižovnická along Karlova over to Mariánské náměstí, the Klementinum's formidable combination of Renaissance, baroque and neoclassical styles covers an area second only to Prague Castle.

Founded by the Jesuits in 1556 to counter the Hussite influence, it now houses the National Library. Besides special exhibitions of library manuscripts,

Betlémské kaple (Bethelehem Chapel), where Jan Hus preached before his martyrdom

Caught in the Act

Less subtle than the Church of sv Jakub's treasures, but a great crowd-pleaser, are the remains of a human forearm (best seen with binoculars) suspended high up on the west wall. The story goes that it was chopped off a thief who got his hand stuck while trying to steal the Madonna's jewels at the high altar – 400 years ago.

two architectural gems are open to the public: the 18th-century **Zrcadlová kaple** (Chapel of Mirrors) during chamber music recitals, and the splendid **Baroque Library Hall** (1727) on guided tours. The **Astronomical Tower**, at the very heart of the complex, has been recording the weather since 1775.

🔲 195 D4 ✉ Karlova (entrance next to church of St Clement) ⚙ Baroque Library Hall: Mon–Fri 2–7, Sat–Sun 10–7, May–Oct; Mon–Fri 2–6, Sat–Sun 11–6, Mar, Apr, Nov, Dec; Astronomical Tower: Mon–Fri 7 pm–8 pm, Sat–Sun 10–8
🚇 Staroměstská

7 Around Mariánské náměstí

Leading up to Mariánské náměstí (Mariánské Square) from the Klem-entinum stands the dům U zlaté studné (House of the Golden Well). This charming Renaissance corner house has bow windows and Ulrich Meyer's baroque stucco sculptures added by the owner in 1701. Saints Sebastian and Roch have an honoured place on the first floor for having, as the owner believed, saved

After 100 years as a warehouse, the Church of St Nicholas is once more a place of worship

him from the plague. (In Christian tradition, the saints are considered as protectors against the plague.)

Besides offering an uncluttered view of the Klementinum, Mariánské náměstí has on its east side the **Nová radnice** (New Town Hall), a stark, late Secessionist work (1910) by Osvald Polívka, a principal architect of the more ornate Obecní dům (Municipal House, ► 138). There is something hypnotically grim about the town hall's corner statues by Ladislav Šaloun – a fierce-looking Iron Knight, patron of the town's armour-ers, and an otherworldly Rabbi Loew, the Jewish community's great 16th-century sage (► 8).

🔲 195 E4 🚇 Staroměstská

8 Church of sv Mikuláš (St Nicholas)

German merchants established the first church of St Nicholas on Old Town Square in the 12th century, using it as a community centre until

the Old Town Hall was built. In 1620, Benedictine monks took it over and subsequently replaced it with the present church. The monastery was closed in 1787 and the church used as a warehouse until 1920. Ironically, the Czech Hussites – so opposed to the pomp of traditional Catholicism – chose this elaborate baroque structure as their main church in Prague rather than the more austere Gothic Týn Church across the square (► 60–62).

It was built in 1735 by Kilián Ignác Dienzenhofer, whose father Kryštof had designed the St Nicholas Church of Malá Strana (► 96). Because of houses once hemming in the church on three sides (removed by slum clearance in the 1890s), the architect gave the main twin-towered façade a southern rather than more conventional western exposure.

The decoration of the lofty interior includes frescoes by Bavarian artist Cosmas Damian Asam of St Nicholas and St Benedict on the arch of the cupola. The painting of the Virgin Mary on the altar is 20th century.

🔲 195 E4 ⊠ Staroměstské náměstí 🔘 Staroměstská

🔟 Dům U zlatého prestenů (House of the Golden Ring)

The Prague City Gallery (also known by its old name Dům U zlatého prestenů, from the Golden Ring emblem it once had) has premises all over town and uses this fine 13th-century mansion for its collections of Czech 20th-century art. Presented on three floors in constantly changing exhibitions, the collections include

Sv Jakub's baroque doorway gives a fore-taste of its ornate interior

symbolists (Bílek and Švabinsky), cubists (Filla and the aptly named Kubišta), realists (Čapek, Zrzavý) and surrealists (Teige, Štyrský) and more recent conceptual artists. Shows of avant garde contemporary works are held in the Gothic-vaulted cellars.

🔲 195 F4 ⊠ Ungelt, Tynská 6
☎ 224 827 022; www.ghmp.cz
🕐 Tue–Sun 10–6 🔘 Náměstí
Republiky 🚊 5, 8, 14 💲 Moderate;
free first Tue of the month

🔟 Church of sv Jakub

The impact of this 14th-century Church of St James, tucked away east of Ungelt, is wonderfully rich and subtle. Total reconstruction in exuberant baroque style after a fire in 1689 does not conceal the church's fundamentally Gothic character. The subdued light, lofty

Getting Lost Around Husova Třída

South of Karlova Street's all too modern tourist traps, the medieval Prague of labyrinthine lanes, cobbled alleys, vaulted passages and cul-de-sacs comes into its own. It is perfectly safe, even desirable, to lose your way here, particularly at night, the best time to go, when the crowds have disappeared and only you and the fabled ghosts walk the streets. You can always scamper back to the safe haven of restaurants and taverns on Husova Street running through the middle of the maze.

Daytime visitors may stumble on such landmarks as the venerable Romanesque **dům U Čapků** (Stork House, on Retězová), now a small museum commemorating the Hussite hero George of Poděbrady, who lived there until he was crowned King of Bohemia in 1458 (► 61) (Retězová 3, open daily 11–6, May–Sep; inexpensive); and the 14th-century Gothic **Church of sv Jiljí** (St Giles, on Husova Street), remodelled on baroque lines in 1733 with fine trompe-l'oeil ceiling frescoes inside.

and narrow nave and extended choir make a delicate counterpoint to the elaborate sculpture and effusive paintings of the altars.

Its acoustics make it an ideal venue for concerts and organ recitals. Reiner's impressive *Martyrdom of St James* adorns the main altar, but the church's undoubted outstanding masterpiece, in the north aisle, is the **tomb of Count Mitrovice** (1714) designed by the great Austrian baroque architect Johann Bernhard Fischer von Erlach and carved by Prague sculptor Ferdinand Maximilian Brokof.

➕ 195 F4
✉ Malá Štupartská
☎ 224 828 816
🚇 Náměstí Republiky 🚊 5, 8, 14

🅱 Celetná ulice

Old Town's most elegant shopping street is an ancient thoroughfare, once

the main medieval trade route between Old Town Square and eastern Europe via the Prašná brána (Powder Gate, ► 152). It was also the beginning of the *Králova Cesta* (Royal Route) for kings' coronation processions to Prague Castle.

Elegant Celetná Street (ulice) winds its way prettily into the old city centre

The colourful baroque façades on originally Romanesque and Gothic houses have been beautifully restored, often with a handsome *pavlač* (balconied courtyard). On the south side of the street, at No 22, look out for the **U Supa** (At the Vulture), a pub installed in one of the street's finest houses. On the north side of the street, two theatres have their premises in historic houses at Nos 13 and 17.

On the corner of Ovocný trh, breaking but not clashing with the prevailing baroque style, the **Dům U černé Matky boží** (House of the Black Madonna, 1912 – Museum of Czech Cubist Art) is a powerful statement of Czech cubist architecture by Josef Gočar. Originally built as a department store, it is now a museum of Czech cubist art, and includes Gočar's superb furniture and porcelain, as well as paintings, sculpture and photographs of Prague's other Cubist buildings at Vyšehrad (➤ 151).

🕂 195 F4 ⊠ Dům U černé Matky boží (Museum of Czech Cubist Art), Ovocný trh 19 ☎ 224 301 003; www.ngprague.cz
🕙 Tue–Sun 10–6 🚇 Náměstí Republiky 🚊 5, 8, 14 💵 Inexpensive

🔟 Karolinum

The redbrick university building running along the north side of the Stavovské divadlo is reserved now for graduation ceremonies. After destruction by Nazi Germany in 1945, only a stone oriel window of the Gothic chapel remains from the original Karolinum founded here by Charles IV in 1348. It was the oldest German university – Vienna

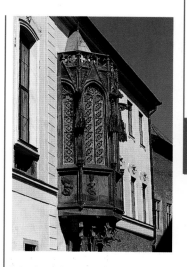

Only this Gothic chapel window survived from the ancient Karolinum University after World War II

and Heidelberg followed later in the same century. Like the town's churches and theatres, the university provided yet another focus for rivalries between the Czech- and German-speaking communities. In 1882, the university formally divided its teaching into separate and parallel faculties. At the end of World War II, the last German-speaking students were driven from the city.

🕂 195 F3 ⊠ Ovocný trh 3 🚇 Můstek

Where to...
Eat and Drink

Prices

Expect to pay per person for a meal, including drinks, tax and service
£ under 350Kč **££** 350–800Kč **£££** over 800Kč

RESTAURANTS

Albio £

Slowly but surely, Prague is catching up with other major European cities in its number of vegetarian restaurants. Albio offers healthy, delicious fare that vegetarians and meat-eaters alike can get excited about. On the menu are large, fresh salads, crispy vegetable stir-fries, innovative tofu and tempeh dishes, soups, organic trout and Norwegian salmon. There is also fresh Bernard beer on tap and several domestic organic wines.

🚹 198 B2 ⊠ Truhlářská 18–20, Nové Město ☎ 222 325 414; www.albiostyl.cz
🕐 Mon–Fri 10–10, Sat 1–10

Brasserie La Provence ££

The owners of this popular restaurant have done their homework, and it shows. This is an authentic Parisienne brasserie – except for the Czech waiters, that is – in every sense: from the old silvered mirrors and red leather booths to the stenciled "huitres" and "vins" on the front doors. The emphasis is on fresh seafood, but there are also

plenty of French favorites like rabbit, roast chicken, and quiche on offer. Half the fun here is gazing about the sparkling *belle epoque* room, or out the massive windows that encase this lovely corner restaurant.

🚹 195 F4 ⊠ Štupartská 9, Staré Město ☎ 257 535 050 🕐 Daily 11 am–1 am 🚇 Náměstí Republiky

Byblos £

Authentic Lebanese specialties, with a secondary menu of Italian favourites, all prepared competently by the generous kitchen in this restaurant just inside the doors of Prague's stock exchange. The regular clientele of Middle Eastern diplomats and journalists attests to this restaurant's authenticity. Many vegetarian options, good Czech wines by the glass, and entertainment by a belly dancer at weekends.

🚹 198 B2 ⊠ Burzovní palác, Rybna 14 (behind Kotva department store) ☎ 221 842 121; www.biblos.cz
🚇 Náměstí Republiky

Dinitz £

The kitchen turns out a delicious international menu of sophisticated but hearty food, with a Middle Eastern slant: crisp Lebanese salad, juicy beef bourguignon, earthy pasta fungi, and succulent pork skewers. Check out the "Jewish menu" for things like gravlax (smoked salmon carpaccio, cream cheese and home-made bread), which reflects the owner's heritage and excellent skills.

🚹 198 B2 ⊠ Na Poříčí 12, Staré Město ☎ 222 313 308; www.dinitz.cz
🕐 Mon–Fri 9 am–1 am, Sat–Sun 10–1 am 🚇 Náměstí Republiky

Don Giovanni £££

Big windows, big photos of Italian celebrities on the pink and white walls – it sounds brash, but the effect works, as does the Italian cuisine, which covers all the major regional specialities with a strong seafood bias. Italian diplomats have made this prime site near Karlův most (Charles Bridge, ► 52) their home from home.

🖅 195 D3 ⊠ Karoliny Světlé 34,
Staré Město ☎ 222 222 062
🕔 Daily 11 am–midnight

Klub Architektů £

Young people pack this stone-vaulted space beneath the Betlémské kaple (Bethlehem Chapel, ▶ 65). The menu offers Czech comfort food: *smažený sýr* (fried cheese), *smažený celer* (fried celery), and *zapečený kuřecí steak s broskví a sýrem* (chicken topped with melted cheese and peaches).

🖅 195 D3 ⊠ Betlémské náměstí 5a,
Staré Město ☎ 224 401 214
🕔 Daily 11:30 am–midnight

Mlynec £££

This is a place for a special meal, so make a reservation and prepare to be pampered. The chef is the only one in the country to receive the Michelin "Bibendum" distinction not once, but three times. Having the grilled monkfish, with sautéed cucumber, spring onion and tomato confit? The 1999 Chablis Mont de

Milieu Premier Cru would be perfect. In warm weather there is seating on the wrought-iron balcony, which looks onto the Charles Bridge.

🖅 195 D3 ⊠ Novotného lávka 9,
Staré Město ☎ 221 082 208;
www.zatisigroup.cz 🚇 Staroměstská

Da Nico Wine Bar and Restaurant £

The Czech-Italian owner of this intimate new wine bar-restaurant takes his cooking seriously, and the pleasure of his guests even more so. Don't be surprised too see him wander out of the kitchen to ask how you liked the risotto or squid-ink pasta, and then bring you something new to taste. The atmosphere is warm and welcoming. This is the kind of place where a meal may last all night, and end up with the chef sitting in the dining room, passing a bottle of grappa around the room.

🖅 195 F4 ⊠ Dlouhá 21 🕔 Mon–
Sun 11 am–1 am ☎ 222 311 807;
www.danico.cz 🚇 Náměstí Republiky

NoStress £

Occupying a corner where three streets converge like some grand sailing ship of old, NoStress is a French-Thai fusion restaurant with a chic interior design gallery tucked into the back. The Belgian chef sends out a variety of hot and cold appetizers, and main dishes like grilled duck breast with plums and fried potatoes, Thai spicy shrimp soup and codfish curry with jasmine rice. Desserts, like the orange and chocolate mousse opera cake, are sublime. There is a laid-back lounge area in the front for those who prefer their calories in liquid form.

🖅 195 E4 ⊠ Dušní 10 ☎ 222 317
007; www.nostress.cz 🕔 Daily
10 am–midnight 🚇 Staroměstská

Orange Moon £

Popadam or spring roll? You can have both in this handsome, two-level restaurant just steps from Old Town Square that serves a decidedly un-Czech menu of spicy Burmese,

Indian and Thai specialties. The curries are a local favorite, but all the stir-fries, soups, and seafood dishes are excellent.

🖅 195 F4 ⊠ Rámová 5, Staré Město
☎ 222 325 119; www.orangemoon.cz
🕔 Daily 11:30–11:30 🚇 Náměstí
Republiky

Palác Kinských £££

An inconspicuous entrance at the back of the National Gallery's main offices leads to this barrel-arched dining room that is lit sufficiently low for discreet conversation while at the same time feeling open and welcoming. An excellent wine list accompanies a menu offering both European and Czech dishes such as *kachna s červeným zelím a knedlíky* (roast duck with red cabbage and dumplings). Tourists, however, will most likely be shown an English menu. The wines can also be sampled at the proprietor's wine bar, **Sekt Bar**, at the front of the Kinsky Palace at 11 Staroměstské náměstí (Old Town Square).

⊞ 195 E4 ⊠ Tynská ulička 3 (off Tynská), Staré Město ☎ 224 810 750; www.palac-kinskych.cz ⊚ Mon–Sat noon–3, 6–11

Pizzeria Rugantino £

Pizza was a rarity in Prague until the changes of 1989 opened the door to more than just political freedom. The pizzas and salads are excellent in this big, busy place, which is popular with everyone from backpackers to local celebrities. Credit cards are not accepted .

⊞ 195 E5 ⊠ Dušní 4, Staré Město ☎ 222 318 172 ⊚ Mon–Sat 11–11, Sun 5–11

Rasoi ££–£££

Informal atmosphere, good service and the city's most authentic Indian cooking to date make this a popular choice – as mild or hot as you like. The same menu is available at lunch upstairs in the saloon-like Bombay Café, where you can also get South Indian "bar food" such as puri cakes to nibble with your Bombay G&T.

⊞ 195 F4 ⊠ Dlouhá 13, Staré Město ☎ Restaurant 222 328 400: Bombay Café 222 222 018 ⊚ Restaurant: daily 11:30–3:30; Bombay Café: daily 11 am–2 am

Ristorante Isabella £££

Celebrity chef Lars Sjöstrand has the king and queen of Sweden's stamp of approval on his ambitious Italian cooking. This cellar restaurant in the boutique Hotel Bellagio on a quiet street a few steps from the river serves some of the best meals in the city. Steak, seafood and pasta are Sjöstrand's specialties, and the Italian-only wine list is impressive and well-priced. Arnold Schwarzenegger, Václav Havel, and Isabella Rosselini have spent many enjoyable hours here.

⊞ 195 E5 ⊠ U Milosrdných 2, Staré Město ☎ 224 819 957; www.ristoranteisabella.cz ⊚ Náměstí Republiky

Rybí trh £££

Unlike the city's older riverside seafood restaurants, Rybí trh (which

means The Fish Market) lies inland amid the recently gentrified confines of the Tyn courtyard, off Staroměstské náměstí (Old Town Square, ▶ 61). A huge selection of seafood is available, some of it swimming in the aquaria scattered around. There are two sparsely decorated dining rooms at the courtyard level and also a brick-arched cellar below.

⊞ 195 F4 ⊠ Týnský Dvůr 5, Staré Město ☎ 224 895 447; www.rybitrh.cz ⊚ Daily 11 am–midnight

Yami £

Korean and Japanese cooking may not appear to have much in common, but the accomplished chefs at this serene Asian restaurant make the pairing of kimchi and smoked eel, or bimbibap and sashimi, work beautifully. Yami has quickly gained a reputation as the best sushi in town; can tables full of Japanese businessmen be wrong?

⊞ 195 F4 ⊠ Masná 3 ☎ 222 312 756 ⊚ Daily Noon–11:30 ⊚ Náměstí Republiky

V Zátiší £££

Winning so much praise and so many awards hasn't spoiled Zátiší, which still seems like an island amid a sea of touristy restaurants. The interior here is low-key elegance, the welcome is unstuffy and hospitable. There's nothing faddish about the cooking – just skilfully prepared European fare with enough Czech touches to remind you that, after all, you're in Prague's Old Town. The menu, like those at owner Sanjiv Suri's other city eateries, now features half a dozen fish dishes, depending on the day's "catch" of imported seafood. If you want local cuisine, try the Bohemian roast goose in honey-lavender sauce. Chocaholics rave over the *čokoládová pěna* (chocolate mousse).

⊞ 195 D3 ⊠ Liliová 1 (at Betlémské náměstí), Staré Město ☎ 222 221 155 ⊚ Daily noon–3, 5:30–11

out to one of Staré Město's newly renovated courtyards. Just a few things are on the menu, including some nice vegetarian dishes and good deserts, like *bábovka* (chocolate cake).

➕ 195 D3 ⊠ Bartolomějská 11, Staré Město ☎ 224 232 427 ⓦ Mon–Fri 9 am–midnight, Sat–Sun 11–midnight

Grand Café Praha

Named after Franz Kafka's girlfriend, this café is run by the Franz Kafka Society, and boasts a spectacular view out onto the Astronomical Clock (▶ 57). The large picture windows put diners directly at eye level with the world-famous figurines, so while the crowds below are jostling for space for the best view, you'll be calmly sipping an espresso and enjoying a private show.

➕ 195 E4 ⊠ Staroměstské náměstí 22 ☎ 221 632 520; www.grandcafe.cz ⓦ Daily 8 am–11 pm

PUBS AND BARS

Bar and Books

The red walls, floor-to-ceiling bookcases, leather banquettes and lots of dark wood create a sophisticated vibe. Not a place for the cigar-phobic: stogies are complimentary for women on Fridays.

➕ 195 E4 ⊠ Týnská 19 ☎ 224 808 250; www.barandbooks.net ⓦ Mon–Fri 2 pm–4 am, Sat 6 pm–4 am, Sun 6 pm–3 am ⓜ Náměstí Republiky

Meloun

The cellar bar at this eclectic music/dance club, attracts more locals than is usual in the heart of the Old Town because it is relatively inexpensive and doesn't tend to go for the tourist crowd. The interior is old, vaulted and brick-lined, more intimate than a typical pub. There's no food, just a short drinks list and beers.

➕ 195 E3 ⊠ Michalská 12, Staré Město ☎ 224 230 127 ⓦ Daily 11 am–midnight

Tretter's

A hangout of visiting movie stars, Tretter's has taken great pains to recreate the swanky feel of a Big Apple cocktail bar during the swing era. Leather booths, candlelight, dark wood tables and black and white photos of singers and movie stars create a sexy atmosphere.

➕ 198 2A ⊠ V Kolkovně 3, Staré Město ☎ 224 811 165; www.tretters.cz ⓦ Daily 7 pm–3 am

U Medvídků

A famous beer hall where the taps dispense a river of mild Budvar from South Bohemia (▶ 25) and there is a well-prepared menu of Czech specialities to soak it all up.

➕ 195 E3 ⊠ Na Perštýně 7, Staré Město ☎ 224 220 930 ⓦ Mon–Sat 11–11, Sun noon–10

U Špirků

At this no-nonsense pub, the house beverage is biting Krušovice – one of the last few big domestic brewers that's still Czech-owned (▶ 24).

➕ 195 E3 ⊠ Kožná 12, Staré Město ☎ 224 238 420 ⓦ Daily 11 am–midnight

U Vejvodů

A former smoky, ancient pub has emerged from reconstruction as a skylit Pilsner palace where visitors won't feel intimidated and locals appreciate the affordable prices.

➕ 195 E3 ⊠ Jilská 4, Staré Město ☎ 224 219 205; www.uvejvodu.cz ⓦ Sun–Thu 11 am–midnight, Fri–Sat 11 am–2 am

CAFÉS AND TEA ROOMS

The resurgence of Prague's café scene (▶ 43) is nowhere more visible than in Staré Město, where delightful coffee houses and tea rooms are dotted about in the winding lanes.

Café Konvikt

Popular with a young, trendy crowd, this inexpensive gathering place has a lofty room with views

Café de Paris

If Obecní dům's (Municipal House, ▶ 138–139) huge café is full on a summer's afternoon, you can often find a seat at this small, equally genuine art nouveau coffee house across the street. Light, international dishes are available, such as pasta, Caesar salad and bagel sandwiches.

+ 195 F4 ☒ Ungelt 2, Staré Město ☎ 224 895 788 ⓖ Daily 9 am–10 pm

Country Life

Dishes at this self-service vegetarian café/healthfood shop are made with only plant-based, and no animal or dairy, products. There are soups, a salad bar, grains and rice, tofu, veggie burgers and fesh juices.

+ 195 E4 ☒ Melantrichova 15, Staré Město ☎ 224 213 366 ⓖ Mon–Thu 9–8, Sun 9–6; closed Sat

Ebel Coffee House

Aromas of freshest coffee emanate from this comfortable, American-style coffee spot for java, bagels and cakes.

The interior is simple, with wooden chairs and small tables, and cases displaying coffee beans and bagels for sale, as well as local Czech and English-language papers to read. The cakes include American brownies and chocolate-chip cookies.

+ 195 F4 ☒ Ungelt 2, Staré Město ☎ 224 895 788 ⓖ Daily 9 am–10 pm

Kavárna Slavia/Café Slavia

The art deco Café Slavia has welcomed just about every notable Prague writer, musician and actor over the past century. You can order the fabled artist's tipple, absinthe, here (it's distilled in the Czech Republic) and examine the haunted devotee of the liqueur staring out from the painting at the far end of the room. Otherwise there's coffees, wine, beer and light meals, including Czech standbys such as *toasty* (toast topped with various meats).

+ 195 D2 ☒ Smetanova nábřeží (at Národní třída), Staré Město ☎ 224 220 957; www.cafeslavia.cz ⓖ Daily 9 am–11 pm

Where to...
Shop

The best way to find the best shopping in Staré Město is to get lost! If it's sold in Prague you'll find it somewhere in this modern-day medieval carnival. The trick is to take your time and enjoy the hunt. In general, prices are far lower than in the West and you can find anything from toiletries to Soviet army medals.

The best thing to do is to venture away from the packed Royal Route (▶ 174–177) and wander amid the alleyways and passages. This way you'll not only escape the crowds, but also come across countless little boutiques, engrossing second-hand bookshops and aromatic bakeries.

For centuries the irre plaza of Staroměstské Town Square) has for and commercial hear

As it's also the focal point ror tou groups and trinket sellers, you may find more attractive shopping opportunities along any of the streets that fan out from the square in all directions.

Fashion

The narrow lane called Tynská, that runs alongside the majestic Tyn church, leads towards Tyn, also known as Ungelt, once decrepit and now a lavishly remodelled Renaissance courtyard turned shopping mall (▶ 60).

In the courtyard, Ivana Follová Art and Fashion (Tyn 1) has locally made jewellery, artworks and women's silk clothing.

Fashion boutiques dot the streets behind Obecní dům (Municipal House, ▶ 138–139).

There's also the department store Kotva at Náměstí Republiky 8.

Two tiny lingerie shops are next door: Dessous Dessous and Judita & Justyna (both at Králodvorská 7).

Look for youthful, but not too radical, women's fashions by a Czech designer at Klára Nademlynská (Dlouhá 7) boutique.

The first street leading off Dlouhá to the left is Dušní, where Boutique Tatiana (Dušní 1) has evening dresses and sophisticated suits.

Books, prints and maps

Anagram Books, in the Ungelt courtyard, stocks history, art, literature and cook books. Antikvariát Ptolomaeus, at Široká 15, has gorgeous old maps, prints and globes. Antik v Dlouhé (Dlouhá 37) has an eclectic mix of items from the 18th and 19th centuries, from clocks to lamps and jewellery. Visit the Prague branch of the Dorotheum auction house, at Ovocny trh 2, for exquisite antique paintings, furniture, and jewellery from all over the region.

General and gifts

On Celetna street, off Staroměstské náměstí, Cristallano (No 12) and Celetná Crystal (No 15) sell crystal, glasswear, garnets and jewellery. Manufaktura, at Melantrichova 17, has lovely Czech-made ceramics, kitchen items, ornaments, and home decor items. Botanicus, in the Ungelt courtyard behind Týn Church, has items made, grown or bottled on an organic farm outside Prague: candles, soaps, specialty oils, vinegars and spices. Next door is Marionety Obchod pod lampou which sells fantastic hand-carved wooden puppets and marionettes. Dr Stuart's Botanicus sells Czech-made gifts such as oils, herb vinegars and hand-made paper.

There's a fascinating curiosity shop, Bric à Brac, in two buildings; one at Tynská 7 and the other behind it in a nameless courtyard.

Just off Dlouhá, Bake Shop Praha (V Kolkovně 4) sells wonderful breads and pastries.

There are two shops worth seek-ing out on Dlouhá: Sejto (No 24) sells linen, silk and cotton textiles (pillows, table-cloths, napkins) screen printed by Czech artists. Bohemia Granat Jewellery (No 28) has silver and gold Bohemian garnet jewellery at factory prices.

A few streets over, Galerie Jakubská (Jakubská 4) exhibits and sells "New Impressionist" paintings by Central and Eastern European artists.

TOWARDS KARLŮV MOST

Antiques

Antique Alma (Valentinská 7) has everything from dolls to furniture, and even a wine bar.

General and gifts

Carefully browse through the hip, angular glassware and accessories by designer Borek Sípek at Arzenal (Valentinská 11). Silk Road, at Kaprova 13, has dazzling home decor items. Next door is Lush, with balms and body ointments.

Towards Nové Město (New Town), look for high-quality contemporary art glass at Galerie Mozart (Uhelný trh 11/Národní třída 73).

For second-hand Eastern European cameras and binoculars, try BS Foto (Betlémské náměstí 7).

Books

The city's best-known antiquarian bookshop, the refined Antikvariát U Karlova mostu, is at Karlova 2.

Art galleries

Three of the best fine art galleries lie on or not too far from quiet little Betlémské náměstí.

Galerie JBK (Betlémské náměstí 8) features works by renowned collage artist Jiří Kolář and other prominent Czech artists.

Nearby Galerie Pallas (Na Perstyně 12) is full of high-quality Czech paintings, and not far away is the Galerie Peithner-Lichtenfels (Michalská 12), which sells high-quality work in all media by leading 20th-century Czech artists.

Where to…
Be Entertained

Jazz in an 800-year-old cellar, a chamber concert amid the luscious statuary of a baroque church, opera "sung" by lifelike marionettes…Staré Město's entertainment is in keeping with its medieval streets and historic architecture.

THEATRE

Divadlo Na Zábradlí

The tiny stage at this influential playhouse ("Theatre on the Balustrade") earned its fame not only for Václav Havel's dramatic works in the 1960s, but also for ground-breaking interpretations of classic and modern drama.

 199 D3 Anenské náměstí 5, Staré Město 222 868 868

Národní divadlo marionet (National Marionette Theatre)

This entertainment for adults and children alike wins kudos for keeping alive the venerable Czech art of puppet opera. *Don Giovanni* has played here since 1991. Younger kids enjoy the antics too, but may get fidgety by the third act.

 199 E4 Žatecká 1, Staré Město 224 819 322; www.mozart.cz

MUSIC

Classical
Klementinum

The lavish 18th-century Chapel of Mirrors is the setting for some memorable chamber music recitals.

 195 D4 Karlova (next to church of St Clement) 272 766 902

Contemporary and jazz
Jazz Club U Staré paní

"The Old Lady" came along in a wave of new jazz and blues clubs in the mid-1990s, and is one of the best for local mainstream bands.

 199 E3 Michalská 9, Staré Město 603 551 680

Reduta

The oldest music club in Prague offers a mix of modern, fusion, Latin, and trumpet jazz.

 195 E2 Národní 20, Nové Město 224 933 487

Roxy

This arts centre provides performance space for top DJs and stars of world music.

 199 E4 Dlouhá 33, Staré Město 224 826 296

Opera
Stavovské divadlo

Buy a ticket for whatever is on at the beautiful Estates Theatre (➤ 63) – the oldest theatre building in Prague – and marvel at the hall where Mozart conducted the first performance of *Don Giovanni*.

The excellent Národní divadlo (National Theatre) opera company (➤ 145) does a couple of Mozart's (as well as Czech and other international) operas in repertory. The box office is across from the back of the theatre in the Kolowrat Palace. Mozart operas aimed at a tourist audience are staged during the summer.

 199 F3 Ovocny trh 1, Staré Město 224 901 448

Blacklight Theatres

Most of this type of theatre is in Staré Město. See page 46 for a description of blacklight theatre, and **Laterna Magika** (➤ 160).

All Colours Theatre (the long-runner here is *Faust*), Rytiřská 31, Staré Město; tel: 221 610 170.

Cerné divadlo image, Pařižská 4, Staré Město; tel: 222 329 191.

Hradčany,
Malá Strana
and Beyond

Getting Your Bearings

Dominating the Vltava River's left bank is the sprawling castle complex and great Gothic cathedral within its walls. Baroque mansions and palaces, many with beautiful gardens, are now embassies, museums, pubs and smart restaurants. Beyond them, bourgeois and working-class neighbourhoods have their share of monuments, revealing the traces, precious and otherwise, left by Mozart and Joseph Stalin.

Hradčany is Prague Castle's neighbourhood. Made a township in the 16th century, it covers the monumental precinct within the castle walls and surrounding gardens, as well as the palaces to the west around Hradčanské náměstí (Castle Square).

Malá Strana (literally "Little Side", as opposed to the bigger right-bank districts) is the old aristocratic district running south of the castle, including the island of Kampa. Its largely unspoiled 18th-century architecture brought Miloš Forman back to his home-town to shoot the film *Amadeus*, his life story of Mozart, in an urban landscape more "Viennese" than Vienna itself. The area includes the wooded park on Petřín Hill.

Further south, Smíchov is a rather ungainly neighbourhood with the saving grace of the Mozart Museum and chamber music concerts at Villa Bertramka.

North and east of the castle are the districts of Bubeneč, Letná and Holešovice, with a modern art museum, a couple of rare relics of the Communist era, and the Metronome (with great views).

Preceding page: A view of Malá Strana and the castle across the Vltava River

Loreta **13**

LORETÁNSKÁ

POHOŘELEC

Strahovský klášter **14**

Strahovská zahrada

15 TROJA
Trojský zámek

Stromovka

DEJVICE BUBENEČ

Veletržní palác **16**

Pražský hrad

JOSEFOV

HRADČANY

Petřín **17**

Strahovský stadion

MALÁ STRANA

Villa Bertramka **18**

0   2 km

0   1 mile

Pražský hrad and Malá Strana bring you to kings on one day and music on the other.

Around Prague Castle and Malá Strana in Two Days

Day One

Morning

Start at **Pražský hrad** (Prague Castle, ➤ 82–85) and visit the main sights – the Old Royal Palace, **St Vitus Cathedral** (➤ 89–91) and **sv Jiří (St George) Basilica** (➤ 100) but save Zlatá ulička (Golden Lane) for an uncrowded visit at the end of the day. Then head for **Malostranské náměstí** (Malá Strana Square, ➤ 95–96) and stroll around the square before visiting the **Church of sv Mikuláš** (St Nicholas Church, left) on the square (➤ 96).

Afternoon

After lunch there's a quick photo-op for Europe's jolliest **Changing of the Castle Guard** (every hour, below) and then relax in **Královská zahrada** (Castle Gardens, ➤ 93) and take in the great views of castle and cathedral from the belvedere's terrace. Head back down to Malostranské náměstí

(Malá Strana Squa...
Then try U hrocha...
Thunovská, an old...
Czech customers...
time to go back to explore the
castle's twilight zone around **Zlatá
ulička** (Golden Lane, ➤ 86–88).

Day Two

Morning
Start the day at **Kampa Island**
(➤ 101) and enjoy a coffee at
eclectic Tato kojkej (➤ 108). On
your way to Strahov Monastery
take a look at **Maltézské náměstí**
(➤ 100) and the **Panna Marie
Vítězná church** (➤ 101). Then
take tram 22 or 23 to Pohořelec
to visit the two beautiful libraries
of **Strahovský klášter** (Strahov
Monastery, left, ➤ 97–98). For
lunch, try the Hradčany restaurant at the Savoy Hotel (➤ 41).

Afternoon
Have a wander round and ride the scenic funicular railway to the top of
Petřín Hill (➤ 104), where there is an observation tower and botanical
gardens. At the bottom of the hill on Újezd Street take tram No 9 to
Bertramka. At the **Villa Bertramka** (➤ 99), you can have tea or coffee in
the courtyard café before the Mozart recital at 5 pm, or visit the museum
and garden. Restaurants are scarce in this part of town, so take tram
No 9 back to Újezd for a meal at Nebozízek (➤ 105).

0

Pražský hrad
(Prague Castle)

The romantic hilltop silhouette beckons wherever you go. Beyond the cool neoclassical façades rise the Gothic spires of St Vitus Cathedral (► 89–91) – enclosed within the castle precincts as the Church was clasped by kings and emperors to support their often precarious power. To wander through the courtyards and palace halls of Prague Castle is to revisit the theatre of Prague's history.

The *hrad*, as the castle is commonly known, has remained the traditional symbol of state power. Kings were crowned here and presidents sworn in. From a first-floor window, Hitler proclaimed the Protectorate of Bohemia and Moravia in 1939. Communist Party bosses kept the people out and President Václav Havel invited them in, for a huge beer-party in 1990.

The first fortress, built in 870 by Duke Bořivoj, was little more than a massive log cabin. Defences of giant wooden beams, earthworks and natural ravines for moats were replaced by stone ramparts in the 11th century. Soběslav I's Romanesque castle of 1135 survives as the "basement" of the largely Gothic and Renaissance Starý královský palác (Old Royal Palace). In 1598, the *hrad* formally assumed its status as Prague's third township (after Old Town and New Town), embracing palaces, churches, chapels, gardens (► 92), aristocratic mansions, even artisans' cottages and workshops in the famous Zlatá ulička (Golden Lane, ► 86–88). Abandoned in the Thirty Years' War (1618–1648), it was given its neoclassical facelift by Empress Maria Theresa in the mid-18th century.

First and Second Courtyards

Flanking the main entrance are modern copies of Ignaz Platzer's two *Conquering Giants* designed in 1768. At the rear of the first courtyard is the **Matyášova brána** (Matthias Gate), a triumphal arch of 1614 now incorporated in the 18th-century neoclassical structure. In the second courtyard to the right is the **Presidential Palace**, with off-limits offices and residential quarters.

To the left are the **Španělský sál** (Spanish Hall) and **Rudolfova galerie** (Rudolf Gallery), 17th-century halls renovated with great neorococo pomp for the aborted

Prague Castle reigns supreme over the Charles River's left bank

Changing of the Guard

If the ceremony of the platoon "guarding" the castle seems faintly comic, it's not wholly unintentional. After Habsburg formality and the grey ritual of the Communists, President Havel gave the show some humour and life: the sentries' blue uniforms, tailored by the Oscar-winning costume designer for *Amadeus*, and a new fanfare for the big noon parade composed by rock musician Michal Kocáb.

Malá Strana Gardens

The rococo terraced palace gardens on the hillside sloping down from Prague Castle have been beautifully restored. With their ornate balustrades, fountains, loggias and arcades, they offer delightful walks and views over Malá Strana and across the Vltava River. They are also magical settings in summer for open-air concerts. Most spectacular is the strictly geometric **Valdštejnská zahrada**, garden of the Wallenstein Palace, with a masterly 17th-century loggia by Giovanni Pieroni, bronze statues by Adriaen de Vries (copies; the originals were looted by the Swedes in 1648) and a posse of peacocks in the aviary. (The palace itself is open only for occasional concerts.) More intimate but just as attractive are the three adjacent **Kolovratská, Ledeburská** and **Pálffyovská** gardens. Entrance: Valdštejnské náměstí 3; open daily Apr–Oct; inexpensive).

coronation of Franz-Josef as King of Bohemia. They open to the public for Prague Spring concerts (➤ 46), otherwise only for official state occasions.

Obrazárna Pražského hradu (Prague Castle Picture Gallery)

On the second courtyard's north side, the gallery exhibits a remnant of the castle's once great art collection; the rest was looted in the Thirty Years' War or carried off by the Habsburgs to palaces in Vienna and Madrid. Among surviving gems are works by Veronese, Tintoretto, Rubens, Cranach and Holbein. Temporary exhibitions are held in the adjacent **Císařská konírna** (Imperial Stables).

Starý královský palác (Old Royal Palace)

The third courtyard, entrance to the home of Bohemia's kings from the 12th to 16th centuries, is on the third floor. Its main feature is the bare but magnificently rib-vaulted **Vladislavský sál** (Vladislav Hall). Completed in 1502, the flamboyant Gothic hall provided a grand setting for the kings' election (by their peers) and, since 1918, the swearing-in of presidents. It was also used for banquets and jousting tournaments, with horses cantering up the ramp of the **Rider's Staircase** on the north side. The intricate rib-vaulting in both hall and staircase transforms the massive stone walls into an arbour of intertwining vines. East of the hall, a spiral staircase leads to a terrace overlooking the city. In the south-west corner, stairs lead down to the Ludvík Wing and the Bohemian Chancellery from where the king's governors were defenestrated in 1618 (➤ 18–19). Two obelisks in the garden moat below mark the spot where they fell.

A spiral staircase in the Old Royal Palace

Vladislav Hall, big enough for jousting tournaments

TAKING A BREAK

The (usually) quietest of many reasonably priced open-air cafés within the castle grounds is tucked away in the northwest corner's **Zahrada na baště** (Garden on the Bastion) to the left of the main entrance as you come in.

➕ 194 A4 ✉ Hradčanské náměstí, Praha 1 ☎ Prague Castle Information Centre tel: 224 373 368; www.hrad.cz 🕐 Castle grounds: 5 am–midnight, Apr–Oct, ticketed areas 9–5; 6 am–11 pm, ticketed areas 9–4, Nov–Mar 🚇 Malostranská 🚊 22, 23 to Pražsky hrad 💲 Grounds: free; buildings/museum: collections moderate

PRAŽSKÝ HRAD: INSIDE INFO

Top tips All approaches involve a fair **walk**.
• For great **views** of the castle above and city below, take Zámecké schody (Castle Staircase) from Nerudova Street (► 102) to the front gate.
• From Malostranská Metro station, Staré zámecké schody (Old Castle Staircase) is a **steep climb** to the rear entrance.
• Changing of the Guard and access to the castle grounds, streets, gardens, plus the cathedral nave (► 90) are **free**. The Information Office in the third courtyard opposite the cathedral sells a ticket (350Kč/175Kč concessions), valid for two days) for the Daliborka Tower, cathedral chancel, ambulatory and crypt, Starý královský palác (Old Royal Palace) and the Basilica of sv Jiří (St George Basilica, ► 100). English-language audio guide costs an extra 100Kč.
• **Separate tickets** (70–100Kč) are necessary for exhibitions at the Obrazárna Pražského hradu (Prague Castle Picture Gallery), Císařská konírna (Imperial Stables), klášter sv Jiří (St George Convent, ► 100) and Lobkovický palác (► 32).

Two to miss Uninformative displays of second-rate collections make the **Muzeum hraček** (Toy Museum) and **Lobcovický palác** (despite replicas of the Bohemian crown jewels) possibles to miss.

2

Zlata ulička
(Golden Lane)

This legendary little street of alchemists, archers, paupers, peddlers and poets squatting in its tiny houses, is best seen not bathed in broad daylight but shrouded in the night's dim lamplight and shadow. The souvenir vendors have gone and the imagination is free to conjure up fantasies of the past.

The Facts...

The lane is tucked away in the castle's northeast corner, beyond klášter sv Jiří (St George Convent, ► 100). It has been here since the 16th century when poor shopkeepers and artisans fled a town fire to settle here. The artisans included goldbeaters, after whom the street was named Zlatnická (Golden Lane).

Today's stone cottages, some of them with an upper floor just 1m (3 feet) high, were erected only in the 18th century. Some 200 years later, the shopkeepers and artisans were joined by a couple of famous writers. In 1916, **Franz Kafka** came to work at night in his sister Ottla's cottage (No 22) and wrote six of his finest short stories. He described the lane in *The Castle* (► 31).

Zlata ulička, a street of legends within the castle precincts

Kafka came to this house to write some of his best work

Jaroslav Seifert lived here in 1929, writing some of the poems that were to win him a Nobel Prize, and in 1952, the Communist regime transformed the cottages into the gaily coloured souvenir shops and craftwork galleries you see today.

...and the Fantasy

It was the German Romantics of the 19th century who decided the artisans working in Golden Lane were alchemists seeking to turn lead into gold for Rudolf II. The emperor posted his guards there not to watch out for foreign enemies but, so legend has it, to make sure the alchemists did not shirk their duties. Hey presto, Zlata ulička became known in German as Alchimistengasse (Alchemist Lane).

But the Czechs also have their Golden Lane legends. One of the prison towers where shopkeepers sold their wares to captives was – and, of course, still is – haunted by the noble knight **Dalibor**, imprisoned for heading a peasant revolt in the 15th century. To fight the boredom of solitude, it is said he learned to play the violin; exquisitely beautiful laments were heard in Zlata ulička even after he had been executed. A pity to spoil a good story, but *housle*, the Czech word for violin, was prison slang for the torturer's rack. Apparently his moans of pain under torture can still be heard on moonlit nights – by some, anyway.

Right: A gable window on one of the artisans' attics

One of several Golden Lane houses promoting the legend of Dalibor

Prison Towers

At the west end of Zlata ulička, take the stairs at **No 24** to a covered walk leading west to the castle's main prison, **Bílá věž** (White Tower). The tower at the other end is the haunted **Daliborka** where Dalibor is said to have played the violin.

TAKING A BREAK

There's an **open-air café** in the courtyard between the Daliborka and Černá věž (Black Tower, not open to the public).

➕ 194 B5 ✉ Zlata ulička ☎ Castle information: 224 373 368
🕐 5 am–midnight, Apr–Oct; 6 am–11 pm, Nov–Mar 🚇 Malostranská 12, 22, 23 💷 Inexpensive

ZLATA ULIČKA: INSIDE INFO

Top tip The **alchemists** of Zlata ulička actually had laboratories in Vikářská, the lane between St Vitus Cathedral and Prašná věž (Powder Tower).

3

Katedrála sv Víta
(St Vitus Cathedral)

It is the steeples of this magnificent Gothic edifice that lend drama to the profile of Prague Castle. As the "parish church" of Bohemian kings and Habsburg emperors, it is the guardian of sacred treasures that were symbols of political struggles. Their architects, from France, Germany and Austria, have created a setting of appropriately regal grandeur. The present church was over 600 years in the making, and master builders completing the work after World War II were strikingly faithful to the original designs of the 14th century.

The cathedral's steeples display a mixture of styles – Gothic, Renaissance and baroque

The Long Haul

Work on the cathedral began in 1344, after Charles IV talked the pope, exiled in Avignon, into granting Prague the status of archdiocese and lending him his architect, Mathieu d'Arras. Mathieu died eight years later, but laid down a distinctively French groundplan derived from his work on Narbonne Cathedral. Immediately, German prodigy Peter Parléř, 23 when he began, came in to give the church its bold Late Flamboyant Gothic character, carried on by his sons until construction was halted by the Hussite troubles of 1420. Successors added incongruous Renaissance and baroque touches until 19th- and 20th-century builders returned to the original plans to complete the church in its Late Gothic form.

The church was officially finished in 1929 for the 1,000th anniversary of the death of St Václav (Wenceslas), the nation's patron saint, but work continued for another 20 years.

Left: A Venetian mosaic over the Zlata brána (Golden Gate)

Exterior
The body of the church is like a huge inverted vessel with flying buttresses and steeply sloping diamond-patterned roof. On the **western façade**, with its three bronze doors, are slender towers flanking a broad rose window over the central portal. Before going inside, pass through to the castle's third courtyard to see the cathedral's spectacular south side. Here, Parléř's great Gothic **South Tower**, 96m (315 feet), is spoiled only at a distance by its baroque onion-bulb dome added in 1770.

To the right of the tower, the German's splendid **Zlata brána** (Golden Gate, 1367), originally the main entrance, is decorated with a Venetian mosaic depicting *The Last Judgment*. Notice, too, the open stone tracery of a spiral staircase on the gate's right wall. With elegant flying buttresses on five polygonal chapels, the **chancel** at the rear is the admirable, very French legacy of Mathieu d'Arras.

Above: A crucifixion carved over the door in the western façade

Interior
There is a striking lofty spaciousness to the nave, colourfully illuminated by the modern stained-glass windows (Parléř had specified clear glass). Fans of art nouveau painter **Alfons Mucha** (► 140) will want to see his 1931 window of *Cyril and Methodius* (Greek Christian missionaries to Bohemia) in the third chapel on the north wall.

The cathedral's most cherished treasure is Parléř's opulently decorated **Chapel of sv Václav** (St Wenceslas) off the south transept. Charles IV wanted this glorification of the country's patron saint to strengthen his fragile hold on the Bohemian crown. Over the site of the saint's grave, he had Parléř design a square gilded chapel bejewelled with jasper, amethyst and blue chalcedony to evoke the New Jerusalem of the Book of Revelations: "four-square – pure

Why St Vitus?
Duke, later Saint, Václav built the first church here in 926 on the site of a shrine to the four-headed Slavic fertility god Svantovit. The church's dedication to St Vitus – *svatý Vít* in Czech – was apparently intended to win over local heathens to the new Christian cult being installed here. Latterday pagans still leave flowers and fruit outside the church to invoke Svantovit's help in having a baby. (St Vitus was a 4th-century martyr invoked against convulsions – whence St Vitus' Dance – and patron saint of dancers and actors.)

KATEDRÁLA SV VÍTA: INSIDE INFO

Hidden gem Off the north aisle, the **Old Sacristy** is an absolute masterpiece of Peter Parléř's gravity-defying Gothic vaulting.

One to miss Crypts can be fun, but not the **Royal Crypt** near the Royal Oratory. The emperors, kings and queens deserved better than to be crammed into this modern restoration of the Romanesque burial chapel.

gold, like unto clear glass". The wall paintings depict episodes from St Václav's life (► 32) above scenes of Jesus Christ's Passion.

To visit the chapels and ambulatory in the **chancel**, you need the Prague Castle ticket. It's worth it. Parléř's intricate patterns of ridge vaulting here revolutionised Gothic design in Central Europe. In the ambulatory on the southeast corner, the extravagant baroque solid silver **Tomb of St John of Nepomuk** (1736) was part of the Jesuits' effort to counter the popular fervour aroused by the Chapel of sv Václav. On the tomb, one of the winged angels is pointing to what was once thought to be the saint's severed tongue (► 32).

South of the choir, the **Royal Oratory**, an elaborate design by Benedikt Ried, was built in 1490 for King Vladislav Jagiello and linked by covered passage to his bedroom in the Old Royal Palace (► 84).

TAKING A BREAK

There's an **outdoor café** in the courtyard at the rear of the church, serving simple snacks and drinks.

Below: The grandiose chapel of sv Václav (St Wenceslas)

🚩 194 A4 ✉ Pražský hrad (Prague Castle) 🕐 Daily 9–5, Apr–Oct; 9–4, Nov–Mar; Sun services only 9–noon 🚇 Malostranská 🚋 22, 23 🎫 Ambulatory, chancel, crypt: moderate (castle ticket); nave, Chapel of sv Václav: free

4

Castle Gardens

The gardens south and north of Pražský hrad (Prague Castle) are a delight both for their charm and for their great views of Prague and of the castle itself. Lovely as they are, the gardens are rarely crowded so they are also ideal for a quick siesta for weary sightseers.

South Gardens

The South Gardens are accessible from the castle via a modern copper-canopied staircase in the southeast corner of the third courtyard. In charge of 20th-century renovations, Slovene architect Josip Plečnik so designed the staircase that its balconies on the way down to the gardens look out in an absolutely straight line over St Nicholas Church of Malá Strana (➤ 96) across the river and down to Vyšehrad Castle (➤ 149).

Tranquillity from another century in the gardens of Prague Castle

Zahrada na valech (Garden on the Ramparts)

What was originally a single stretch of formal geometric baroque garden running the length of the castle's south façade has been re-landscaped as a charming, more varied little park. From the staircase, an esplanade leads across to a large semicircular observation terrace. In front of the Old Royal Palace (➤ 84) a monument marks the spot where the Defenestrated governors landed in 1618 (➤ 18). You will also see an Alpine arboretum, an aviary, pergola and other

Politically Correct

During his restoration work on the Míčovna pavilion in 1950, at the height of the Stalinist era, Pavel Janák added a nice touch to the row of allegorical figures flanking the sandstone pilasters. Between Peace and Justice, the fellow representing "Industry" is holding a hammer and sickle.

pavilions. At the west end, a piece of the baroque garden has been preserved with a sculpture of Samson at the centre of an 18th-century fountain.

Rajská zahrada (Paradise Garden)

Beyond the Samson Fountain, the smaller garden has at the centre of its immaculate green lawn a giant granite basin made from one monolithic slab. At the far end, a monumental staircase leads to Hradčanské náměstí (Castle Square, ➤ 102).

Královská zahrada (Royal Gardens)

These most luxuriant of the castle's gardens lie north of the hrad across the 16th-century Pražný most (Powder Bridge), accessible from the north gate

The entrance to Emperor Rudolf's indoor tennis court

of the castle's second courtyard. The bridge spans the **Jelení příkop** (Stag Moat), a broad wooded ditch in which the Habsburgs planted groves of lemon and fig trees and kept wild game for their hunts.

Across the street from the garden entrance is the 17th-century **Jízdárna** (Riding School), baroque but in simple, sober style, now an art gallery used for occasional exhibitions.

Created by Ferdinand I in 1534, the gardens have an appropriately regal air – fountains playing among impeccable green lawns surrounded by almond trees, azaleas and a spectacular spring display of tulips. Tulips made their appearance here in 1551 (some 10 years before the Dutch got hold of them), grown from Turkish seeds brought back by the Austrian ambassador to the Ottoman Court.

The veranda view across the Belvedere's garden terrace to the cathedral

On the south terrace is the 16th-century **Míčovna**, a Renaissance pavilion for Emperor Rudolf's real (royal) tennis court and now occasionally used for concerts. The façade is decorated with *sgraffiti* and a frieze of allegorical figures. In front is Matyáš Braun's sculpture of *The Night* (1734).

Best Vantage Points

Most of the Royal Gardens offer fine views of the castle, but the **Belvedere's garden terrace** is the best place from which to see the fortifications, Daliborka and White Towers (➤ 88), and above all, the north side and chancel of Katedrála sv Víta (St Vitus Cathedral, ➤ 89–91). You also get a great view over the bridges on the Vltava River.

To the right of the pavilion is a summer villa of the Czech president, Václav Havel, the **Zahradní dům** (Royal House), which is 18th century with some modern additions (unfortunately it is closed to the public).

At the east end of the gardens, the **Belvedere** is an exquisite example of pure Italian Renaissance style, probably the finest in Central Europe. Ferdinand I built this summer palace in 1537. In the middle of the garden terrace, a Renaissance *giardinetto*, is Francesco Terzio's **Zpívající fontána** (Singing Fountain, 1568). Its music can be heard as the water drips from one basin to the other.

TAKING A BREAK

Lví dvůr (Lion's Court) restaurant (➤ 179), at the entrance to the Royal Gardens, is housed in Rudolf II's private zoo, where the emperor heated the cages in wintertime for his beloved lynxes, leopards, lions and wolves. Today's restaurant guests are served at tables.

Top: Queen Anna never lived to enjoy the Belvedere, built for her by her husband Ferdinand Above: Mythological heroes on the Singing Fountain

➕ 194 B4/5 ✉ Pražský hrad ☎ 224 373 368 🕐 Daily Apr–Oct (Belvedere year-round) 🚇 South Gardens, Malostranská; Royal Gardens, Hradčanská 🚋 South Gardens, 12, 22, 23 Malostranské náměstí; Royal Gardens, 2, 8, 18 Pražný most 🎫 Free, except for concerts and exhibitions

CASTLE GARDENS: INSIDE INFO

Top tip Concerts and exhibitions in the gardens are usually inexpensive. For latest programmes check with the Information Centre in the third courtyard at Prague Castle (tel: 224 373 368).

6

Malostranské náměstí

(Malá Strana Square)

The bustling centre of public life in the Malá Strana district, this cobbled square is a major landmark on the Royal Route that brought Bohemia's kings from the Old Town across Charles Bridge up to their castle. In effect, the square is divided in two by the magnificent Church of sv Mikuláš (St Nicholas) Malá Strana.

A fire in 1541 destroyed the square's modest medieval houses, largely the homes of Protestants later expelled in the Thirty Years' War. Reasserting Catholic influence at the end of the 17th century, the Jesuits and their supporters at court began turning Malostranské náměstí into a triumphant spiritual fortress of the Counter-Reformation. They created the square's dramatic décor of predominantly neoclassical façades around an exultant baroque church adjoining what was then a Jesuit college.

Lichtenštejnský palác (Liechtenstein Palace)

Looking down on Malá Strana Square from St Nicholas church tower

Occupying the west side of the square, the Lichtenštejnský palác houses the university's music faculty, offering occasional concerts, exhibitions and a pleasant café. Its place in Prague's history is less agreeable. The palace's first owner was Karl von Liechtenstein, the Habsburgs' imperial governor who ordered

the execution of 27 Czech Protestants in 1621 (► 57). In 1648, it was occupied by commanders of the invading Swedish army who fought the last battle of the Thirty Years' War on Charles Bridge. Exactly 200 years later, it was the HQ of Austro-Hungarian Field Marshal Alfred Windisch-grätz, brought in to crush the Prague revolt of 1848.

Church of sv Mikuláš (St Nicholas) Malá Strana

As the centrepiece of Malá Strana, the 18th-century church is the finest jewel of Prague's many baroque monuments. Its blend of power and elegance can be seen in

The belfry and dome of St Nicholas hug each other like newlyweds

the gently curving western façade and the dome and bell-tower. The design was a family affair. Bavarian-born Kryštof Dienzenhofer built the façade and nave. His son, Kilián Ignác, began the nave ceiling, choir and dome in 1737, and the bell-tower was added in 1755 by Anselmo Lurago (Ignác's son-in-law).

The interior is a jubilant symphony of light and colour. The nave and choir are formed by a succession of ellipses and their arches, columns, larger-than-life sculptures and altars all carry the eye up to the ceiling frescoes. Above the nave is Johann Lukas Kracker's vast painting, *Apotheosis of St Nicholas*.

TAKING A BREAK

Among the many bars and cafés, the stylish **Square** is a decidedly chic place in which to stop and refuel. Facing out on to Malostranské náměstí, it has a big international menu and a late night bar. Alternatively, you can join the sophisticates at **St Nicholas Café** on nearby Tržiště Street.

➕ 194 B4 ✉ Malostranské náměstí 🕐 St Nicholas Church: 9–5, Apr–Sep; 9–4, Oct–Mar; bell-tower: 10–6, Apr–Oct; 10–5, Nov–Mar 🚇 Malostranská 🚋 12, 22 💶 St Nicholas Church: inexpensive; bell-tower: inexpensive

---

MALOSTRANSKÉ NÁMĚSTÍ: INSIDE INFO

Top tip Many of the patrician palaces surrounding the square have been converted into restaurants and Gothic-vaulted basement bars.

Hidden gem At the corner of Mostecká Street on the square's south side (No 1), the Renaissance **dům U petržílka** (Parsley House) has a fine example of a typical Prague *pavlač* (balconied courtyard).

14

Strahovský klášter
(Strahov Monastery)

Not one but two of the most beautiful libraries in Europe make this monastery stand out among Prague's great baroque monuments. Vladislav II had the monastery built in 1140, prompted by Moravian Bishop of Olomouc, Jindřich Zdík, and as testimony of its status as a scholarly institution, the libraries saved the monastery from dissolution by Emperor Joseph II in 1783. It was closed under the Communists, but monks are back in residence now and have revived the abbey church, refectories and gardens.

Vladislav II located the monastery on the road to Pražský hrad (Prague Castle) so that it doubled as a useful defensive outpost. It served the Premonstratensian order, whose founder, St Norbert (1080–1134), had placed study of the scriptures at the centre of monastic life.

At the entrance on the western edge of Hradčany, **St Norbert's statue** stands over the baroque gates (1742). Just inside the entrance, the small, late Renaissance parish **Church of St Roch** (1612) is an art gallery that shows temporary exhibitions of religious art.

Strahov's Philosophical Hall is a glorious architectural ode to wisdom

Across the courtyard is the 12th-century abbey-church, **Nanebezvetí Panny Marie** (Virgin Mary of the Assumption) transformed into its present baroque form in 1744. Vividly restored frescoes recount the life of St Norbert. Mozart played the organ here in 1787, creating his *Fantasy in G Minor*.

The Libraries

Upstairs, the first and bigger of the two libraries is the **Filosofický sál** (Philosophical Hall). It was built to house the collections – scientific and religious – of the Louka monastery library in Moravia, closed by Joseph II in the 1780s. Indeed its construction was dictated by the dimensions of Louka's magnificently carved floor-to-ceiling walnut bookcases. The ceiling frescoes (1794) by Austria's Franz Anton Maulbertsch are an allegorical tribute to humanity's *Quest For Truth*. Further examples of the quest for truth are displayed in the glass cabinets: ancient insects, dessicated marine life – turtles, lobsters and crabs – and two whale penises exhibited in a narwhal horn.

The bejewelled cover to the monastery's 9th-century New Testament

The older, low-ceilinged **Teologický sál** (Theological Hall) was built in 1671 to replace the library destroyed by the Swedish army. Looking down on the lecterns and globes of the world are Friar Siard Nosecký's frescoes proclaiming the superiority of divine wisdom over the wisdom of rational study.

The monastery's oldest and greatest treasure is the bejewelled 9th-century *Strahov Gospel* from the German School of Trier, its Latin text in gold lettering exhibited in a glass case in the corridor.

TAKING A BREAK

Stroll back to Loretánské náměstí for a hearty meal at **U Ševce Matouše** (► 106).

➕ 196 C1 ✉ Strahovské nádvoří 1/132, Praha 1 ☎ 233 107 711; libraries 233 107 708 🕐 Libraries: daily 9–12, 1–5 🚋 22/23 Pohořelec 💰 Inexpensive

---

STRAHOVSKÝ KLÁŠTER: INSIDE INFO

Hidden gem A door in the monastery's east wall leads to **Strahovská zahrada**, Strahov's gardens and orchards at the northern end of Petřín Hill (► 104). From here there is a fine panoramic view of the city.

One to miss After the splendours of the libraries – unless you're crazy about church gold, silver plate and reliquaries – the unimaginative **Strahovská obrazárna** (Strahov Gallery) over the cloisters is not worth the entrance fee.

18

Villa Bertramka

In an industrial district with traffic roaring by, some greenery remains to remind you that the place where Mozart added the finishing touches to his opera *Don Giovanni* (➤ 21) was once a charming house in the country. It has been lovingly restored to something like the haven of peace it was in 1787. A recital here of Mozart's chamber music is one of the more delightful moments Prague has to offer.

Tonight, Josefina?

Hostess Josefina Dušek, 20 years younger than her husband, was only two years older than Wolfgang Amadeus. They flirted outrageously and Mozart composed a concert aria for her: *Bella mia fiamma, addio* ("My beautiful flame, goodbye").

South of Malá Strana, in what is now the working-class district of Smíchov, the house originally stood amid vineyards. It was bought (from one Mr Bertram) by composer-pianist František Dušek and his wife Josefina, a concert soprano, who invited Mozart to the villa to prepare *Don Giovanni* for its world première. After Dušek's death in 1799, subsequent owners neglected the house until 1838 when a Mozart Society was founded. Fire gutted the villa in 1871, but with great good taste spared Mozart's apartment, enough for the house to be rebuilt as a museum.

It has been tastefully restored with an exterior double staircase leading to the upper-floor gallery, loggia and recital room. The memorabilia include a harpsichord in Mozart's sitting room that he played for his patron, Count Nostic. In the garden, a lovely setting for concerts, are Tomás Seidan's 19th-century bust of the composer and bronze statues of Papagena and Papageno from *The Magic Flute*.

TAKING A BREAK

Café **Bertramka** in the villa's courtyard is a good place to stop for lunch or a snack.

Wolfgang Amadeus played on that harpsichord

✚ 200 A2 ✉ Mozartova 169, Praha 5 ☎ 257 316 753 ⏰ Daily 9–6, Apr–Oct; 9:30–4, Nov–Mar; chamber music Wed and Sat 5 pm 🚇 Anděl 🚊 9 💵 Museum: moderate; concerts: expensive

At Your Leisure

5 Klášter sv Jiří (St George Basilica and Convent)

Behind its handsome, russet-hued baroque façade, Prague Castle's second church reveals itself as in fact much older than the Gothic St Vitus Cathedral. The basilica's interior is a beautifully restored and well-preserved Romanesque structure dating to 1142. The long, narrow nave leads to the choir via an unusual but strangely not incongruous double baroque staircase. To the right of the choir is the **burial chapel of St Ludmila**, Bohemia's first Christian martyr and grandmother of St Václav (Wenceslas). Beneath the choir, the **crypt** contains the tombs of the convent's first abbesses. On the altar to the right is a macabre 16th-century allegorical sculpture of Vanitas, showing snakes and lizards crawling through a saint's entrails.

The convent, **klášter sv Jiří**, founded·in 973 and closed by

St George Basilica is the last resting place of Good King Wenceslas' grandmother

Emperor Joseph II in 1782, is now a **Museum of Baroque Art in Bohemia**, with paintings by Bartholomeus Spranger, Hans von Aachen, Karel Škréta, Petr Brandl and major sculpture by Matyáš Braun and Ferdinand Maximilian Brokof.

➕ 194 B5 ✉ Jiřské náměstí 33, Pražský hrad ☎ 224 372 434
🕐 Tue–Sun 10–6 🚊 22, 23 Pražský hrad 🎟 Inexpensive

7 Malá Strana Bridge Towers

The fortified gate-arch on the left bank of the Karlův most (Charles Bridge, ► 52–55) is flanked by two towers. The shorter one, built in 1166, was part of the earlier Judith Bridge, with *sgraffiti* decoration and Renaissance gables added in the 16th century. The taller tower (1464) matches the right bank's bridge tower with its similar chisel-blade roof, turrets and battlemented gallery. Besides an impressive view over Malá Strana and the river, the tower has a display relating the history of the bridge and the myth-laden life of John of Nepomuk (► 32).

➕ 194 C4 ✉ Karlův most 🕐 Tower: daily 10–6, Apr–Oct 🚊 12, 22, 23
🎟 Tower: inexpensive

8 Maltézské náměstí (Maltese Square)

This L-shaped square named after the Maltese Knights (medieval guardians of the old Judith Bridge) is surrounded by some characteristic baroque palaces now transformed into embassies. On the south side of the square (No 1) is the grandiose **Nostic palác** (1670) with a splendid central doorway added a century later. Once the home of the family who owned what is now the Stavovské divadlo (► 63), it has undergone a recent restoration. Around the corner at No 6 is the elegant rococo **Turba palác** (1768), now the Japanese Embassy.

➕ 194 B3 🚊 12, 22

❾ Kampa Island

Any time a place has a couple of waterways around some houses, it is likely to be dubbed the Venice of somewhere. So this quaint little river island, reached from Charles Bridge by a double flight of stairs, is known as the "Venice of Prague". It is separated from Malá Strana by an arm of the Vltava River called the Čertovka (Devil's Channel) which used to activate mill-wheels – still there but non-functional.

Na Kampě, the square running north of Charles Bridge, is bordered by some pretty 18th-century houses, notably No 7, **dům U zlatého lva** (the Golden Lion).

➕ 194 C3 🚊 12, 22, 23

❿ Panna Marie Vítězná (Our Lady of Victory Church)

This unprepossessing 17th-century church is one of Malá Strana's great tourist attractions. Originally built by German Lutherans, it was handed over in 1624 to the Carmelite Order, which made it a monument to the victory at Bílá Hora (White Mountain, ➤ 62). But what really draws both devout pilgrims and disrespectful fans of high kitsch is the **Pražské Jezulátko**

The baroque nave of the pilgrimage Church of Our Lady of Victory

(Infant Jesus of Prague). This wax-covered wooden figure, brought to Prague in 1628 as part of the dowry of a Spanish bride, is said to have miraculous powers, in honour of which scores of luxurious little costumes have been sent here from all over the world. The silk, satin, velvet and lace clothing is displayed, along with some astonishing jewellery, in a little museum on a spiral staircase in the south aisle of the church.

➕ 194 B3 ✉ Karmelitská 9
🕐 Mon–Sat 10–5:30, Sun 1–5
🚊 12, 22 🏛 Museum: inexpensive

History in an Embassy Garden

The splendid 18th-century baroque Lobkovický palác at Vlašská ulice 19, now the German Embassy, witnessed in the summer of 1989 a turning point in history. Thousands of East Germans "on holiday" climbed into the embassy garden and camped there while seeking West German citizenship. They left their rickety Trabant cars in surrounding streets. The Czechoslovak government was obliged to lay on trains to take them into West Germany, and the flood of refugees led to the fall of the Berlin Wall. Today, from behind the embassy in Petřín Park, you can see Giovanni Battista Alliprandi's beautiful undulating rear façade of 1713. And in the garden stands David Černy's modern sculpture, *Quo Vadis?*, a gold-painted Trabant raised on legs.

⓫ Nerudova Street

Once the main thoroughfare linking the castle to the town, Nerudova Street has some of the city's finest baroque palaces and mansions. It is named after Jan Neruda, a prominent 19th-century Czech writer famous for his portraits of life in Malá Strana's artists' quarter. This activity has been revived in recent years as galleries and studios have reappeared along the street. Coming from Malostranské náměstí (Malá Strana Square), look on the left for the elegant **Morzinský palác** (No 5, now the Romanian Embassy) with Ferdinand Maximilian Brokof's sculptures of two giant Moors holding up its ornate

The palaces on Nerudova Street have been turned into Embassy Row

balcony. Across the street at No 20 is the Italian Embassy, housed in the imposing **Thun-Hohenšteinský palác** (1725). Flanking the doorway are two great eagles by Matyáš Braun.

➕ 194 A4 🔲 12, 22

⓬ Hradčanské náměstí (Castle Square)

The great fire of 1541 cleared away Castle Square's artisans' homes, workshops and butchers' shops, to be replaced by the palaces of Czech and foreign nobility. On the south side of the square, notice the highly decorative **Schwarzenberský palác** with its stepped gables and elaborate *sgraffiti* imitating Italian diamond-point masonry, a whimsical design for the Military History Museum now there. It makes a sharp contrast with the severe **Thun-Hohenšteinský palác** of the dukes of Tuscany (now housing the Czech Foreign Ministry) at the west end of the square.

The **Martinický palác** in the northwest corner is a quaint Renaissance reworking of three Gothic houses, with *sgraffiti* biblical and mythological scenes between the first-floor windows. On the north side, the 18th-century **Šternberský palác** houses the National Gallery's small collection of European masters, including Albrecht Dürer's *Feast of the Rosary* and works by Bernardo Daddi, Tintoretto, Bronzino, Simon Vouet, El Greco, Goya, Rembrandt, Rubens, Frans Hals, Jan van Goyen and Jan Steen.

➕ 194 A4 📷 Šternberský palác museum: 233 350 068 🕐 Tue–Sun 10–6 🔲 22, 23 💷 Inexpensive

🔢 Loreta

The Loreta pilgrimage sanctuary, one of 50 throughout Bohemia, was founded here in 1626 in a concerted campaign to re-Catholicise the country after the Protestant defeat at Bílá Hora (White Mountain, ➤ 62).

Within a cloister, **Mary's Santa Casa** (sacred home) is reproduced, miraculously transported first to Italy (after the Crusades, by the Angeli family) and thence, as replicas, to wherever the faith needed to be bolstered. Inside the shrine is a wooden *Black Madonna and Child* and beside the shrine a Nativity Church displaying the gruesome martyrdoms of various female saints.

Krýstof Dienzenhofer and his son Kilián Ignác added the cloister's monumental baroque façade facing the square in 1722.

Get there on the hour to hear the bells in the tower, which play hymns on the hour throughout the day.

➕ 200 A4 ✉ Loretánské náměstí 7
☎ 220 516 740 🕓 Tue–Sun 9–12:15, 1–4:30 🚃 22, 23 💷 Inexpensive

🔢 Trojský zámek (Villa Troja)

This French-style baroque château out in the northern suburbs was built by Jean-Baptiste Mathey for the Šternberk family in 1685. Surrounded by French-style formal gardens, the villa is in a charming country setting, most agreeably reached in summer by boat along the Vltava River. Mathey designed a handsome monumental double staircase modelled on that of Fontainebleau in France and enlivened by heroic sculptures of fighting giants by Georg and Paul

Trojský zámek (Villa Troja) is a country chateau outside the northern suburbs of the city

...ne interior has some ...gant ceiling frescoes celebrating ...absburg victories over the Turks in a style compatible with the Hermann sculptures of giants.

🔲 197 E5 ✉ U trojského zámku 6
🕐 Tue–Sun 10–6, Apr–Oct; Sat and
Sun 10–5, Nov–Mar 🚇 Nádraží
Holešovice, then 🚌 112, or Vltava River
boat from mooring near Palackého most
👆 Moderate

16 Veletržní palác (Trade Fair Palace)

The huge Functionalist building built in 1928 has been transformed into a **Museum of Contemporary Art** – mainly from 1900 to the present day. On six floors, accessible by lift, are works by the major Czech painters, sculptors, decorative and applied arts designers and architects, in addition to several temporary exhibitions. Artists include abstract master František Kupka, sculptor František

Bílek, cubists Emil Filla, Bohumil Kubišta and Josef Čapek. Other European artists exhibited include Rodin, Renoir, Van Gogh, Henri Rousseau, Picasso, Matisse, Klimt, Schiele and Munch.

🔲 198 B3 ✉ Dukelských hrdinů 47,
Holešovice ☎ 224 301 122
🕐 Tue–Sun 10–6, Thu 10–9 🚌 5, 12,
17 👆 Three floors expensive; two
floors moderate; one floor inexpensive

17 Petřín

Prague's biggest park is a wooded hill extending southeast from Strahov Monastery (► 97–98) to Malá Strana. From the monastery garden, follow the old **Hladová zed** (Hunger Wall) begun in the 15th century to mark the southern boundary of the old city – and provide employment for the poor. As it winds southeast, the wall passes the **Rozhledna**, a miniature 1891 version of the Eiffel Tower, and **Bludiště**, a mini-Gothic castle with a Mirror Maze inside. Just beyond the funicular railway are the **Růžový sad** (rose garden) and **Štefánikova hvězdárna** (observatory). The funicular railway, for which normal public transport tickets and passes are valid, takes you down to Malá Strana and buses back into the city centre.

🔲 194 A2 🕐 Tower (Rozhledna)
and observatory: daily 10–7, Apr
and Sep; daily 10–10, May–Aug;
daily 10–6 Oct; Sat–Sun 10–5,
Nov–Mar. Maze: daily 10–6, Apr–Oct.
Funicular railway: daily 9–11:30,
Apr–Oct; 9–11:20, Nov–Mar
🚌 22, 23 👆 Funicular railway:
inexpensive

Petřín's mini Eiffel Tower was completed in 1891, just two years after the original in Paris

Where to...
Eat and Drink

Prices

Expect to pay per person for a meal, including drinks, tax and service
£ under 350Kč **££** 350–800Kč **£££** over 800Kč

RESTAURANTS

Černý orel ££

Italian wines and Czech Pilsner accompany their respective cuisines in the two comfortably luxurious low-ceilinged rooms. The popularity of this neighbourhood among Italian tourists ensures that plenty of their nation's favourite dishes (generous and inexpensive portions) appear on the menu here, along with traditional Czech cuisine.

⊞ 194 B4 **⊠** Malostranské náměstí 14, Malá Strana **☎** 257 533 207; www.cernyorel.com **⊘** Daily 11–11

Baráčnická rychta £

Climb the twisting street above the American embassy to find this quintessential Czech *hospoda*: dark, warm, welcoming, with lots of wood, perfunctory but professional service, and all the pork knuckle and beer you can down. The fruit dumplings are excellent. A very comfortable and inexpensive place for a good meal. There's often a Moravian band on Friday and Saturday nights.

⊞ 194 A4 **⊠** Tržiště 23 **☎** 257 532 461 **⊘** Daily noon–midnight **⊚** Malostranská

Gitanes ££

Gitane's specialises in Balkan specialities. Seafood and roasted meat dishes dominate the menu: *čevapčiči* for beef-lovers, or the simmered pork dish, *mučkalica*. There's plenty for the non-meat eater, too: stuffed peppers, feta, olive and cucumber salad, roasted beans simmered with spices. There are wines from the former Yugoslavia, France and the Czech Republic.

⊞ 194 B4 **⊠** Tržiště 7, Malá Strana **☎** 257 530 163; www.gitanes.cz **⊘** Daily noon–midnight **⊚** Malostranská

Hergetova Cihelná £££

This restaurant on Kampa Island features a terrace with gorgeous views across the river and what some would call the best wood-fired gourmet pizzas in the city. The large menu also features plenty of excellent salads, meat and fish entrées. The BBQ burger with bacon and cheddar cheese is a very popular choice. Reservations are recommended, and essential if you want a seat on the terrace in summertime.

⊞ 194 4C **⊠** Cihelná 2b, Malá Strana **☎** 257 535 534 **⊘** Daily noon–2 am

Nebozízek ££

This historic restaurant serves fine examples of the national cuisine: game, duck, pork, fruit-based sauces, and pancakes for dessert. But the main reason to dine here is the view over Prague and onto the castle. Reservations essential.

⊞ 194 B2 **⊠** Petřínské sady 411, Malá Strana **⊘** Daily noon–11 **☎** 257 315 329; www.nebozizek.cz **⊚** Tram 9 to Újezd, then funicular to halfway up Petřín

Pálffy Palác ££

The Pálffy's charmingly shabby palace houses the most romantic dining room in the city, decorated with subdued colours and old prints. It is a favourite brunch spot, as much for the mood as the food. At dinner the menu is contemporary, such as shiitake mushroom-stuffed chicken breast in tarragon sauce, and salmon baked in Brie.

🏠 194 C4 ⊠ Valdštejnská 14, Malá Strana ☎ 257 533 322; www.zlatastudna.cz
🕐 Daily 7 am–11 pm

Rybářský klub £–££

If it swims in a Czech river or pond, they serve it here. The pike in black sauce and the river eel are local favourites. Or try the national fish, carp (breaded and fried, it's the traditional Christmas Eve supper), although this bony beast is something of an acquired taste. The interior has the comfortable, solid feel of a fisherman's club room. In the summer a few small tables at the back make for splendid riverside dining.

🏠 194 C3 ⊠ U Sovových mlýnů 1, Kampa, Malá Strana ☎ 257 534 200
🕐 Daily noon–11

Sovový Mlýny ££

This riverfront restaurant is located inside Kampa Museum, a showcase for modern Central and Eastern European art. From the Staré Město side of the river, the 4-story white building on the opposite shore is impossible to miss. The restaurant specialises in excellent Czech cooking: leg of duck with sautéed red cabbage and apples, roasted pork joint with crisped potatoes. There's a fine selection of Moravian wines, and tables by the window (and outside on warm nights) give a spectacular view across the river to the National Theatre.

🏠 194 C3 ⊠ U Sovových mlýnů ☎ 257 535 900; www.sovovymlyny.cz
🕐 Daily 9 am–midnight
🚇 Malostranská

Sushi Bar ££

This little California-esque bar, minimalistically decorated in pale laminated tables and chairs, split off from the fish shop next door, is helping to lead the way for a rising tide of sushi restaurants. Seafood is delivered twice weekly, so you might want to call ahead to make sure of getting fresh eel, scallops, seabass or crab, then watch the Czech chefs whip up sushi rolls, sashimi or tempura.

🏠 194 C2 ⊠ Zborovská 49, Smíchov ☎ 603 244 882 🕐 Daily noon–midnight

U Labutí ££

Translated as "At the Swans", this establishment, which is more of a club than a restaurant, has comfortable seating with antique tables and chairs. The chef produces traditional Czech cuisine, with some international dishes as well, including steaks and chicken.

🏠 194 A4 ⊠ Hradčanské náměstí 11 ☎ 220 511 191 🕐 Daily noon–4, 6–midnight

U malířů £££

Visitors to Prague used to be taken to gawk at "the most expensive restaurant in town" – imagine charging £10 for a piece of beef! This is classic French cuisine overseen by a master French chef. The main dining room re-creates a Bohemian Renaissance princely hall.

🏠 194 B3 ⊠ Maltézské náměstí 11, Malá Strana ☎ 222 776 003
🕐 Daily 11:30 am–midnight

U Ševce Matouše ££

You can easily guess that this long-established steakhouse under the arches of Loreto Square was once a cobbler's shop from the ancient bronzed shoes that decorate the entrance and perch on stands in the dining room. The décor is simple, and the food is, of course, steaks with many different sauces, although poultry and fish are also served.

🏠 196 C2 ⊠ Loretánské náměstí 4, Hradčany ☎ 220 514 536
🕐 Daily 11–11

U Zlaté hrušky £££

Leg of venison, duck with peas and barley, suckling pig: classic Bohemian meals in a classic Bohemian house. Four centuries ago, when the astronomer Tycho Brahe (▶ 8) lived next door, he probably dined on food very much like this.

✚ 196 C2 ⊠ Nový svět 3, Hradčany
☎ 220 514 778 ⏰ Daily 11:30–3,
6:30–midnight

U Zlaté studně £££

Opinion is divided on whether the
food at this stylish restaurant matches
the view. Most would say it doesn't,
but that's nothing against the food,
for the view – Malá Strana roofs
breaking into red-tiled waves at
your feet – will knock your socks
off. The cuisine is international, and
the menu lists some specialities that
are still hard to come by in Prague,
like baked goose liver. Don't try to
find this place without a good map;
it's hidden in a cul-de-sac above
Valdštejnské náměstí.

✚ 194 B4 ⊠ U Zlaté studně 166/4
(off the north end of Sněmovní),
Malá Strana ☎ 257 011 213
⏰ Daily noon–4, 6–11

Waldštejnská hospoda ££

The medieval "House of the Three
Storks" received its present façade
in the 18th century, and inside

rather resembles a hunting lodge of
that era. The cooking follows in the
same vein, leaning towards game,
fowl and traditional Czech dishes –
rich pork recipes swimming in
even richer sauces.

✚ 194 B4 ⊠ Valdštejnské
náměstí 7, Malá Strana ☎ 257 532
195 ⏰ Daily 11:30–11:30

PUBS AND BARS

BarBar

Step gingerly down the stairs and
watch your head as you enter this
friendly cellar bar-restaurant popular with ex-pats and locals from the
surrounding neighbourhood. Sweet
and savory crêpes and Czech comfort food like *halušky* and *gulaš* is
served in the back room.

✚ 194 B3 ⊠ Všehrdova 17 ☎ 257
312 246; www.bar-bar.cz
🚇 Malostranská

Hostinec Na Kampě

Pilsner Urquell is the draught beer
at this Kampa pub. It's popular with

tourists, with its carefully selected,
well-used wooden furniture and old
photos. There's a restaurant and a
small, fairly expensive pension.

✚ 194 C3 ⊠ Na Kampě 15, Malá
Strana ☎ 257 531 432 ⏰ Daily
11–11

Královská Šatlava

Near Charles Bridge, but generally
immune to foreign influence, this
comfortable pub has a couple of
unsteady pool tables and walls
decorated with kitsch paintings of
duelling swordsmen. The taps
dispense Bernard, a fine, light lager
from a small, family owned brewery.

✚ 194 B4 ⊠ Saská (between
Lázeňská and the Charles Bridge
stairs), Malá Strana ☎ No phone
⏰ Daily 6 pm–2 am

St Nicholas

This is most people's idea of a
perfect cellar bar. Arched stone
ceilings and rough walls, tiny lights
on cosy tables, efficient service,
strong drinks, some tasty snacks on

the menu, and always great music
playing – David Bowie to Bob
Marley.

✚ 194 B4 ⊠ Tržiště 10, Malá Strana
☎ No phone ⏰ Mon–Fri
12 pm– 1am, Sat–Sun 4 pm–1 am

U Černého orla

Look for the namesake black eagle
clutching a mug of beer above the
doorway to find the venerable pub
that makes no concessions to
modernity. A few footballs and
trophies comprise the décor. There's
classic pub grub, and locally brewed
Staropramen beer on tap.

✚ 194 B3 ⊠ Újezd 33, Malá Strana
☎ 290 003 957 ⏰ Mon–Fri 10–10,
Sat–Sun 11–10

U Černého vola

Unlike the U Černého orla (above),
the entrance at the Black Ox depicts
not the pub's animal symbol, but a
trio of holy figures sculpted in stucco
on the façade of this rococo house.
The small beer hall inside is famous
for its Velkopopovicky Kozel beer.

The light variety has a slight fruity finish; the dark is very sweet.

⊞ 196 C2 ⊠ Loretánské náměstí 1, Hradčany ☎ 220 513 481 🕙 Daily 10–10

U Malého Glena

There's no cover charge for the bar at this popular jazz and rock music club. Funky mismatched furnishings and a big wooden bar make for a comfortable drinking space.

⊞ 194 B4 ⊠ Karmelitská 23, Malá Strana ☎ 257 531 717; www.malyglen.cz 🕙 Fri–Sat 10 am–3 am, Sun–Thu 10 am–2 am

U Maltéze

Under the arcades of Maltese Square is this little indoor and outdoor pub with Budvar – the original Budweiser (▶ 25) – on tap and classic pub snacks like the pickled sausages known as *utopenci* – "drowned men" – named presumably because they float in a large jar of pickling sauce.

⊞ 194 B3 ⊠ Maltézské náměstí 15,

Malá Strana ☎ 257 531 324 🕙 Daily noon–midnight

U sedmi Švábů

The best time to visit many Czech pubs is summer – beer garden time – but here the open hearth is particularly welcome when it's cold. It's a bit on the kitsch side, but the hearty Bohemian food, costumed staff and environment are most entertaining.

⊞ 194 A4 ⊠ Jánský vršek 14, Malá Strana ☎ 257 531 455 🕙 Daily 11–11

CAFÉS AND TEA ROOMS

Caffeteria

This soothing, street-level café, near to Charles Bridge, it has much to recommend it. It is non-smoking, has free wi-fi, plays low, relaxing music, and offers a daily selection of fabulous home-made cakes, in addition to fresh salads, crêpes, panini and toasted sandwiches.

⊞ 194 B4 ⊠ Tržiště 12 🕙 Mon–Fri 7 am–8 pm, Sat–Sun 8 am–8 pm

☎ 608 707 137; www.caffeteria.cz 🚇 Malostranská

Kavárna Akvarel

Inexpensive coffees, cocktails and snacks are served in this gallery overlooking the Wallenstein Riding School's main hall.

⊞ 194 C4 ⊠ Valdštejnská at Klárov, Malá Strana ☎ 257 073 139 🕙 Tue–Sun 10–10

Malý Buddha

A soothing tearoom serving simple Chinese and Vietnamese vegetarian "temple foods" based on rice or glass noodles. The heady aroma from the many steaming teapots providing Tibetan clove, Royal Nepalese and Hong Kong-style fruit teas promotes a meditative mood. Reservations.

⊞ 194 A4 ⊠ Úvoz 46 (off Pohořelec), Hradčany ☎ 220 513 894 🕙 Tue–Sun 1–10.30

Sternberg Palace

The proprietors of this refreshment room at the National Gallery had

the idea of removing the canvases from the ornate frames lining the walls, so that visitors can imagine their own masterpieces while they are enjoying a selection of drinks, sandwiches and desserts.

⊞ 194 A4 ⊠ Hradčanské náměstí 15, Hradčany ☎ 220 514 634 🕙 Tue–Sun 10–5.30

Tato Kojkej

Situated at the end of Kampa Park, complete with a paddlewheel out front, this is an eclectic place to have a coffee, cocktail or glass of wine.

⊞ 194 C3 ⊠ Kampa Park, Mala Strana ☎ 257 323 102 🕙 Daily 10–midnight

U Zavěšenýho Kafe

This version of the literary coffee house is usually jammed with students and the type of Prague intellectual who thrives on beer, cheap and filling traditional food, tobacco fumes and endless discussion.

⊞ 194 A4 ⊠ Radnické schody 7, Hradčany 🕙 Daily 11 am–midnight

Where to...
Shop

Shopping opportunities in lower Malá Strana are best where Karlův most (Charles Bridge) merges into Mostecká Street. Interesting shops selling locally made goods and crafts can also be found to the north and south of Mostecká Street.

On the hill running up towards the castle, Nerudova is the main street (▶ 102). At Pražský hrad (Prague Castle), nearly all the shops are crammed onto Zlata ulička (Golden Lane).

Behind Pražský hrad there are several quirky shops and arty galleries that are good for gifts around Pohořelec Square and in the rather twee neighbourhood of Nový Svět.

LOWER MALÁ STRANA

Curio-seekers should try Vetešnictví (Vítězná between nos 14 and 18) – a browser's paradise.

Inexpensive housewares and fabrics are available at Atelier Trnka (Újezd 46), while near by, Antikvariát U Pražského Jezulátka (Karmelitská 16) sells an odd array of English-language books among the Czech second-hand titles.

More shops huddle on the ground floors of the looming baroque palaces on Maltézské náměstí, a couple of blocks towards the river. Old dolls, 19th-century landscapes, and walking sticks are specialities at Galerie-Antique Na Staré Poště (Maltézské náměstí 8).

Just off the square at Antique Ahasver (Prokopská 3) you'll find a selection of old textiles and the excellent contemporary photographs of Pavel Ahasver.

From Karmelitská, head up Tržiště and follow it to the left, where it becomes Vlašská. At No

13, tiny Pavla & Olga is brimming with fantastic one-of-a-kind dresses, costume jewellery, skirts and shirts for women. A few steps on is Signet (Vlašská 15), where you'll find rare and special old Czech, German and Russian books and maps. North of the bridge, U Lužického seminaře Street has a wide variety of possibilities. Look at the contemporary glassware at Galerie Z (No 7) and the faux-historical goblets at Krámek "U Škopků" (No 22).

UPPER MALÁ STRANA

Picture-perfect Nerudova Street oozes alluring little shops such as La Candela (No 7), which makes colourful candles that look like old-fashioned ribbon candy.

Just next door, there are fanciful Czech puppets and marionettes at Handmade (No 11). Walk a few more steps up this steep street and take a rest at the charming U Zeleného čaje (No 19), where you can buy Czech ceramics and order

gourmet coffees, 150 kinds of tea and delicious sweets.

Browse through old books, postcards, stamps and prints at Antikvariát U Zlaté Číše (No 16).

On the same side of the street, go through a passage selling tourist souvenirs and emerge into the courtyard of Romen: The Little Shop (No 34), a nonprofit showcase for the work of Roma, or gypsy, artisans, which carries colourful jewellery, gypsy music CDs, paintings, scarves, books and baskets.

PRAŽSKÝ HRAD AND HRADČANY

Fortunately, the castle's keepers have not allowed the sacred precinct to become over-commercialised.

The Museum Store (off Zlata ulička, also accessible by a stairway from Jiřská) is the most comprehensive shop of its kind in town, full of replicas, books and toys inspired by the castle's art and historical collections.

Where to...
Be Entertained

The shops in Hradčany are, if anything, more minute and idiosyncratic than those in Malá Strana. **Galerie Gambra** (Černínská 5) is the headquarters of the Czech Surrealist movement and the sales point for head-spinning art, ceramics and books by animator Jan Švankmajer and other members of the group.

Nearby **Galerie Nový Svět** (Nový Svět 5) has a wider selection of contemporary Czech art.

If it's Picasso, Braque or living artists in the same price range you want, have a look at the changing sales exhibitions mounted by **Galerie Miro** (Strahovské nádvoří 1), in the grounds of the Strahov Monastery.

Tasteful art, candles and silk scarves made by nuns can be found at **Galerie Karmel** (Radnické schody 3), on the staircase linking Loretánská with Nerudova).

Locally made wooden and tin toys are available at **Hračky** (Pohořelec 24).

MUSIC

Classical
Villa Bertramka

Concerts of Mozart's music are performed year-round at the Mozart Museum, installed in the villa where Wolfgang Amadeus used to stay (▶ 99).

🕂 204 A2 ⊠ Mozartova 169, Smíchov ☎ 257 317 465 🕘 9:30–6, Apr–Oct; chamber music Wed and Sat 5 pm 🖐 Expensive

Lichtenštejnský palác

During the summer lively operatic productions are staged in the courtyard of this palace opposite Malá Strana's Church of St Nicholas (▶ 96). The palace is the seat of the Prague music academy, and faculty

and students perform regularly. There are also regular concerts of contemporary classical music.

🕂 198 B4 ⊠ Malostranské náměstí 13, Malá Strana ☎ 257 534 206

Contemporary and jazz
Malostranská beseda

When you want to hear Czech rock, folk or blues, this spacious club is a good bet. Jazz and swing bands also play here.

🕂 198 B4 ⊠ Malostranské náměstí 21, Malá Strana ☎ 257 532 092

Paegas Arena

Big-name rockers and top Czech ice-hockey stars do their stuff here.

🕂 202 B4 ⊠ Výstaviště (Fairgrounds), Holešovice ☎ 233 379 248

SPORT

Sparta Stadium

This is the home of Prague's top soccer team, Sparta Praha. The season runs from August to December and February to May. Tickets are easily obtainable at the gate. Sparta Praha regularly tops the Czech league table and takes part in European competitions.

🕂 201 E3 ⊠ Milady Horákové 98, Letná ☎ 220 570 323

FAMILY ENTERTAINMENT

Výstaviště Fairgrounds

This a 100-year-old amusement park with an exhibition hall and a small funfair. Two modern theatres stage Czech-language musicals, and the low-budget replica of the Globe Theatre in London stages summer Shakespeare in both Czech and English.

🕂 202 B4 ⊠ Výstaviště (at the eastern end of Stromovka Park), Holešovice 🕘 Daily 10–7

Josefov
(Old Jewish Quarter)

Getting Your Bearings

Josefov, the neighbourhood of the Old Jewish Quarter, is compact and easy to get around in one day. Enough of the ghetto has been preserved to get a feeling for the particular role Jewish people played in the life of the city. They have gone but their monuments remain as rich and often moving reminders of their vibrant contribution.

With nimble footwork and an occasional blind eye, you can avoid the surfeit of touristy souvenir shops and pathos-laden memorabilia, and witness the sheer beauty of Starý židovský hřbitov (Old Jewish Cemetery) and Staronová synagoga (Old-New Synagogue).

Roughly speaking, the neighbourhood fills the corner of the right bank's river bend. From Old Town Square, it extends northeast to Anežský klášter (Convent of St Agnes) and west to the Rudolfinum. Most of the synagogues and the cemetery cluster on either side of Maiselova Street. The Spanish Synagogue is over to the east, closer to the quarter's other main thoroughfare, Pařížská třída (Paris Boulevard).

There are plenty of cafés and restaurants, even a couple that are kosher.

★ Don't Miss

- **3** Pinkasova synagoga (Pinkas Synagogue) ➤ 116
- **5** Starý židovský hřbitov (Old Jewish Cemetery) ➤ 118
- **7** Staronová synagoga (Old-New Synagogue) ➤ 121

Starý židovský hřbitov **5**

Rudolfinum **1**

Obřadní síň **4**

Uměleckoprůmyslové Muzeum (UPM) **2**

Pinkasova synagoga **3**

DVOŘÁKOVO NÁBŘEŽÍ

17 LISTOPADU

MÁNESŮV MOST

NÁMĚSTÍ JANA PALACHA

ŠIROKÁ

0 ____ 200 metres

0 ____ 200 yards

Tickets for the Jewish Museum

The Jewish Museum includes Starý židovský hřbitov (Old Jewish Cemetery), Obřadní síň (Ceremonial Hall) and four of Josefov's five synagogues. The fifth synagogue, Staronová (Old-New Synagogue), is separate. Tickets are available at the synagogues or tourist agencies around Maiselova Street. To avoid crowding, tickets specify a timetable granting about 20 minutes for each "sight", but this is quite flexible.

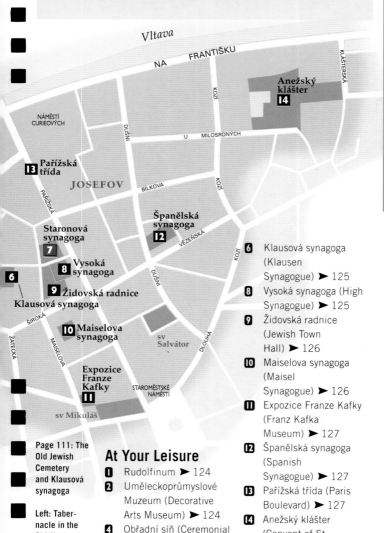

Vltava

NA FRANTIŠKU

KLÁŠTERSKÁ

Anežský klášter
14

NÁMĚSTÍ CURIEOVYCH

DUŠNÍ

KOZÍ

U MILOSRDNÝCH

Pařížská třída
13

JOSEFOV

BÍLKOVA

KOZÍ

PAŘÍŽSKÁ

Španělská synagoga
12

VĚZEŇSKÁ

Staronová synagoga
7

Vysoká synagoga
8

DUŠNÍ

KOZÍ

6

9 **Židovská radnice**

Klausová synagoga

ŠIROKÁ

ŽATECKÁ

MAISELOVA

10 **Maiselova synagoga**

sv Salvátor

DLOUHÁ

Expozice Franze Kafky
11

STAROMĚSTSKÉ NÁMĚSTÍ

sv Mikuláš

Page 111: The Old Jewish Cemetery and Klausová synagoga

Left: Tabernacle in the Old-New Synagogue

At Your Leisure

- **1** Rudolfinum ► 124
- **2** Uměleckoprůmyslové Muzeum (Decorative Arts Museum) ► 124
- **4** Obřadní síň (Ceremonial Hall) ► 124

Take a poignant trip back into Prague's Jewish past, including five synagogues, the Old Jewish Cemetery and a decorative arts museum.

Around Josefov in a Day

Crowds on the **Jewish Museum tour** (➤ 113) can be a real problem. The best chance of avoiding them is to visit some of the neighbourhood's other sights in the morning and then head over to the synagogues and cemetery during (most people's) lunch hour. This also gives you more flexibility with the itinerary as specified on the tour ticket.

10:00 am
Start at the **Rudolfinum** (➤ 124) to enjoy the 1900s décor of its café. You might also take in one of the usually excellent temporary art exhibitions.

11:00 am
Take a look on náměstí Jana Palacha at the Dvořák statue, then make for the **Decorative Arts Museum** (➤ 124). While most people are still doing the Jewish Museum tour, have an early lunch at either Café Colonial (➤ 129) or kosher King Solomon (➤ 129).

1:00 pm
With, hopefully, most of the crowd now at lunch, you are ready to start the Jewish Museum tour. At this time of day, you can start out at **Pinkasova synagoga** (above, ➤ 116–117). The exhibit here is worth the full 20 minutes or more (timing is not as strict as the ticket suggests).

1:30 pm
Don't be hurried on your walk through the **Starý židovký hřbitov** (Old Jewish Cemetery, detail left, ➤ 118–120). There is plenty to see here, and most of all a unique atmosphere to take in.

2:00 pm

On either side of the cemetery exit, the exhibits at the **Obřadní síň** (Ceremonial Hall, ➤ 124) and the **Klausová synagoga** (➤ 125) should take about half an hour between them.

2:30 pm

Give yourself more time for the **Staro-nová synagoga** (Old-New Synagogue, detail left, ➤ 121), the most impor-tant stop after the cemetery. Stroll around the **Židovská radnice** (Jewish Town Hall, ➤ 126), check the time – backwards and forwards – on the Hebrew and Roman-numeral clocks, and walk south to **Maiselova synagoga** (➤ 126).

3:30 pm

Double back north on Maiselova and head east along Siroka to end the museum tour at the spectacular **Španělská synagoga** (➤ 127).

4:00 pm

Coming back west on Široka, it's time for some chic profanity at **Pařížská třída** (Paris Boulevard, below, ➤ 127). You may have done enough architec-tural sightseeing by now, so this is the place to stop at one of the cafés before some window-shopping and people-watching.

6:00 pm

Before the evening starts, head back to the heart of Josefov for a beer at U pivrnce, an honest-to-goodness old-fashioned pub at Maiselova 3 (➤ 130).

③

Pinkasova synagoga
(Pinkas Synagogue)

The Renaissance synagogue, built in the 16th century as a private synagogue, is now a sober memorial to the Czechoslovak Jews killed in World War II.

The synagogue was founded in 1479 by Rabbi Pinkas and enlarged by his great-nephew Aaron Meshullam Horowitz. It was then taken over in 1535 by Žalman Horowitz and integrated into the family residence abutting directly on the south side of the Old Jewish Cemetery (► 118–120). The original late Gothic building was remodelled a century later in its present Renaissance style with the addition of a women's gallery in the 17th century, vestibule and council room, creating a charming inner courtyard for the entrance. It has been rebuilt many times over the centuries.

The Interior
Inside the synagogue is an interesting blend of the two styles, with richly coloured Renaissance motifs edging the Flamboyant Gothic rib-vaulting. There is no attempt here, as in the Staronová synagoga (► 121–123), to avoid ribs forming a cross. The central *bima* (pulpit for leading the service) has kept its rococo

Above: A few hundred of the 77,297 names of the dead

wrought, iron grille on gilded spiral supports.

Memorial 77,297 is the title of the wall-monument to Czechslovak Jewish victims in the Nazi concentration camps. It took Václav Boštík and Jiří John five years (1954–59) to cover the synagogue's walls with all 77,297 names, dates of birth and dates of death written in simple black and red

A child's painting from the Theresienstadt concentration camp

letters. In 1968, the synagogue was closed and the names removed, as the Communist authorities insisted, because of the deteriorating state of the building. The Communist regime's Czech critics say the decision was strictly political, in the heated "anti-Zionist" atmosphere following Israel's victory in the Six-Day War in 1967.

The synagogue was renovated in the 1990s and the Memorial names were restored. Against the east wall, around the Tabernacle that once held the scrolls of the Law and the Prophets, are written the names of the principal concentration camps where the Czechoslovak Jews died.

"Children's Drawings From Terezín (1942–1944)"
A permanent exhibition in an upstairs gallery is devoted to drawings by Jewish children in the German concentration camp of Theresienstadt, an hour's drive from Prague (► 170–172). The Jewish Museum keeps in the synagogue a collection of 4,500 drawings saved and hidden by the children's art teacher, Bauhaus painter Friedl Dicker-Brandeisová. The children continued to draw, mostly pictures of a fantasy world outside the camp, until they, like their teacher, were deported to Auschwitz.

Left: The *bima* pulpit with wrought-iron grille in Pinkasova Synagoga

TAKING A BREAK
Get away from it all at the delightful first-floor 19th-century café in the **Rudolfinum concert hall** on the Vltava River embankment, Alšovo nábřeží 12 (► 124), or you could try the Starbucks-inspired **Coffee Heaven** (► 131).

195 D4 U Staré Školy 1 Jewish Museum: 221 711 511; reservations 222 317 191 9–6, Apr–Oct, 9–4:30, Nov–Mar; closed Sat and Jewish holidays Staroměstská 17, 18 Jewish Museum ticket: expensive

PINKASOVA SYNAGOGA: INSIDE INFO
Top tip Excavations in the synagogue basement in the 1970s uncovered a **ritual bath** (*mikveh*) dating back to the 15th century, at least 100 years before the present synagogue was built.

5

Starý židovský hřbitov

(Old Jewish Cemetery)

There is a chaotic beauty here that gives particular meaning to the Hebrew name for a cemetery, *beit hayim* (House of Life). With Prague's Jewish population all but gone – of the 56,000 in 1939, approximately 1,500 remain – their cemetery sustains the memory of the community. The monumental tombs of the proud and the simple stones of the humble crowd together in a glorious, disorderly affirmation of life.

Founded in the first half of the 15th century and closed to new burials in 1787, the cemetery today numbers around 12,000 tombs on the surface and tens of thousands more in uncounted layers beneath. Subsidence, erosion and the weathering of the ages have created an undulating landscape of crooked and tottering tombstones. The cemetery's oldest tomb is dated 1439 – a few older stones brought here from other cemeteries are inserted in a wall by the Klausová synagoga (► 125), while some wooden burial-tablets are displayed in the museum of the Obřadní síň (Ceremonial Hall, ► 124).

Tomb Styles

You can practically date the tombstones according to their style. After the first simple flat limestone or granite markers of the 15th century, rounded or pointed red and white marble tombs appear in the 16th century, more ornate, with carved Hebrew inscriptions. Poems or passages from the Bible extol the virtues of the deceased, and homage is paid to worldly success or scholarship. In the 17th century, wealthier Jews

Stones and More

As a sign of respect, it is the Jewish custom to place on a tomb not flowers but a small stone. Formerly, visitors would also put coins on the tombs of the rabbis. The destitute would visit the cemetery at night to collect the money as alms.

Pictorial Symbols

Animals or other emblems are often carved on tombstones as visual puns on the Hebrew or German name of the deceased or in order to symbolise a profession. Thus there may be a lion for Yehuda, Loeb or Loewe; two hands in blessing for the priestly family of Cohen; a pitcher for their temple assistants, the Levites and thus Levy; a deer for Hirsch; a cockerel for Hahn; a mouse for Maisel; a violin for a musician; scissors for a tailor, etc.

followed the Christian fashion for monumental baroque sepul-chres simulating a miniature chapel.

Household Names in the Ghetto

The tombstones express the Jews' 11th Commandment – "Remember"

Best known of the people buried here, and the most visited tomb, is that of the community's most revered scholar, **Rabbi Yehuda Loew ben Bezalel**, who died in 1609 (➤ 8). His monumental double tomb (shared with his wife Perl) was remodelled in the 18th century with a lion for his name, beneath a bunch of grapes to symbolise his ripe old age of 96.

STARÝ ŽIDOVSKÝ HŘBITOV: INSIDE INFO

Top tips Entrance to the cemetery, as part of the Jewish Museum tour, is from the Pinkasova synagoga (► 116–117) on Siroka Street with the exit by the Klausová synagoga on U Starého hřbitova (► 125).

• A cemetery **map** is provided with the Museum's tour brochure showing the location of its most famous tombs.

• Men **cover their heads**, just as in a synagogue, as a Jewish cemetery is considered holy ground.

• Orthodox Jewish **Cohens** (*kohanim*), forbidden by religious law to set foot in the cemetery, can view Rabbi Loew's monumental tomb from a window between the ground and the first floor in the Klausová synagoga (► 125).

Visitors place pebbles on his grave as a mark of respect. Just across the way, his contemporary, financier **Mordechai Maisel** (died 1601), was the mayor of what was then known as the Jewish Town and one of its greatest benefactors. Don't look here for the tomb of **Franz Kafka**. He is buried in the Jewish section of Olšanské Cemetery over in Žižkov (► 155).

In the male-dominated world of Orthodox Jewry, **Hendel Bashevi** (died 1628) stands out as the only woman here to have a truly monumental tomb of her own. Indeed, in its sheer size and the splendour of its late Renaissance decoration, it outshines that of the sages and rabbis around her. The wife of wealthy community leader Jacob Bashevi, whose letters of nobility won her the right to place two heraldic lions on her monument, she was renowned for her work with the poor of Josefov.

The **oldest tomb** is said to be that of writer Rabbi Avigdor Kara, who died in 1439.

TAKING A BREAK

Head over to the Vltava River and relax at one of the outdoor **cafés on the Vltava embankment** (Alšovo nábreží), or go to **King Solomon** (► 129) for something kosher.

One of the proud lions on Hendel Bashevi's tomb

🔹 195 D4 ⬛ Entrance by Pinkasova synagoga, Siroká 3
☎ Jewish Museum 221 711 511; reservations 222 317 191 🕐 9–6, Apr–Oct; 9–4:30, Nov–Mar; closed Sat and Jewish holidays 🔲 Staroměstská
🚊 17, 18 🎟 Jewish Museum ticket: expensive

7

Staronová synagoga
(Old-New Synagogue)

The city's oldest synagogue (1275) is also the oldest in Europe still being used regularly for worship. Quite apart from being a treasure for Prague's dwindling Jewish community, it is a significant monument for anyone interested in what makes Prague such a special city.

The Old-New Synagogue's steep gabled roof creates one of the city's most distinctive silhouettes

Architecture being a profession denied to Jews at the time, the Staronová was probably erected by master builders and masons from the site of the nearby Anežský klášter (Convent of St Agnes, ➤ 128). Deceptively small on the outside, the synagogue is simple in form, distinguished only by the crenellated, steeply sloping brick gable of its façade. The entrance is on the south side through a Gothic portal. The finely carved stone

pediment's stylised vine has 12 roots and 12 bunches of grapes – symbolic of the 12 tribes of Israel.

On sabbaths and holy days, Orthodox Jews are called to this *bima* pulpit to read a portion of the Torah

The Interior

The long vestibule and a parallel area along the other side of the hall of worship have window-slits through which women, separated from the men in Orthodox Judaism, could follow the service. The hall itself is unexpectedly loftier because the floor's level is today so much lower than that of the improved street outside. Marrying function and faith, the Gothic vaults each have five load-bearing ribs rather than four so as not to form a cross, forbidden in a Jewish house of worship. Sturdy octagonal pillars with the *bima* (a rectangular platform-like pulpit), between them divide the hall into twin naves, unique among Bohemia's medieval religious buildings. Above the elegant wrought-iron frame of the *bima* is the Jewish community's red banner (1716) with a Star of David and the traditional hat then worn in public.

The Tabernacle

Built into the east wall in the 16th century, the Tabernacle (*aron ha-kodesh*) houses the scrolls of the Law (Torah, the first five books of the Bible) and the books of the Prophets (Haftarah). During the sabbath service (Saturday), the two scrolls are carried ceremonially to the *bima*, where seven members of the congregation are called up in turn to share in the reading of a chapter from the Prophets. A quorum

So What's New?

The story of the synagogue's name sounds like a Jewish joke. When it was first built, the community already had an Old Synagogue – Altschul in Yiddish – so they called this one Neuschul, New Synagogue. In the 16th century, the wealthy and powerful Wechsler family built another synagogue and told the rabbis: "We're calling it the New Synagogue. Yours is old now. You'll have to find a different name." "But," said the rabbis, "we have an Old Synagogue already. What do we do?" Every Jewish community has a Solomon and, whoever he was, he came up with the name Old-New Synagogue. He had God on his side: in the slum-clearance of 1900 (▶ 127), the Old Synagogue and Wechslers' New Synagogue disappeared. The Old-New Synagogue survived.

(*minyan*) of at least ten men must be present for a properly constituted service to be held.

Survival

In a town where so many of its older buildings have had to be reconstructed after devastating fires over the centuries, the Staronová has escaped unscathed, blessed, say the faithful, by the most revered of its sages, Rabbi Loew (► 8). Perversely, it also benefited from the personal decision of Adolf Hitler to preserve it and the other synagogues of Josefov as what he called an "Exotic Museum for an Extinct Race". The Nazis had treasures from synagogues all over Bohemia transported to Prague. Today they are exhibited in testimony to a people still very much alive.

TAKING A BREAK

For a culinary break, head over to the Belgian café **Les Moules** (► 129) for excellent people-watching and fresh seafood.

➕ 195 E4 ✉ Červená ulice ☎ Reservations 224 800 812 ◑ Sun–Fri 9:30–6, Apr–Oct; Sun–Thu 9:30–5, Fri 9:30–2, Nov–Mar ; closed Sat and Jewish holidays Ⓠ Staroměstská 🚎 17, 18 💳 Special ticket: expensive

STARONOVÁ SYNAGOGA: INSIDE INFO

Top tips People are expected to **dress appropriately** for a house of worship. Men are requested to cover their heads – paper *kippah* are available at the ticket office or synagogue entrance.
• Staronová is separate from the Jewish Museum ticket. Be sure to have the right **ticket** (► 113).

Hidden gem In the little park north of the synagogue is Symbolist (and Protestant) sculptor František Bílek's 1905 **statue of Moses**, at his feet the fragments of his shattered tablets of the Law. Read into this what you will – like beauty, the meaning of a symbol is in the eye of the beholder.

At Your Leisure

❶ Rudolfinum

The imposing 19th-century neo-Renaissance concert hall is home to the great Czech Philharmonic Orchestra, and a main venue for the annual Prague Spring Music Festival. Besides the orchestra's splendid Dvořák Hall (the composer's statue is in the square outside), its galleries host prestigious temporary art exhibitions and there is a delightful spacious café on the first floor. The building served as the first Czechoslovak parliament (1918–38) and the German Army HQ in World War II. The hall faces onto náměstí Jana Palacha, the square honouring Jan Palach, the Czech student-martyr who committed suicide to try to rouse the people from their apathy (► 143).

➕ 195 D4 ✉ Alšovo nábřeží 12
☎ Concerts: 227 059 227; tours: 12 444; www.czechphilharmonic.cz
🕐 Café Tue–Sun 10–6
🚇 Staroměstská 🚊 18 💷 Moderate

❷ Uměleckoprůmyslové Muzeum (Decorative Arts Museum)

Even the Czechs admit this museum's name may be hard to say and simplify it from Uměleckoprůmyslové Muzeum to UPM. The 19th-century building (many parts of which have undergone a thorough restoration) houses first-rate Bohemian and European glass, porcelain, ceramics, furniture and metalware collections from the 16th to the 20th century. There is a special emphasis on art nouveau and Czech cubism, but not all of the exhibits are always on display. The ground-floor Espresso UPM is also worth a visit.

➕ 195 D4 ✉ 17 listopadu 2 ☎ 251 093 111; www.upm.cz 🕐 Tue 10–7, Wed–Sun 10–6 🚇 Staroměstská
🚊 17, 18 💷 Moderate

❹ Obřadní síň (Ceremonial Hall)

On the left as you leave the Old Jewish Cemetery, the stone neo-Romanesque building (1908), with its little round corner turret, was once the ceremonial hall of the Jewish Burial Society. Until the 1920s, bodies were prepared here for burial in the New Jewish Cemetery over in Žižkov (► 155). Don't let the hall's appearance put you off visiting its intriguing exhibition of Jewish burial customs and its explanations of the tombstone imagery and inscriptions.

➕ 195 D4 ✉ U starého hřbitova 3
☎ Jewish Museum 222 317 191
🕐 9–6, Apr–Oct; 9–4:30, Nov–Mar; closed Sat and Jewish holidays 🚇 Staroměstská
🚊 17, 18 💷 Jewish Museum ticket: expensive

Statues of composers and artists adorn the façade of the Rudolfinum concert hall

6 Klausová synagoga (Klausen Synagogue)

To the right of the cemetery exit, the Klausen Synagogue, created by Mordechai Maisel in 1573, originally consisted of three smaller buildings (Klausen in German) – a synagogue, *mikveh* ritual bath, and *yeshiva* Talmudic school. Destroyed by fire in 1689, they were replaced five years later by the present synagogue, second in importance only to the Staronová synagoga (► 121–123). It was used for the funeral ceremonies of the adjacent cemetery, of which there is a fine view from upstairs windows. The handsomely restored baroque interior today houses an exhibition of **Hebrew manuscripts** and traditional artefacts of everyday Jewish life.

➕ 195 E4 ✉ U starého hřbitova 4 ☎ Jewish Museum 222 317 191; reservations 222 317 191 🕐 9–6, Apr–Oct; 9–4:30, Nov–Mar; closed Sat and Jewish holidays 🚇 Staroměstská 🚋 17, 18 🎫 Jewish Museum ticket: expensive

8 Vysoká synagoga (High Synagogue)

Next door to the Židovská radnice (Jewish Town Hall), the High Synagogue's plain grey building con-

The Klausová Synagogue conducted funeral services for people buried in the Old Jewish Cemetery

ceals in its interior an ornate hall of worship located upstairs – hence the name. The decoration, restored after the fire of 1689, makes an elegant adaptation in Renaissance style of the building's original Gothic ribbed-vaulting. The synagogue is generally reserved for non-Orthodox Jewish services and is only open to worshippers.

➕ 195 E4 ✉ Červená 4 🕐 Fri–Sat (sabbath services), Jewish holidays 🚇 Staroměstská 🚋 17, 18

The Jewish community's greatest benefactor, Mordechai Maisel, left his name on this synagogue

🎵 Židovská radnice (Jewish Town Hall)

The baroque town hall and clock-tower were reconstructed in 1765 on the site of an earlier building founded in the 1560s by its mayor, Mordechai Maisel. It brought the ghetto's administration into line with those of the Old Town, New Town and Malá Strana. Besides the four Roman-numeral clocks, there is a **Hebrew clock** on which the hands run "counter-clockwise". Over the main entrance on Maiselova is the Jewish Town's coat of arms, a Star of David with a traditional Jewish hat. Use of the emblem, also on the clocktower, was granted by Ferdinand III after the Jews had fought against Swedish troops on Charles Bridge in 1648 (➤ 52–55). The assembly rooms are used for Jewish festivals and other community activities but are otherwise closed to the public.

➕ 195 E4 ✉ Maiselova 18
Ⓢ Staroměstská
🚊 17, 18

🔟 Maiselova synagoga (Maisel Synagogue)

Halfway up Maiselova Street, Maisel Synagogue is often the first one visited on the Jewish Museum tour for anyone coming from Staroměsté náměstí (Old Town Square). When the Jewish Town's illustrious and very wealthy 16th-century mayor, Mordechai Maisel, built this syna-gogue in 1592, towards the end of his life, it was the most lavishly decorated building the Prague ghetto had ever seen. The simpler neo-Gothic structure you see today is the result of frequent remodelling after a devastating fire in 1689. The hall of worship and upstairs women's gallery are now used as an exhibition space for some beau-tiful **silver and gold ritual objects** collected from various disbanded Czechoslovak Jewish commmunities. They include wine goblets, spice caskets (*besamim*) and intricately patterned plaques and crowns that adorned scrolls of the Torah. These are treasures originally assembled, not by the Jewish community itself, but by the German Nazis in the 1940s for their own aborted "Exotic Museum for an Extinct Race" (➤ 123).

➕ 195 E4 ✉ Maiselova 10 ☎ Jewish Museum: office 221 711 511; reserva-tions 222 317 191 🕐 9–6, Apr–Oct; 9–4:30, Nov–Mar; closed Sat and Jewish holidays Ⓢ Staroměstská 🚊 17, 18
🎫 Jewish Museum ticket: expensive

⑪ Expozice Franze Kafky (Franz Kafka Museum)

Near the western façade of the Church of St Nicholas, a small museum is installed in the building standing on the site of Franz Kafka's birthplace. The bronze bust on the corner was mounted during a brief 1960s thaw in the general Communist hostility to this profoundly subversive writer (➤ 30–31). Today, his rehabilitation is such that the little square in front of the museum has been given his name. The exhibits include photographs of him and his family, his many homes around the city, and copies of his manuscripts and drawings. (Make sure you don't confuse this with the Gallery Franz Kafka, which is devoted to temporary art exhibitions.)

➕ 195 E4 ✉ Náměstí Franze Kafky
☎ 222 321 675 🕐 Tue–Fri 10–6, Sat 10–5 🚇 Staroměstská 🚋 17, 18
💷 Inexpensive

⑫ Španělská synagoga (Spanish Synagogue)

On the east side of the neighbourhood, the most recent of Josefov's synagogues, the Spanish Synagogue, is also the most lavish. It was built in 1868 in Moorish style, with an interior inspired by Spain's Alhambra Palace. It stands on the site of the Altschul (Old Synagogue), house of worship of a Byzantine Jewish community arriving in the 11th century. The interior is a riot of gilded geometric and floral motifs in bright but subtle reds, blues and greens. Its exhibits document the history of Czech Jews from the 19th century to the present. Up in the women's gallery are some remarkable photos of the ghetto before and after its demolition in the 1900s.

➕ 195 E4 ✉ Vězeňská 1 ☎ Jewish Museum 221 711 511; reservations 222 317 191 🕐 9–6, Apr–Oct; 9–4:30, Nov–Mar; closed Sat and Jewish holidays 🚇 Staroměstská 🚋 17, 18
💷 Jewish Museum ticket: expensive; individual entry: inexpensive

⑬ Pařížská třída (Paris Boulevard)

Elegant and leafy Paris Boulevard is an urban showpiece epitomising the neighbourhood's brash break with the past. In the 1900s, ruthless slum clearance in dank and overcrowded Josefov made way for the new boulevard (➤ 122). Today, exuberant neo-baroque and art nouveau architecture, fashionable shops, cafés and chic restaurants amply justify its name.

Ornate façades like this one characterise the exuberant architecture of Pařížská třída (Paris Boulevard)

It runs straight from Staroměstské náměstí (Old Town Square) to Čechův most (bridge) at the Vltava River. Starting at Old Town Square, the grand four-storey neo-baroque house on the northeast corner was the home of the Kafka family in 1913. (Next door is the Image Theatre, which puts on flashy shows of pantomime, dance and "blacklight theatre", ▶ 46.) Across the street are two fine houses, Nos 7 and 9, on opposite corners of Jáchymova Street. Peek into Matej Blecha's ornate neo-Gothic building at No 15 (corner of Široká) to see its splendid art nouveau oval stairwell. Two other art nouveau gems are at Nos 28 and 19, the latter by Bedřich Bendelmayer, designer of the Grand Hotel Evropa on Václavské náměstí (Wenceslas Square, ▶ 141–144).

Reflecting a lingering need to latch on to the past, the street began as Mikulášska třída (Nicholas Boulevard), named after the nearby church (▶ 66) on Staroměstské náměstí (Old Town Square). In 1926, when the French capital was very much in vogue, the street became what it most looked like: Pařížská třída (Paris Boulevard). Then, under German occupation during World War II, SS commanders renamed it Nuremberg Avenue after their favourite town back home. Today, the name is once more reminiscent of France.

➕ 195 E5 🚇 Staroměstská 🚃 17

🄸🄸 Anežský klášter (Convent of St Agnes)

On the northeast edge of Josefov, the 13th-century Convent of St Agnes holds a place of honour in the life of the Old Jewish Town inasmuch as its master builders and masons also worked on the Staronová synagoga (▶ 121–123).

It is one of Prague's earliest Gothic buildings, built in 1280 for the Order of Poor Clares founded by

A sober Gothic cloister leads to St Agnes' Convent Museum of Medieval and Renaissance Art

Agnes, daughter of King Přemysl Otakar I. The convent was closed in 1782, but was restored and reopened in November 2000 as a **Museum of Medieval and Renaissance Art**. German art at present exhibited here includes works by Holbein, Altdorfer, Cranach and Baldung-Grien.

➕ 195 F5 ✉ U Milosrdných 17
☎ 224 810 628; www.ngprague.cz
🕐 Tue–Sun 10–6 🚇 Náměstí Republiky 🚃 5, 8, 14 💷 Inexpensive

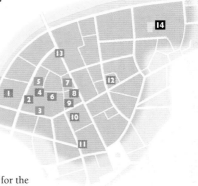

Where to...
Eat and Drink

Prices
Expect to pay per person for a meal, including drinks, tax and service
£ under 350Kč **££** 350–800Kč **£££** over 800Kč

RESTAURANTS

Café Colonial ££
French colonial cuisine is served here in this inviting set of rooms. This place buzzes with both drinkers and diners all day long, which is a record most other local eateries could envy, in fact eateries the world over. The menu is eclectic, ranging from tandoori salad or steamed blue mussels to start, to main courses like beef fondue, ginger duck or sea bass.

🚇 195 D4 ⊠ Široká 6 ☎ 224 818 322 🕐 Daily 10–midnight

Cafe La Veranda ££
Chef Radek David was named Czech Chef of the Year in 2003. Lunches and dinners here are exquisitely and carefully prepared, with a focus on intense flavours. So whether you choose the baked duck breast with thyme, cannelini beans, carmelised shallots or the tuna "grillé-cru" with roasted mushrooms and spinach, chances are you'll be well pleased.

🚇 195 E4 ⊠ Elišky Krásnohorské 2, Josefov 🕐 Mon–Sat 11 am–midnight, Sun Noon–10 pm ☎ 224 814 733; www.laveranda.cz 🚇 Staroměstská

Chez Marcel £–££
If your languages run to French rather than Czech, no problem! The same goes for the staff and much of the regular crowd at Chez Marcel's. They dine and drink with insouciance, but at Czech prices. Jazz tunes and old French advertising posters add to the bistro atmosphere as patrons dine on steaks, *poulet frite* (chicken and chips), or a simple *croque monsieur* (ham and cheese toasted sandwich). The crème caramel is not bad either. No credit cards.

🚇 195 F4 ⊠ Haštalské náměstí 12, Staré Město ☎ 222 315 676 🕐 Mon–Fri 8–1 am, Sat–Sun 9–1 am

King Solomon £££–£££
This kosher restaurant holds true to its name with a warm interior intended to resemble the Temple of Jerusalem. If that's not your preferred environment in which to dig into *gefilte fisch* or *blintzes*, ask to be seated in the glazed atrium. They'll also send a sabbath lunch box to your hotel on request.

🚇 195 D4 ⊠ Široká 8, Josefov ☎ 224 818 752 🕐 Sun–Thu noon–11 pm. Fri dinner and Sat lunch by reservation only

Les Moules ££
You can get mussels in coconut milk with chilli and fresh coriander and a side of *pommes frites* at this brasserie. The stunning double-height windows that look out onto the Old-New Synagogue and Pařížská Boulevard make the view here so pleasant that it's easy to overlook the restaurant's inner charms: traditional dark wood panelling, comfortable tables and ornate light fixtures.

🚇 201 E4 ⊠ Pařížská 19/203, Josefov ☎ 222 315 022 🕐 Mon–Fri 8:30–midnight; Sat–Sun 9–midnight

Pravda £££
The restaurant/club called "The Truth" feels like a stray from some glitzy Mediterranean port. Indeed, Prague's is the offspring of the original in Marbella, part of owner

is not the only way to treat a filet mignon. If you've less red-blooded appetites, try the classically Czech roast duck.

🚇 195 F5 ☒ Anezská 2, Staré Město ☎ 224 811 118 ⓒ Daily 11–11

PUBS AND BARS

Although the demolition of the old quarter a century ago swept away the notorious night-time establishments of Josefov, this neighbourhood is richer in drinking places than restaurants. Westernised bars and cafés cluster around Pařížská třída (Paris Boulevard). Look for relatively untouched pubs on Dušní and Kozi streets, a few blocks to the east.

Alcohol Bar

A night here is a bit more sophisticated than in other cocktail spots in Prague, but "professional" doesn't equal "pretentious." You're apt to get a smile and a greeting from the staff as you descend to this modern cellar bar, and the prompt service doesn't stop when it's busy. A nightly DJ spinning popular euro-hits, imaginative cocktails and a ventilation system that keeps the air remarkably smoke-free makes this a fine place to spend a few hours.

🚇 195 E4 ☒ Dušní 6, Josefov ☎ 224 811 744 ⓒ Daily 7 pm–3 am; www.alcoholbar.cz ⓜ Staroměstská

Barock

From the people who brought Pravda (▶ 129) to Prague comes this très chic joint across the street. The staff are friendly and cool, the patrons just plain cool. Why not order a rather good salad, sushi or Thai-style fish to accompany your cold drink?

🚇 195 E5 ☒ Pařížská 24, Josefov ☎ 222 329 221 ⓒ Mon–Fri 8:30 am–1 am, Sat–Sun 10 am–1 am

Česká vinoteka

Taste the bottled fruits of northern Bohemia's wine region at this

Tommy Sjoo's string of restaurants. The lunchtime scene is relaxed, reflecting the many walk-ins strolling near Staronová synagoga (Old-New Synagogue), so an order of just salad and water won't ruffle the feathers of the amiable, attentive staff. Dinner becomes a more glamorous affair – although still relaxed by European standards. The food is eclectic world food – adventurous for Prague – including Vietnamese spring rolls, lobster soup and tacos.

🚇 195 E5 ☒ Pařížská 17, Josefov ☎ 222 326 203; www.pravda-restaurant.cz ⓒ Daily 11:30 am–1 am

U Červeného kola ££

Steaks are the forte at "The Red Wheel", an old inn with a rustic air whose existence you'd never suspect from the street. The interior maintains a touch of pre-revolutionary days with bizarre rounded chandeliers in the best socialist-realist taste. Fortunately, Prague chefs have learned since then that "well done"

minuscule wine bar by the Anežsky klášter (St Agnes Convent). The best-known regional labels are Melnik and Zernoseky, both of which produce reliable reds such as the dry, tannic Frankovka and the smoother Svatovavrinecke.

🚇 195 F5 ☒ Anezská 3, Staré Město ☎ 222 311 293 ⓒ Mon–Fri 11 am–midnight

Molly Malone's

The crackling fireplace and menu of Irish favourites are two reasons to call on this friendly pub; Guiness on draught and the convivial mix of ex-pats and locals are two more. Try to get the cosy table tucked into the upstairs nook.

🚇 195 F5 ☒ U Obecního dvora 4, Josefov ☎ 224 818 851; www.mollymalones.cz ⓒ Daily 9 am–1 am ⓜ Náměstí Republiky

U Pivrnce

The ancient vaulted ceilings of this pub are decorated with contemporary and explicitly naughty scenes by well-known cartoonist Urban. There's an extensive menu of beef, chicken and pork dishes. Try "Mydlář the Executioner's Sword", a beef and pork skewer commemorating the famous Prague executioner.

⊞ 195 E4 ⊠ Maiselova 3, Josefov ☎ 222 329 404 ⓒ Daily 11 am–midnight

Zlatá Praha

In summer, the ninth-floor terrace bar attached to the Inter-Continental Hotel's high-class restaurant commands an unbeatable panorama of the Old Town. And you can order drinks and light meals to complement the view.

⊞ 195 E5 ⊠ Náměstí Curieových 43/5, Staré Město ☎ 296 630 914 ⓒ Daily noon–3, 6–11:30 pm; Sun brunch 11–3 pm

CAFÉS

Coffee Heaven

Bright, busy and brimming with delicious treats – fresh *panini*,

baguette sandwiches, cakes and pastries – to go with excellent coffee.

⊞ 195 E4 ⊠ Pařížská 1, Staré Mesto ☎ 222 311 967; www.coffee-heaven.eu.com ⓒ Staroměstská

Dolce Vita

This reasonably genuine Italian café has a small upper gallery for an intimate grappa, a busy street level and a few outdoor tables. On the menu are *panini* (Italian sandwiches), cakes and *tiramisu*.

⊞ 195 D4 ⊠ Široká 15, Josefov ☎ 222 329 192 ⓒ Daily 7:30 am–11:30 pm

Kavárna Rudolfinum

You can always find plenty of soft seating in this amply proportioned, elegantly dressed room in the Rudolfinum (▶124). No other café in town has such gentlemanly waiters, even if they do offer only a limited selection of drinks and snacks.

⊞ 195 D4 ⊠ Alšovo nábřeží at Náměstí Jana Palacha, Staré Město ☎ 224 893 317 ⓒ Exhibitions only Tue–Sun 10–6

Where to...
Shop

Shopping in the old Jewish quarter centres on the neighbourhood's parallel main streets, Pařížská and Maiselova. You can find excellent antiques, old books and prints, and boutique fashions here, though price tags are high by local standards.

PAŘÍŽSKÁ TŘÍDA

A century on from the massive urban development scheme that created "Paris Boulevard", this short street boasts the highest density of chic boutiques in town, as Christian Dior, Louis Vuitton, Hermès and even Pringle of Scotland vie for your custom. A few locally owned shops remain, such as the factory store

for the established Karlovy Vary (Karlsbad) porcelain maker, Thun (Pařížská 2), and one of the city's few specialist coin dealers, Obchod s mincemi Zlatá Koruna (Pařížská 8). Philharmonia (Pařížská 13) has a large selection of classical CDs.

AROUND JOSEFOV

Heading away from the thoroughly tourist-friendly heart of the quarter, the shops become fewer but show more character. The three-block stretch of Bilkova between Pařížská and Kozí is developing a certain chic. A number of furniture/design shops have opened here, including **Design by Donlič** (Bilkova 13). Near by, **Galerie Behémót** (Elišky Krásnohorské 6) puts on tiny, influential sales exhibitions of cutting-edge Czech visual artists. **Galerie La Femme** (Bilkova 2) specialises in renderings of the female form by mid-range Czech artists of both sexes. **Prague House** of Photography (Haštalská 1) has an excellent selection of books covering all aspects of Czech photography. Dekomania (Haštalská 1) sells imported fabrics, candles and the cast-iron domestic accessories so popular among upwardly mobile Praguers. The cramped Decorative Arts Museum gift shop (▶ 124) stocks very interesting goods related to its collections: replica glassware, books, cards, etc.

JEWISH HERITAGE

The small gift shop at the Maisel Synagogue (Maiselova 10, ▶ 126) stocks a comparatively dignified selection of replicas, such as wooden and silver Torah pointers.

For inexpensive gifts, try the Franz Kafka Museum (Náměstí Franze Kafky 3, ▶ 127).

Antikvariát V Široké (Široká 7) sells new and second-hand books on Judaism, a few guides to the Jewish Quarter, and some old prints and modern artworks.

Where to...
Be Entertained

Prague has always been known for its artistic heritage. Many concerts are performed in churches and palaces and are extremely popular. Sometimes it is the only way to see the church, which may be closed to the public otherwise.

MUSIC

Classical
Rudolfinum

The Dvořák Hall is a jewel of an auditorium where the best local and visiting musical talent performs. This is home to the Czech Philharmonic Orchestra, the country's best travelled, most respected cultural institution, which proudly upholds the great musical traditions of Central Europe. The excellent Prague Philharmonia Chamber Orchestra and the Czech National Symphony Orchestra make regular appearances. Chamber concerts take place in the Suk Hall.

🚏 199 D4 ✉ Alšovo nábřeží at Náměstí Jana Palacha, Staré Město ☎ 227 059 227

Klášter sv Anežký České (St Agnes Convent)

The historic St Agnes Convent complex includes a concert hall built in the 1980s from the ruins of an early Gothic church. It is one of the better venues in town for serious classical music, and one of the few where Praguers outnumber tourists.

🚏 199 F5 ✉ U Milosrdných 17, Staré Město ☎ 224 810 628

Kostel sv Šimona a Judy (Church of SS Simon and Jude)

High-quality chamber concerts take place in this large baroque Church of SS Simon and Jude. Advance tickets are sold at the FOK agency, U Obecního domu 2, in Staré Město (Old Town).

🚏 199 E5 ✉ Dušní at U Milosrdných, Staré Město ☎ 222 002 336 (FOK); www.fok.cz

BOAT RIDES

Excursion boats dock at the quayside below Na Františku Street, across from the Inter-Continental Hotel. You can simply pick from the available craft or reserve through the largest tour operator, EVD (from the booth on the quay or telephone 224 810 030; www.evd.cz), which runs brief sightseeing rides, lunch trips and evening cruises.

EVD also operates the Jazzissimo jazz cruise several times weekly from April to November.

Nové Město
(New Town)
and Beyond

Getting Your Bearings

Despite its name and modern buildings, Nové Město (New Town) has a place well anchored in history. If its monuments proudly proclaim the Czechs' rise to nationhood, Vyšehrad Castle is bathed in the legendary mists of Prague's medieval beginnings. And from Vltava Embankment you can enjoy the blithely unhistoric pleasures of open-air cafés and dancing.

With the art nouveau Obecní dům (Municipal House) as its bright beacon on the southeast corner of Staré Město (Old Town), Nové Město (New Town) extends from the avenues of Na příkopě and Národní south along the Vltava River to the heights of Vyšehrad. To the east lie the airy bourgeois residential neighbourhood of Vinohrady and more working-class district of Žižkov.

This is the liveliest part of modern Prague. With its shops and cinemas, Václavské náměstí (Wenceslas Square) is the bright and busy centre where young and old like to stroll. Národní třída has two cultural monuments, the august Národní divadlo (National Theatre) and, opposite, Café Slavia, renowned haunt of artists and their groupies.

Preceding page: The café in the Obecní dům

Above: Obecní dům, Prague's favourite meeting place

★ Don't Miss

1 Obecní dům (Municipal House) ➤ 138

4 Mucha Muzeum ➤ 140

7 Václavské náměstí (Wenceslas Square) ➤ 141

10 Národní divadlo (National Theatre) ➤ 145

12 Vltava Embankment ➤ 147

13 Vyšehrad Castle and Cubist buildings ➤ 149

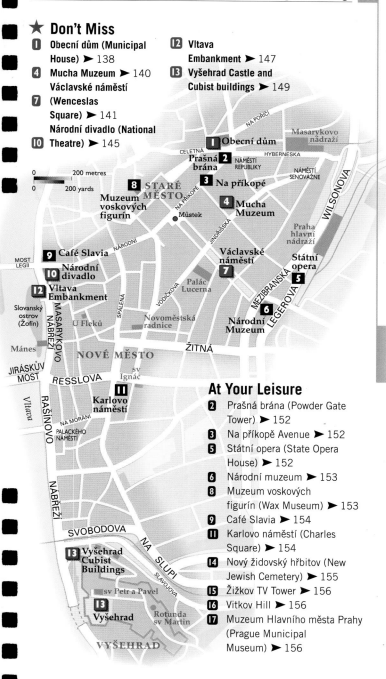

At Your Leisure

2 Prašná brána (Powder Gate Tower) ➤ 152

3 Na příkopě Avenue ➤ 152

5 Státní opera (State Opera House) ➤ 152

6 Národní muzeum ➤ 153

8 Muzeum voskových figurín (Wax Museum) ➤ 153

9 Café Slavia ➤ 154

11 Karlovo náměstí (Charles Square) ➤ 154

14 Nový židovský hřbitov (New Jewish Cemetery) ➤ 155

15 Žižkov TV Tower ➤ 156

16 Vitkov Hill ➤ 156

17 Muzeum Hlavního města Prahy (Prague Municipal Museum) ➤ 156

The New Town is where the Czechs hang out.
Ancient meets modern in areas less frequented by tourists.

Around Nové Město in a Day

10:00 am
Make a bright start at **Obecní dům**
(Municipal House, right, ► 138–139) and
maybe visit the café. At the southern end of
the building, climb the **Prašná brána** (Powder
Gate Tower, ► 152) for a good rooftop view
of the monuments you'll be visiting.

11:00 am
Stroll west along **Na příkopě** (► 152)
and maybe do some shopping before
heading south on Panská to the
Mucha Muzeum (► 140).

12:00 noon
Cut over on Jindřišská west to **Václavské náměstí** (Wenceslas Square,
► 141–144). Walk up to the Wenceslas Monument and then back down,
ending up at the truly grand Grand Hotel Evropa for a pre-lunch cocktail
in its elegant café (► 142).

1:00 pm
At the Vodičkova junction
with Václavské náměstí,
hop on the No 9 tram,
which turns north and west
to run along Národní třída
to the **Vltava Embankment**
(left, ► 147–148). From
Masarykovo nábřeží, walk
down the causeway over to
Žofín Island (► 148) for
lunch at one of the restaurants (► 157), perhaps out
on the terrace. After lunch,
choose between a siesta
in the garden and hiring a
rowing boat for a closer
look at the river.

3:00 pm

Back up on Masarykovo nábřeží, walk south to **Mánes Gallery** to see one of its excellent temporary exhibitions of modern art (► 147). Then continue south along the embankment to look at Frank Gehry's wild **Ginger and Fred building** (► 148) before hopping on a No 17 or 21 tram down to Vyšehrad.

4:00 pm

This is the ideal time to explore the grounds of **Vyšehrad Castle** (► 149), pay your respects to Dvořák (right) and Smetana in the cemetery and take in the late afternoon view from the ramparts. Leave yourself time to see Josef Chochol's unique **cubist buildings** (► 151).

5:30 pm

From the embankment – Rašínovo nábřeží – take the No 17 or 21 tram back north to Národní and tea or an apéritif in Café Slavia (► 154).

7:00 pm

Round off the evening with some opera or ballet at **Národní divadlo** (National Theatre, below, ► 145–146).

Obecní dům
(Municipal House)

For many people, this masterpiece of art nouveau architecture is the city's grandest 20th-century building. Its ornate café and restaurants and splendid concert hall, all lovingly renovated, certainly make it one of the most popular.

Art nouveau design at its most exuberant

Long before the word "multi-functional" had entered the modern urban planner's vocabulary, the city of Prague was commissioning its architects to design a home for art exhibitions, classical music concerts and a traditional coffee house with good cuisine to add a touch of class to the municipal offices. In an unabashed expression of the Czech national revival that rejected the Habsburg past, it replaced an old royal palace turned military academy. It was completed in 1911 and independent Czechoslovakia was proclaimed there seven years later, on 28 October, 1918.

On the Square
Antonín Balšánek and Osvald Polívka erected a lofty domed rotunda from which two bold wings spread to embrace the west side of busy náměstí Republiky (Republican Square). In the archway over the rotunda's entrance is Karel Špillar's mosaic, a somewhat pompous allegorical *Homage to Prague*.

The Interior
The building's artwork inside has a much lighter touch. Lobbies, cloakrooms, elevators and stairways are all decorated with art nouveau floral motifs or the geometric patterns of the Czech *secesní* (Secession/art nouveau). Leading artists competed to contribute – Jan Preisler, Max Švabinský, Mikoláš

Aleš and sculptor Ladislav Šaloun. **Alfons Mucha**, most famous
of them all since moving to Paris (► 140), wanted to do all the
interior painting himself, and did a grand job on the **Mayoral
Hall**, but had to accept his colleagues' participation in the café
and restaurants. Exhibitions, often of the artists who decorated
the Obecní dům, are held on upper floors.

*Smetana Hall
traditionally
hosts the
opening
concert of the
Prague Spring
Music Festival*

Smetanova sín (Smetana Hall)
On the first floor, this is the city's largest concert hall with
a monumental elliptical glazed dome. It is principally the
home of the **Prague Symphony Orchestra**, though the Czech
Philharmonic plays here during the annual Prague Spring
Music Festival (► 46).

A traditional – and highly emotional – event is the festival's
opening night when Smetana's *Má vlast* (*My Country*) is played
in the presence of the president. On either side of the stage,
Šaloun's sculptures represent *Má vlast* on the left and Dvořák's
Slavonic Dances on the right.

TAKING A BREAK
The grand **café** is good for morning or late afternoon coffee;
for lunch there's French cuisine in the elegant surroundings of
Francouzská (► 157); and in the evening Czech specialities
and beer in the tavern-like basement **Plzeňská** (► 158).

✚ 195 F4 ✉ Náměstí Republiky 5 ☎ 222 002 101 ⊕ Ticket/information
office 10–6 Ⓜ Náměstí Republiky 🚊 3, 5, 14, 24 🎟 Free; tours moderate

OBECNÍ DŮM: INSIDE INFO

Hidden gem Just off the ground-floor café is a charming art nouveau **billiard
hall**, which can also be reached by a side staircase from a rear entrance on
U Prašne brány Street.

4

Mucha Muzeum

This museum of works by art nouveau master Alphonse Mucha (1860–1939) is one of the most popular in Prague. Yet the artist who made his name in Paris during the Belle Époque with his highly decorative poster art remains more appreciated by visitors than by his fellow countrymen. Inaugurated in 1998, the collection lets you decide.

Housed in the Kaunický palác south of Na příkopě Avenue, the museum presents Mucha's paintings, lithographs, drawings, pastels, sculpture and personal memorabilia. Best known are his theatre posters for the great actress Sarah Bernhardt – *Gismonda, Médée, Lorenzaccio* and *La Samaritaine* – guaranteeing his commercial success in the 1890s. Mucha served Parisian society and the design departments for Nestlé's baby food and Moët et Chandon champagne.

In 1910, after a spell in Chicago and New York, Mucha was desperate to prove himself a truly Czech painter. Back in Prague, he painted lofty allegorical themes for the Obecní dům (Municipal House, ► 138–139) as well as stained-glass windows for St Vitus Cathedral (► 89–91).

Slav Epic

In an English-language video, the museum tells the story of Mucha's most ambitious work – the *Slovaská epopej* (*Slav Epic*) of 20 giant canvases, which took him 18 years to complete. The solemn patriotic paintings are exhibited in his hometown, Moravský Krumlov (in Moravia, 180km/112 miles southwest of Prague).

TAKING A BREAK

In memory of Mucha's good times, have a good French coffee at **Paris-Praha** on Jindřišská.

➕ 195 F3 ✉ Panská 7 ☎ 224 216 415 🕐 10–6, Mar–Dec; 11–5, Jan–Feb 🚇 Můstek 🚊 3, 9, 14, 24 💲 Moderate

---

MUCHA MUZEUM: INSIDE INFO

Top tip Be sure to see Mucha's collection of **personal snapshots** of models and famous friends – including fellow painter Paul Gauguin playing the harmonium in his underwear.

❼
Václavské náměstí
(Wenceslas Square)

The unquestioned centre of modern Prague bustles night and day. Czechs and tourists alike flock here, drawn by the cinemas, restaurants, casinos and shopping arcades. In the past, they came here, often in their thousands, to witness some of the most dramatic events in modern Czech history.

Opposite: Mucha's Paris theatre poster for Sarah Bernhardt's *Gismonda* launched his international career

Less a square, more of a long and broad sloping esplanade, Václavské náměstí (Wenceslas Square) was originally created by Charles IV in 1348 as the New Town's Horse Market. It extends from Národní muzeum (➤ 153) down to Můstek Metro station on Na příkopě Avenue (➤ 152).

Wenceslas Monument

At the top of the square, the equestrian **statue** of patron saint sv Václav (Wenceslas) is surrounded by four other national saints – his grandmother Ludmila, Vojtěk, Prokop and Anežska (Agnes). Sculptor Josef Myslbek took 25 years to complete the monument, in 1912, of the man who led the Christian conversion of the Czechs (➤ 32) and it immediately became a natural focus for Prague's most fervent popular demonstrations.

Václavské náměstí (Wenceslas Square) slopes away from the Wenceslas Monument

The Buildings

Blending innovative use of steel and glass with more ornate art nouveau façades, Václavské náměstí epitomises the Czechs' early enthusiastic embrace of modernity in the 20th century.

Visit the Evropa
Hotel and the
Café Evropa
within

The 1920s and 1930s were boom years for big stores and
cinemas. For a state funeral, die-hard traditionalists had the
neon signs draped in black. Spared bombardment in World War
II, the square is a living museum of 20th-century architecture.

Downhill from Wenceslas Monument on the right, the **Jalta
Hotel** (No 45) is a classical piece of 1950s Stalinist design,
bleak and charmless. Much more attractive, on the left at
the corner of Stepanská, is the imposing rotunda of the old
Moravian Bank building (1916). Next door (No 36) is the
historic **Melantrich** publishing house
where, on its balcony in 1989, Václav
Havel joined the beloved but hapless
Alexander Dubček who tried 20 years
before to introduce "Socialism with a
human face".

Directly opposite, the **Grand Hotel
Evropa** (1906) by Bendřich Bendelmayer
and Alois Dryák is a landmark among art
nouveau buildings on the square. Besides
the façade's splendid double bay windows,
notice, perhaps on your way into the
ornately decorated restaurants or café,
the lofty oval gallery around the hotel's
stairwell. Down the street on the other
side of Jindřišská, Osvald Polívka's neo-
baroque corner building (No 19), now

Tourist's Lament
The fourth verse of the Christmas
carol *Good King Wenceslas*
might well have been written for a
footsore sightseer:
"Sire, the night is darker now,
And the wind blows stronger.
Fails my heart, I know not how.
I can go no longer."
"Mark my footsteps, my good page,
Tread thou in them boldly:
Thou shalt find the winter's rage
Freeze thy blood less co-oldly."

housing the Polish Cultural Institute, is best known as the **Assicurazione Generali** where Franz Kafka got his first job as an insurance clerk.

The square's other art nouveau jewel is across the street at No 12, the **Peterka House**, a subtle design by Jan Kotěra, a pupil of Vienna's Secession master, Otto Wagner. Side by side at the bottom end are the famous shops of **Bata Shoes** (No 6) and **Lindt Chocolate** (No 4), both pioneering buildings for their 1920s functionalist design in steel and glass on a reinforced concrete frame. (A great patron of Czech art before World War II, Tomás Bata fled when his shoe factories and shops were expropriated by the Communists in 1948. His family retrieved the business in 1989.)

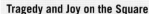

Tragedy and Joy on the Square

1848 Crowds met here to celebrate an open-air Mass before their abortive revolt, the first "Prague Spring", was brutally repressed by Austrian artillery. Overnight, the Horse Market became Václavské náměstí (Wenceslas Square).

1918 Thousands gathered at the foot of the Wenceslas Monument to celebrate the proclamation of the new Czechoslovak Republic.

1939 A demonstration against the German occupation ended in the fatal shooting of medical student Jan Opletal.

1948 Armed factory workers paraded here in support of the Communist Party's February coup d'état.

1968 The new "Prague Spring" of social reforms was ended in August by Soviet tanks. They fired at the Národní muzeum, mistaking it – according to conflicting reports – either for the Czechoslovak Parliament or the Czechoslovak Radio Station. Five months later, philosophy student Jan Palach burned himself alive near the Wenceslas Monument in protest at the people's lethargy and apathy. His gesture is marked by a small memorial.

1989 Hundreds of thousands staged the Velvet Revolution's candlelit demonstration to force the end of the Communist regime and call for Václav Havel to become President.

Two figures of classical mythology bear the weight of a bay window

In its time, Palác Koruna was a beacon of modernity

Opposite, **Palác Koruna** offers the square a fitting, if somewhat overpoweringly monumental No 1. The majestic tower's spangled crown (*koruna*) lights up at night. When it was first built, Ladislav Machoň designed a Cubist cinema in the basement, a fast-food restaurant on the ground floor – Europe's first – and an apartment for himself at the top of the tower.

TAKING A BREAK

This is a good place to try out one of Prague's teahouses, the easygoing **Dobrá čajovna** (literally "good teahouse"), on Václavské náměstí 14, next to the Peterka House (► 158).

🕂 195 F3 ⊠ Václavské náměstí 🚇 Muzeum, Můstek 🚃 3, 9, 14, 24

VÁCLAVSKÉ NÁMĚSTÍ: INSIDE INFO

Top tip The **lower end** of the square is popular in the early evening, especially with the young crowd, for the Czechs' equivalent of the Spanish *paseo* or Italian *passeggiata*. Apart from cars serving big hotels, the square is a pedestrian zone.

Národní divadlo
(National Theatre)

Like a cathedral or royal palace, this theatre is a veritable
national shrine, paid for by the Czech people themselves.
The massive, long-domed building is Nové Město's most
prominent landmark overlooking the Vltava River. Profit from
an evening at the opera here, both for the festive atmosphere
and a close-up view of the grand interior.

**The National
Theatre towers
over the Vltava
River like a
grand ocean
liner**

The imposing neo-Renaissance building was designed by Josef
Zítek, architect of the Rudolfinum (► 124). Above the stately
portico at the entrance are Bohuslav Schnirch's statues of Apollo
and the nine Muses.

The Interior

Paintings and sculptures in the sumptuous interior are by leading artists later known collectively as "The Generation of the
National Theatre". For the lobby, Mikoláš Aleš and František
Ženíšek painted 14 scenes inspired by Smetana's symphonic
poem *Má vlast* (*My Country*). Many of the sculptures are by
Josef Myslbek, creator of the Wenceslas Monument (► 141).
The majestic, four-tiered auditorium is lavishly decorated in
gold and red. Voytěch Hynais created the spectacular allegorical
painting for the safety curtain. Written in gold over the arch is
the theatre's aspiration: *Národ sobě* (*The Nation to Itself*).

The People's Theatre

At the height of the Czech nationalist movement in the 19th century, the Národní was built as a Czech counterpoint to the German-speaking community's Stavovské divadlo (Estates Theatre, ► 63). The people wanted a theatre specifically for Czech opera and drama. Under Austrian pressure, parliament refused funds, but a public subscription raised donations. Over 50,000 people brought the foundation stones to the building site in 1868. The stones came from historic sites in Bohemia and Moravia – but also from Chicago, sent by Czechoslovak émigrés with the inscription: "What blood unites, the sea will not sunder". The theatre opened in June 1881 with Smetana's patriotic opera *Libuše* and, just two months later, after only 12 performances, was gutted by fire. It was rebuilt with a public subscription, this time with a donation by Emperor Franz Joseph, who was conscious of the need to keep his subjects happy.

TAKING A BREAK

You can have a cocktail in the elegant and historic Café Slavia (► 74); or, at the other end of the scale, but no less fun, have a beer in U Zpěváčků, a noisy workers' pub behind the theatre on Na Struze (► 158).

Audiences here have heard some of the most sublime acoustics in European music

➕ 195 D2 ✉ Národní třída 2 ☎ 224 901 377 🕐 Box office: daily 10–6; also open 45 minutes before performances 🚇 Národní třída 🚃 6, 9, 17, 18, 22, 23 💷 Opera: moderate–expensive

NÁRODNÍ DIVADLO: INSIDE INFO

Top tip At the interval in the theatre bar, try the **Czech champagne – Bohemia sekt** – it's really pretty good.

One to miss People who may find the Národní divadlo's architecture pompous are immediately reconciled when they see the starkly modern, almost brutally cold glass box of the **Nová scéna** (New Stage) next door. Devoted principally to the National Theatre's repertoire of modern Czech drama, it was designed by Karel Prager in 1983 while he was renovating the Národní.

⑫

Vltava Embankment

Take a riverside walk beside some of Nové Město's most elegant buildings, including Národní divadlo (National Theatre). Then step out onto Žofín Island, with its cafés, concerts and open-air balls, to compare styles with two startling, modern office towers, Ginger and Fred, "dancing" together further down the embankment.

South of Národní divadlo (National Theatre, ► 145–146), the buildings on **Masarykovo nábřeží** (Masaryk Embankment) offer showcases of early 20th-century architecture, an eclectic mixture of art nouveau, historicist and modern functionalist styles. On the corner of Na Struze, at No 32, the Goethe-Institut (German Cultural Centre) occupies the attractive building that was the East German Embassy. The art nouveau ornament is by Ladislav Šaloun. No 16 is the concert hall (1906) of the historic **Hlahol Choral Society**, a major contributor to the Czech national revival. With its sculpture by Josef Pékarek and an allegorical mosaic of "Music" in the gable, the façade bears a characteristic inscription: *Zpěvem k srdci – srdcm k vlasti* ("Let the song reach the heart, let the heart reach the homeland").

Mánes Art Gallery

Mánes Art Gallery's watermill tower looks across the handsome buildings of Masaryk Embankment

Forming a bridge between the embankment and Žofín Island, the gallery is housed in Otakar Novotný's handsome, white, concrete and glass functionalist building of the 1920s, in sharp contrast to the adjoining black onion-domed tower of the old Šítek watermill. The gallery, founded by the Josef Mánes Arts Association, exhibits major contemporary art rather than the 19th-century folksy genre painting associated with Mánes. The gallery's café and restaurant look out over the river.

The Palacký Monument

On a square beside the bridge is a gigantic monument to František Palacký, 19th-century historian, politician and leader of the Czech national movement. "Father of the Nation" (*Otek národy*), Palacký produced the five-volume *History of the Czech Nation* at a time when the Austro-Hungarian Empire had almost obliterated the Czechs as a separate entity. Palacký fought Engels' contemptuous dismissal of the Czechs as "an absolutely non-existent nation" who "have never had a history of their own".

Žofín Island

The island is known by the name of its popular concert hall, Palác Žofín, which honours Archduchess Sophie, mother of Emperor Franz-Joseph. Officially, it is Slovanský ostrov (Slavonic Island). Formed by a sandbank and landfill, the island has been a favourite pleasure park for nearly 200 years. Facilities include **rowing boats** in the summer (May–Oct), open-air cafés, restaurants, concerts – jazz and classical – and dancing (mostly ballroom) in the gardens.

Ginger and Fred

On the embankment just south of Jiráskův most (Jiraský Bridge) is one of the city's more imaginative edifices, two modern towers clinging to each other in a dancers' embrace. The Dutch company offices were built in 1996 by maverick California architect Frank Gehry and his Yugoslav associate Vlado Milunič. The building is known variously as *tančící dům* (Dancing House) and "Ginger and Fred", after Ginger Rogers and Fred Astaire.

A peaceful end to the day floating across the Vltava River

Nestling up against the thoroughly modern couple is a now inevitably quaint-looking 1900s apartment building. It was built by Václav Havel, grandfather of the Czech president. The latter lived in the top-floor apartment with his first wife, Olga.

TAKING A BREAK

There are several cafés and restaurants in the **Mánes Gallery** or on **Žofín Island**, but you might like to duck away from the embankment to the city's most historic pub, U Fleků (► 158).

🕂 195 D2 ⬚ Mánes, Masarykovo nábřeží 250; Palác Žofín, Slovanský ostrov 226 ☎ Mánes 224 930 754; www.galeriemanes.cz ⏱ Tue–Sun 10–6 🚋 17, 21 💷 Mánes Gallery: free

VLTAVA EMBANKMENT: INSIDE INFO

Top tip At weekends the Mánes Art Gallery has become a favourite rendezvous for **Latin American dancing**.

Vyšehrad Castle and Cubist Buildings

The castle rock at the southern edge of Nové Město is a place bathed in myth as much as in reality. It is the romantic site of an 11th-century clifftop fortress above the Vltava River – Vyšehrad means "Castle on the Heights". Redbrick ramparts enclose vestiges of its ancient buildings and a national cemetery honouring the country's creative genius. The gardens are ideal for picnics – with wonderful views at sunset.

The Fortress

Castle signposts from Vyšehrad Metro station lead along V Pevnosti Street to the southeast entrance, through the **Leopoldova brána** (Leopold Gate). Fork right to the **sv Martin Rotunda**, one of the few structures remaining from the original castle. This 11th-century chapel, restored in 1878 and used now only for funeral services for Vyšehrad Cemetery, is the city's oldest surviving Romanesque building. Over to the left, on Soběslavova Street, archaeologists have excavated foundations of the even older **Basilica of sv Vavřince** (St Lawrence), built before the castle. The **Church of sv Petr a Pavel** (SS Peter and Paul) is a neo-Gothic reconstruction (1887, towers 1903).

The Rotunda of sv Martin is the funeral chapel for Vyšehrad Cemetery

In a garden, Vyšehrad's fanciful origins are reinforced by Josef Myslbek's 19th-century statues of mythical couples. Closest to the river are *Libuše and Přemysl*, the prophetess and her husband, and *Lumír and Píseň*, a legendary singer with his muse. At the other end of the garden are *Šárka and Ctirad*, a woman warrior and her lover, and another couple of warriors, *Záboj and Slavoj*, pure concoctions of a spurious legend forged for the nationalist cause in 1816.

The Czechs' revered artists are buried in this arcaded portico

The Cemetery

North and east of SS Peter and Paul Church, the medieval cemetery became in 1869, as part of Vyšehrad's nationalist mission, a Pantheon for Czech musicians, opera singers, actors, writers, painters and sculptors. Here, the country celebrates its artists, not its politicians and generals. Surrounded by Antonín Wiehl's neo-Renaissance arcaded portico, their graves are shown on a map at the entrance next to the church.

Designed by Ladislav Šaloun, the monumental **tomb of Antonín Dvořák** is set in the arcade behind a wrought-iron railing. The more modest **tomb of Bedřich Smetana** stands near the formidable **Slavín Monument**. Also designed by Wiehl, the column and sarcophagus mark a communal tomb for 50 artists, including painter Alfons Mucha and sculptors Šaloun and Myslbek.

The Dungeons

Beside Vyšehrad's north entrance/exit, **Cihelná brána** (Brick Gate), a guided tour takes you under the ramparts into the castle dungeons and Gorlice Hall, housing original baroque statues from Charles Bridge.

The Myth

The Vyšehrad cliff was discovered by Princess Libuše, legendary heroine celebrated in Smetana's opera. Standing with her husband Přemysl, she looked across the river at where Prague Castle now stands and prophesied: "I see a great city whose fame will touch the stars." They hurried over and found an old man already building the threshhold – *prah* (hence the city's name). A mosaic designed by Mikuláš Aleš depicts the myth in the lobby of the Old Town Hall (► 57).

The Reality

Right: Legendary Šárka and Ctirad vow eternal love in the Vysehrad gardens

A church and fortified trading post were built on the heights of Vyšehrad in the 10th century, 70 years after the establishment of Prague Castle. To counter his rivals, Vratislav II, a prince of Bohemia's founding Přemyslid dynasty, built a castle here in 1085. Forty years

later, his successors returned to Prague Castle and Vyšehrad was abandoned until restored by Charles IV. The fortress was destroyed by the Hussites and later the Habsburgs left only the redbrick ramparts.

Vyšehrad Cubist Buildings

Prague offers Europe's only examples of cubist art applied to architecture. Along with the Black Madonna House on Staré Město's Celetná Street (➤ 69), the finest are Josef Chochol's two villas and an apartment building (1912–14) north of Vyšehrad.

From the north side of the castle, cut through to Neklanova to see the great **Hodek Apartment House** on the corner of Hostivitova. In characteristic cubist style, the prismatic shapes of balconies and windows make an intricate play of light and shade beneath a dramatically projecting cornice. In the **Villa Kovařovič**, set back in a garden facing Rašínovo nábřeží (embankment), Chochol uses more restrained cubist shapes to create the appearance of an elegant country manor. South along the embankment, his **Three-Family House** (Rodinný trojdům) is an elongated building with handsomely framed windows and cubist gables for the upper floors. They are private homes and not open to the public, but their main interest is their exterior.

Joseph Chochol's Hodek Apartment House is an outstanding example of Prague's unique cubist architecture

TAKING A BREAK

If you haven't brought your own picnic, **Na Vyšehradě** near SS Peter and Paul Church is a pleasant little wine bar serving good snacks.

Vyšehrad Castle
➕ 201 D1 ✉ V Pevnosti 159/5 ☎ 241 410 348; www.praha-vysehrad.cz
🕐 Grounds dawn to sunset; exhibits daily 9:30–6, Apr–Oct; daily 9:30–5, Nov–Mar 🚇 Vyšehrad 🚋 7, 8, 24 to Albertov 💷 Dungeons: inexpensive

Cubist Buildings
➕ 201 D2 ✉ Hodek: Neklanova 30; Kovařovič: Libušina 3 (rear); Three-Family House: Rašínovo nábřeží 6–10 🚋 3, 6, 14, 18, 21, 22

VYŠEHRAD CASTLE: INSIDE INFO

Top tip The best **view** over New Town, Old Town and across the river to Prague Castle is up on the ramparts on the north side of the fortress.

One to miss A banal exhibition of **historical drawings** in the southwest bastion (Hradební věž).

At Your Leisure

❷ Prašná brána (Powder Gate Tower)

Looming dark and incongruous on the edge of the garish modern náměstí Republiky (Republican Square), this sturdy, 15th-century Gothic tower was the starting point for the grand procession of kings along the *králova cesta* (Royal Route) over to Prague Castle. When the Habsburgs abandoned this tradition, the tower served as a gunpowder store. It blew up in the Prussian siege of 1757 and was restored in the late 19th century. It is well worth going up the tower for the rooftop **view** across Old and New Town's domes and spires.

➕ 195 F4 ✉ Na příkopě ⏰ Daily 10–6, Apr–Oct 🚇 Náměstí Republiky 🚃 5, 8, 14, 24 🎟 Inexpensive

❸ Na příkopě Avenue

Bordering the Staré Město and Nové Město (Old and New Town) districts, this popular pedestrianised shopping street was, during its fashionable heyday nearly 150 years ago, the German-speaking community's favourite avenue. Known then as Am Graben (meaning, like Na příkopě, "On the Moat"), it competed with the equally emphatically Czech atmosphere of Národní třída.

At the centre, on the south side facing Havířská Street, the splendid **baroque palace** at No 10 was once the German bourgeoisie's social headquarters, the "Deutsches Kasino". Designed by Kilián Ignac Dienzenhofer in 1743, today it serves once more as a casino.

Apart from two noteworthy adjacent bank buildings (Nos 18 and 20) by Osvald Polívka, mixing art nouveau and neo-Renaissance, the street succumbed to the functionalist building boom of the 1930s.

➕ 195 F3 🚇 Můstek

❺ Státní opera (State Opera House)

Opened in 1888 as the Neues Deutsches Theater (New German Theatre), the imposing neoclassical building serves as Prague's third opera house, though that is by no means a value judgement.

Many musicians regard the acoustics of its neorococo auditorium as even better than those of the Národní divadlo (National Theatre, ► 145–146) and Stavovské divadlo (Estates

Prašná brána (Powder Gate Tower) has recovered well from its gunpowder explosion

Modern and traditional meet on Na
Příkopě Avenue

Theatre, ► 63). Given the freeway
traffic outside, this is really nothing
short of a miracle.

**➕ 201 E4 ✉ Wilsonova 4 ☎ 224 227
266; www.statniopera.cz 🚇 Muzeum**

6 Národní muzeum

The colossal pile at the top of
Václavské náměstí (Wenceslas Square)
is a deliberate but clumsy expression of
the 19th-century movement for Czech
national renewal. The neo-Renaissance
building, designed by Josef Schulz,
was opened in 1890 as a monumental
companion-piece to the Národní
divadlo (National Theatre).

The museum does have a vast
collection of plants, minerals, fossils,
insects, animals and human prehistoric stones and bones, but for most
people the real interest is at the top of
the ceremonial staircase leading from
the grand marble entrance hall.

There, under the great glass dome,
are the statues of those who led the
way to Czechoslovakia's national
independence – a display that many
young Czechs regard as the monumental fossil of a bygone age.

**➕ 201 E3 ✉ Václavské náměstí 68
☎ 224 497 111; www.nm.cz 🕐 Daily
10–6, May– Sep; 9–5, Oct–Apr. Closed
first Tue of month 🚇 Muzeum 🚌 6, 11
✋ Moderate**

8 Muzeum voskových figurín (Wax Museum)

Close to Václavské náměstí
(Wenceslas Square), this popular
museum requires a certain knowledge
of Czech history – or willingness to
learn – in order to appreciate the
scenes of famous characters. The
most easily recognisable figures are
from the 20th century – Soviet leaders, their Czechoslovak underlings
and their (generally) more democratic
successors. Feel free to ask the Czech
visitors what they are laughing at –

The Wax Museum's trio: Havel, Klaus and Dubček

the young ones especially will be happy to explain in English.

➕ 195 E3 ✉ Melantrichova 5 ☎ 224 229 852; www.waxmuseumprague.cz
🕐 Daily 9–8 🚇 Můstek 💷 Moderate

9 Café Slavia

This landmark café opposite Národní divadlo (National Theatre) has been a meeting place for artists, writers and political dissidents from the 1920s to the Velvet Revolution of the 1990s (➤ 14).

They included Karel Teige's avant-garde Devětsil group, poet Jaroslav Seifert, cubist architect Josef Chochol and journalists Milena Jesenská and Egon Erwin Kisch. During easier times, the intellectuals complain that gentrification destroys the old atmosphere, but the cosmopolitan mix of coffee, apple strudel and foreign newspapers remains.

Enjoy the view from the riverside tables or, on the Národní třída side, watch the beautiful people arrive for the opera.

➕ 195 D2
✉ Národní třída 1 ☎ 224 218 493; www.cafeslavia.cz
🕐 Daily 8 am–midnight
🚇 Národní třída
🚌 6, 9, 18, 21, 22

11 Karlovo náměstí (Charles Square)

Its extended, tree-lined gardens now give Prague's biggest square more the appearance of a public park than the city square it was in the 18th century. It was originally a cattle market, set up by Charles IV when he created Nové Město (New Town) in 1348 – along with the horse market at Václavské náměstí (Wenceslas Square, ➤ 141–144) and a hay market farther east (náměstí Senovážné).

In the northeast corner, the well-restored Gothic gabled building,

largely 15th century, is **Nové Město's town hall**, the scene of Prague's first Defenestration (► 18). On the east side, next to the old Jesuit college, now a hospital, is the 17th-century **Church of sv Ignác** (St Ignatius). It is built on the classic Jesuit model of the Gesù church in Rome, except for the portico added to the façade. Inside, the baroque interior is particularly lavish. On the southwest corner of the square, a baroque building associated with several alchemists, including the Englishman Edward Kelley (► 8), is fancifully known as the **Faustův dům** (Faust House).

✚ 195 E1 🚇 Karlovo náměstí
🚃 4, 6, 10, 22, 23

🔟 Nový židovský hřbitov (New Jewish Cemetery)

East of Olšanské municipal cemeteries, tombstones in the New Jewish Cemetery tell the story of the community's last years. Laid out in the 1890s, it is a place of pilgrimage not just for the (signposted) **grave of Franz Kafka**, but also for the tombs and memorials of Prague's Jewish citizens, prominent and otherwise, with tombstones bearing the inscription *1944 v Osvietimi* ("1944 in Auschwitz").

On the simple tomb of Kafka and his parents is a plaque in memory of his three sisters, who died in concentration camps. On a wall opposite is a tribute to Kafka's friend **Max Brod**, "born in Prague, writer and thinker who carried Czech culture abroad" – among the first to champion Jaroslav Hašek, author of *Good Soldier Švejk*, and composer Leoš Janáček.

✚ 201 C4 ✉ Izraelská 🕐 Daily 9–4:30, Apr–Sep; Sun–Fri 9–3:30, Oct–Mar 🚇 Želivského 🚃 10, 11, 16
💰 Inexpensive

Monumental Architecture

A monument among Prague's classical hotels, the **Hotel Paříž** (tel: 222 195 195) stands behind the Obecní dům (Municipal House, ► 138). Its architecture (1907) is a palatial combination of neo-Gothic and art nouveau. In the elegant café, bar and restaurant, everything is designed with exquisite attention to detail.

Praha hlavní nádraží (Main Station) on Wilsonova (below) is a slice of history. With some art nouveau frills, Josef Fanta's grand design of 1909 was appropriate to what began as Franz-Joseph Station, Prague's swansong for the Habsburg Empire. Nine years later, in gratitude for the American president's help in gaining independence, the Czechs renamed it Woodrow Wilson Station. Ideologies came and went, renovations added two formidable glass structures, and it is now just Prague Main Station.

Žižkov TV Tower, the Communist regime's belated unwelcome legacy

15 Žižkov TV Tower

Completed in the early 1990s after its Communist builders had left power, the tower is 260m (853 feet) above sea level and the view from the observation deck at 100m (328 feet) is spectacular. On a clear day you can see a distance of 100km (62 miles). Don't miss the surreal giant bronze babies, by local artist David Černy, that "climb" up the sides. There is a restaurant up on the fifth floor, at 63m (207 feet) high.

🔲 201 A4 ✉ Mahlerovy sady 1
☎ 267 005 778; www.tower.cz 🕐 Daily
10 am–11 pm 🚇 Jiřího z Poděbrad
💵 Inexpensive

16 Vitkov Hill

On the north side of the working-class neighbourhood of Žižkov, overlooking the city centre, a monument building was erected in 1932 on the hilltop site of a famous Hussite victory over papal forces in 1420. Created by Bohumil Kafka (no relation), the gigantic **bronze equestrian statue** of the Hussites' one-eyed general, Jan Žižka, was added in 1950. Originally honouring the Czechoslovak fight against the Habsburgs, the monument building served as an arsenal during the German occupation as well as as a mausoleum for Czech Communist leaders after World War II.

Party leader Klement Gottwald's body was embalmed, like Lenin's in Moscow, but less expertly, so that its badly deteriorated remains had to be cremated. All were moved to Žižkov's Olšanské Cemetery in 1990. Surrounded by tanks and artillery, the hillside Armádní Muzeum (Army Museum) is devoted to the country's military history during the two world wars.

🔲 199 D2 ✉ U památníku 2
Žižkov 🕐 Army Museum: Tue–Sun
10–6 ☎ 973 204 924;
www.militarymuseum.cz 🚇 Jiřího z
Poděbrad 💵 Army Museum: inexpensive (Tue free)

17 Muzeum Hlavního města Prahy (Prague Municipal Museum)

Off the beaten track, but well worth seeking out, the Prague Municipal Museum traces the city's story from prehistoric times to the present. Its superb collection of Gothic, Renaissance and baroque sculptures and painting are beautifully displayed. Of particular interest are the scale-model of 19th-century Prague and fine architectural models of major monuments that have now disappeared.

🔲 198 C2 ✉ Na Poříčí 52 Karlin
☎ 224 816 773; www.muzeumprahy.cz
🕐 Tue–Sun 9–6 🚌 8, 25 🚇 Florenc
💵 Inexpensive

Where to...
Eat and Drink

Prices

Expect to pay per person for a meal, including drinks, tax and service
£ under 350Kč   ££ 350–800Kč   £££ over 800Kč

RESTAURANTS

Aromi ££

The perfect neighbourhood Italian restaurant, the service is warm and the dining room inviting. Try sea bass in white wine sauce, with olives and potatoes, and the ravioli with truffle and cheese-truffle fondue or the three-pasta sampler, chosen by the chef.

➕ 201 F3 ⊠ Mánesova 78, Vinohrady ☎ 222 713 222; www.aromi.cz ⓞ Sun–Thu 11 am–10 pm; Fri–Sat 11 am–11 pm ⓜ Jiřího z Poděbrad

Červená Tabulka ££

Tucked away on a side-street, this place has a cosy, cottage feel. The food isn't country fare, though. It's sophisticated and carefully prepared. A complimentary warm loaf of rustic bread with herb butter and a large wine list complete a highly enjoyable dining experience. Reservations.

➕ 201 E5 ⊠ Lodecka 4, Nové Město ☎ 222 716 003 ⓞ Daily 11:30–11

Don Pedro's ££

This cheery restaurant on the river serves excellent Columbian food: empanadas, churrasco, steaks, thick stews, and much more. Try the agua de panela – a refreshing drink made from lemons and limes. Wines from Uruguay, Argentina and Chile.

➕ 195 D2 ⊠ Masarykovo Nábřeži 2, Nové Mesto ☎ 224 923 505; www.donpedro.cz ⓞ Daily 11–11:30 ⓜ Národní trída

Francouzská Restaurace £££

All glistening brass and exquisite woodwork, the restaurant on the ground floor of Obecní dům (Municipal House, ▶ 138–139) is a spacious, stylish spot for French cuisine or Bohemian duck.

➕ 198 B2 ⊠ Náměstí Republiky 5, Nové Město ☎ 222 002 770 ⓞ Daily noon–4, 6–11 pm

Íver £–££

Spicy Slovak cooking (not a good choice for vegetarians). Italian and Mexican dishes, and a raucous gypsy band in the evenings are the specialities of this lively place.

➕ 195 E2 ⊠ Purkyňova 4, Nové Město ☎ 224 946 071

ⓞ Restaurant: daily 11 am–midnight; wine bar: daily 4 pm–3 am

Mánes £

The terrace of this 1930s art gallery makes one of the better spots in town for a budget Czech meal with river view. Try the pork knuckle (vepřové koleno) or grilled trout (pstruh). The indoor dining room is well proportioned, in keeping with the functional style of the gallery.

➕ 195 E2 ⊠ Masarykovo nábřeži 250, Nové Město ☎ 224 930 516; www.restaurant-manes.cz ⓞ Daily 11–11

Restaurant Žofín ££

An attractive room at the ballroom on the island, dominated by bright brass chandeliers. Kulajda is a filling potato soup, and lamb cutlets and steak in vine leaves are other menu regulars. There's a spacious terrace with a river view and a small, less expensive menu.

➕ 195 D2 ⊠ Žofín 226, Slovanský ostrov ☎ 224 919 139 ⓞ Daily 6:30–11

Šuteren £££

One of the city's new dining stars, this is a favourite of gourmets. The continental menu specialises in fresh seafood, some prepared with an Asian twist, and local game. Pheasant with plum sauce and salmon with baby spinach and wild rice are two standouts.

⊞ 195 D1 ⊠ Masarykovo nábrezi 26, Nové Město ☎ 224 933 657
⊕ Mon–Fri 11:30–midnight, Sat 6 pm–midnight Ⓜ Národní třída

Tamada £

At this rustic restaurant in the shadow of the Tančíci dům, just off the river, you can sample delights like *adžharian khachapuri* (melted cheese and a soft-boiled egg tucked into buttery bread), *chakhokhbili* (spicy minced pork and beef baked in dough), and the zesty *kutaisi salad* (tomato, cucumber, walnuts, onion and spices).

⊞ 195 D1 ⊠ Jenštejnská 2, Nové Město ☎ 224 913 810 ⊕ Daily 11 am–midnight Ⓜ Karlovo náměstí

Universal £

This restaurant's inexpensive French and Mediterranean dishes, as well as huge helpings of scalloped potatoes and large salads, keep the mostly young regulars coming back for more. No credit cards.

⊞ 195 D2 ⊠ V Jirchářích 6, Nové Město ☎ 224 918 182 ⊕ Daily 11:30 am–midnight

U Šemíka £

This warm restaurant has booklined walls and leather sofas, adding atmosphere to an extensive menu of Czech fare.

⊞ 201 D2 ⊠ Vratislavova 36, Nové Město ☎ 224 911 330; www.usemika.ca ⊕ Daily 11:30–11:30

Pivovarský dům

A Czech emigré from America brews his own Bohemian-style light and dark beers in sight of drinkers at this cheerful pub-restaurant. Try home-made banana beer, a few

speciality imports, and Czech liqueurs such as *medovina* (mead).

⊞ 201 D3 ⊠ Lípová 15, Nové Město ☎ 296 216 666 ⊕ Daily 11–11:30

Plzeňská Restaurace

This basement tavern is an extravagant piece of art nouveau design. Ceramic murals by leading Czech artists glow in the dim lighting. The food is standard pub fare such as goulash and *svičková na smetaně* (thin-sliced sirloin in cream sauce).

⊞ 198 B2 ⊠ Náměstí Republiky 5, Nové Město ☎ 222 002 780 ⊕ Daily 11:30–11

U Fleků

Two spacious beer halls and an even roomier beer garden ensure plenty of space at this famous beer palace. They've been brewing rich, dark beer here since 1499. Come and dig into steaming plates of "Fleck's treat" – duck, pork and sausages.

⊞ 195 D2 ⊠ Křemencova 11, Nové Město ☎ 224 934 019; www.ufleku.cz ⊕ Daily 9 am–11 pm

Café Louvre

A grand café of Prague's heyday that reopened once Communism was banished, the Louvre offers a range of Czech dishes, salads and home-made ice-cream as well as billiards and, rare for Prague, a non-smoking room. The Louvre is open for breakfast every day.

⊞ 195 E2 ⊠ Národní třída 20, Nové Město ☎ 224 930 949; www.cafelouvre.cz ⊕ Daily 8 am–11 pm

Dobrá Čajovna

A Czech gift to the world of serious relaxing was born in the early 1990s here at the "Good Tea room". Teas from the world over are brewed here with an almost spiritual devotion. a limited menu is available. No mobile phones or smoking.

⊞ 195 F3 ⊠ Václavské náměstí 14, Nové Město ☎ 224 231 480 ⊕ Mon–Fri 10–9:30, Sat–Sun 3–9:30

Where to...
Shop

Bigger stores, lots of familiar brand names and the hustle and bustle of city life – shopping in Nové Město (New Town) certainly feels different from shopping in some of the older historic districts.

Václavské náměstí (Wenceslas Square) forms the area's main artery and, with a mix of department stores and shops offering *levné* (cheap) goods, is the one place in Prague that's never short of people buying and selling. At the bottom of Wenceslas Square runs the crowded pedestrian zone on Na příkopě, which leads via 28 Října into another major shopping street, Národní třída.

VÁCLAVSKÉ NÁMĚSTÍ

Among the gauds and baubles of this long "square", look for the fine selection of traditionally painted Easter eggs at Original Souvenir (Václavské náměstí 12).

In the mazelike Lucerna Arcade, between Vodičkova and Štěpánská streets, shops worth seeking out include Galerie Mody (upstairs opposite the cinema), which stocks fashions and accessories by half a dozen Czech designers; Beruška for the clever wooden toys and dolls; and Cellarius, for both Czech and imported wines and spirits.

AROUND VÁCLAVSKÉ NÁMĚSTÍ

Offices, government ministries and shops pack the grid of streets either side of Václavské náměstí (Wenceslas Square). The densest concentration of shops lies on Vodičkova Street. On the right hand side of the bottom of the square is Bontonland Megastore (Václavské náměstí 1), a massive CD store that covers all genres of music in depth, and has a brilliant selection of Czech and Eastern European music. The Mucha Museum gift shop, naturally, features items inspired by Alphonse Mucha's work (Panská 7, ▶ 140).

A few blocks off the square's upper end, Dům Porcelánu Praha (Jugoslávská 16, Vinohrády, near I P Pavlova Metro station) has two floors of Czech porcelain from most of the major factories.

NA PŘÍKOPĚ

One end of this shopping magnet is anchored by the extraordinary Obecní dům (Municipal House, ▶ 138).

Expensive shops line three sides of the building, but better, and less expensive, is the replica art nouveau jewellery and glassware at Art Décoratif (U Obecního domu).

Closer to Václavské náměstí (Wenceslas Square) is a shop worth making a detour for, Moser (Na příkopě 12), which has been displaying its timeless lead-free glassware in these sumptuous surroundings since 1925.

AROUND NÁRODNÍ TŘÍDA

One of the city's largest musical-instrument emporia is Hudební nástroje Kliment (Jungmannovo náměstí 17).

Folk crafts from the eastern Czech Republic's distinctive Valašsko region are at Tamaša (Charvátova 9).

The Platýz Courtyard at Národní třída 37 offers a row of shops with classy Czech and imported women's fashions and shoes, and a friendly Seattle-style coffee house.

A good stop for glass and small sculptures in other media is Galerie Pyramida (Národní třída 11).

Look for delightful wooden toys, puzzles and trains at Kid-Trnka (Ostrovní 21).

Finally, for emergencies, there's even a Tesco supermarket (Národní třída at Spálená).

Where to...
Be Entertained

THEATRE

Animato

This theatre offers a show called *Rock Therapy* inspired by the Beatles' *Yellow Submarine*.

➕ 199 F3 ⊠ Savarin Palace, Na příkopě 10 ☎ 281 932 665

Archa

Prague's all-purpose stage for avant-garde drama, music, dance, film – you name it. Tickets are scarce, but worth the trouble to find.

➕ 205 E5 ⊠ Na Poříčí 26 ☎ 221 716 333

Laterna Magika

The Magic Latern is the most famous of the blacklight (mime, clowning and lighting effects in

front of a black screen) and multi-media theatres.

➕ 199 E2 ⊠ Národní třída 4 ☎ 224 914 129

MUSIC

Classical
Smetanova síň (Smetana Hall)

Home to the Prague Symphony Orchestra, this hall is a work of art in its own right.

➕ 205 E4 ⊠ Náměstí Republiky 5, Staré Město ☎ 222 002 101

Contemporary and jazz
Lucerna Music Bar

A cavernous club hosting touring bands and Saturday night DJs.

➕ 195 D2 ⊠ Vodičkova 36, Nové Město ☎ 224 217 108 Ⓜ Můstek

Palác Akropolis

Czech underground rock, world music, jazz and alternative sounds from major artists and local acts make this funky concert hall and club deservedly popular.

➕ 206 A4 ⊠ Kubelíkova 27, Žižkov ☎ 296 330 911

Radost FX

Trendies flock here to dance, mingle and eat in the all-night veggie café.

➕ 205 F2 ⊠ Bělehradská 120, Vinohrády ☎ 224 254 776

Reduta

The oldest music club in Prague offering a mix of modern, fusion, Latin, and trumpet jazz.

➕ 199 E2 ⊠ Národní třída 20 ☎ 224 912 246

Opera
Národní divadlo (National Theatre)

The singers and orchestra perform to very high standards in this beloved and beautiful hall. Czech

operas are the speciality. Good seats can sometimes be had from the box office for around 250Kč. You can book by post, email or Internet three months in advance, for any show here or at the Stavovské divadlo (▶ 63).

➕ 199 D2 ⊠ Národní třída 2 ☎ 224 931 544; advance booking: 224 901 487; ntprague@narodni-divadlo.cz; www.narodni-divadlo.cz

Státní opera Praha

At the ornately gilded and painted State Opera House, Verdi is the thing. Adventurous contemporary works are also regulars, along with ballet. Note that rear seats in the boxes have poor views of the stage.

➕ 205 E3 ⊠ Wilsonova 4 ☎ 224 227 266

FILM

Most of the cinemas line Václavské náměstí (Wenceslas Square) or Na příkopě. Try Slovanskdum for Hollywood releases (Na příkopě 22).

Excursions

Three places to discover on day-trips from Prague: Kutná Hora – glorious vestiges of a silver-mining boom town; good cheer in Mělník's castle wine cellars; and the heart-rending Terezín (Theresienstadt) concentration camp.

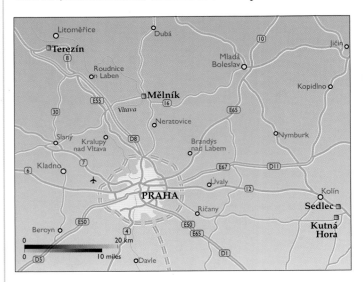

Kutná Hora

Its silver mines made Kutná Hora the second most important town in the old kingdom of Bohemia – economic, political and cultural rival to Prague. The silver has gone but not the unique beauty of its great Church of St Barbara. At the mining museum, put on a traditional white uniform to explore disused shafts and galleries; and enjoy a gruesome thrill in a Cistercian cemetery chapel where the baroque décor is fashioned from human bones.

1–2

From the Na Valech car-park, walk east along Husova Street to the Rejskovo náměstí (Rejsek Square). The **Kamenná kašna** here is a handsomely carved Gothic polygonal stone well, designed in 1495 by Matyáš Rejsek, one of the architects of the Church of St Barbara. Continue east on Husova and turn uphill at the second left, Šultysova.

2–3

Stop on the corner of Husova and Šultysova. At the beginning of the sloping street is the **Morový sloup** (Plague Column) carved in 1715 by František Baugut, sculptor of the parade of statues in front of the Jesuit College. It was a votive offering

Page 161: Excursions outside Prague offer many interesting streets to explore

following an epidemic which killed 6,000 townspeople. Go on up Šultysova to **U Haviŕu** (No 154) a pleasant wine cellar/restaurant where you may want to reserve a table for lunch. Continue to Václavské náměstí (Wenceslas Square).

3–4

Like Prague's square of the same name, Václavské náměstí is more of a sprawling esplanade than a square. On the north side over to the left, just past the corner of Česká Street, is the imposing **Kamenný dům**

(Stone House). Its ornate Gothic gabled façade was added in 1489 for a recently ennobled mining magnate. Notice the coat of arms carved in the gable – Adam and Eve under the Tree of the Knowledge of Good and Evil.

4–5

Double back along the south side of Václavské náměstí and turn right down Kollárova to the city's main square, Palackého náměstí. Turn left across the square to the patrician mansions on the east side.

If you need extra details for your trip, the **tourist information office** (tel: 0327 512 378) is located in the Sankturinovský dům, a baroque reconstruction of one of the town's oldest houses. The square also offers an authentic pizzeria, **Piazza Navona**, as a good lunch alternative (➤ 166).

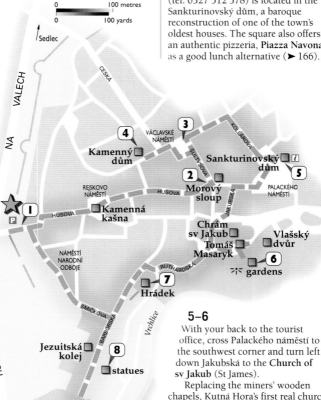

| 0 | 100 metres |
| 0 | 100 yards |

5–6

With your back to the tourist office, cross Palackého náměstí to the southwest corner and turn left down Jakubská to the **Church of sv Jakub** (St James).

Replacing the miners' wooden chapels, Kutná Hora's first real church was begun in 1330, but ran into trouble when the first of its two planned towers began, as you can see, to lean, Pisa-like, because of subsidence in

A statue of a Kutná Hora silver miner in Vlašský dvůr (Italian Court)

abandoned mining tunnels. (Access only during church services.)

On the south side of the church is a **statue of Tomáš Masaryk**, first president of Czechoslovakia, resurrected after its successive removals by the Germans and Communists.

Behind him is the sprawling **Vlašský dvůr** (Italian Court), where for 250 years the coveted Prague Groschen coins were minted (until they were replaced by the *Thaler*, "dollar"). Understandably, the place was heavily fortified with moats and

ramparts, and the king used it as a residence on visits to Kutná Hora. The guided tour visits the royal treasury, with its warning over the door *Noli me tangere* ("Don't touch me"), and the palace's chapel and audience halls.

At the rear of the Vlašský dvůr, stroll out onto the **gardens** sloping down to the Vrchlice River for a spectacular **view** across the hillside to the chram sv Barbora (Church of St Barbora).

6–7

Back at the front of the Vlašský dvůr, turn left past the Church of sv Jakub and along the narrow, cobbled street of **Ruthardská**, a wonderful relic of the medieval town. This follows the city wall west to the **Hrádek**, an old fortress, silver-smelting factory and now a **Mining Museum**. It is located directly over old mineshafts and tunnels which you can visit after putting on a miner's traditional white tunic and helmet with (modern) lamp.

7–8

From the Hrádek, walk up Barborská beside the former **Jesuit College**, founded as part of the Catholic Counter-Reformation in 1667. Along the parapet overlooking the valley are 18th-century baroque **statues** of church saints by František Baugut, that were inspired by the statues on Prague's Karlův most (Charles Bridge, ► 52–55).

Hi Ho, Silver!

Lured by reports of silver, German monks from Waldsassen came to stake the first claim. They founded a Cistercian monastery in 1142 at Sedlec (► 166), now a suburb of Kutná Hora. No silver turned up for 100 years until, so the story goes, Brother Antoň woke from a siesta in the monastery vineyard to discover the precious ore near his head, "sprouting" from the stony ground. He marked the spot with his habit (*kutna*) and scampered home in his breeches to tell the tale. Thus were born a town's fortune – and its name. The Hussite Wars stopped the city's growth in the 1420s, and a century later, the mines could no longer compete with silver flooding the market from the Americas and rival mines in Germany. Mining ground to a halt in the Thirty Years' War (1618–48). The arrival of the Jesuits left only a few baroque monuments to sustain the city's pride as it settled for a quiet life, with some golden or silver memories.

Rent a car rather than face the hassle of the bus and train connections (➤ 37 for telephone numbers).
AA Auto: www.aa-auto.cz
Czechocar: www.czechocar.cz
Dvořák: www.dvorak-rentacar.cz
Vecar: www.vecar.cz.

8–9

At the top of Barborská, on the left of the forecourt of St Barbara's Church, is the recently restored 14th-century **Kaple Božího těla** (Chapel of Corpus Christi). This is a two-storey cemetery chapel that originally served as an ossuary in deliberate competition with the more famous "bone chapel" of Sedlec (➤ 166).

Dedicated to the patron saint of miners, the **Church of sv Barbora** (St Barbara) is one of the great treasures of the nation. Its dramatic, tent-like silhouette is without parallel in Gothic architecture (and reminiscent of the Munich Olympic Stadium).

Seeking independence from the Cistercian abbey of Sedlec, the miners brought in master builders from Prague's St Vitus Cathedral (➤ 89–91).

The mining magnates paid for the Church of sv Barbora from their own pockets

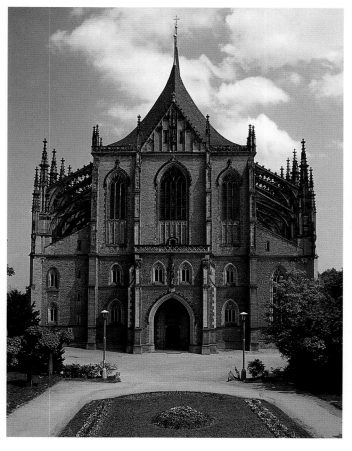

Sedlec

If you have time, drive the 3km
(2 miles) to the suburb of Sedlec. The
route takes you straight to Sedlec's
former monastery church of Panna
Maria (St Mary). As the church is
likely to be closed for its prolonged
restoration (the monastery itself is
now a Philip Morris tobacco factory),
turn left up Zámecká to the monks'
cemetery and **Kostnice** (Ossuary)
(there's parking near by).

Over 600 years, the subterranean
"bone chapel" accumulated 40,000
skeletons. In 1870, František Rint,
a woodcarver by trade, was hired to
fashion the bones into a décor for
the chapel: the result is huge bells,
chandelier, chalices, even the coat-of-
arms of the Schwarzenberg family,
former owners of the chapel.

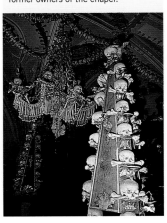

Begun in 1380 but halted by the
Hussite Wars, the church achieved its
present unique shape under Benedikt
Ried (builder of Prague Castle's
Vladislav Hall, ➤ 84) in the 16th
century. As you can see in the interior,
it was his lofty rib-vaulting that
created the need for the roof's fascinating canopy of cones. Also worth
a look are the **Gothic frescoes** of
mining and minting in the Hašplířská
(or Winchers') chapel and Mincířská
(Minters') Chapel.

TAKING A BREAK

Try **U Havíru** (Sultysova 154, tel: 327
513 997) a wine cellar/restaurant, or
Piazza Navona (Palackého náměstí
90, tel: 03 275 125 88) a pizzeria.

Tourist Information Office
➕ 201 off C3 ✉ Palackého náměstí 377
☎ 03 275 123 78; www.kutnahora.cz 🕐 Daily
9–6, Apr–Sep; Mon–Fri 9–5, Sat–Sun 10–4,
Oct–Mar

Vlašský dvůr (Italian Court)
➕ 201 off C3 ☎ 03 275 128 73 🕐 Daily
9–6, Apr–Sep; daily 10–5, Mar & Oct; daily
10–4, Nov–Feb 💰 Inexpensive

Hrádek Mining Museum
➕ 201 off C3 ☎ 03 275 121 59 🕐 Tue–Sun
10–6, Jul–Aug; Tue–Sun 9–6, May, Jun & Sep;
Tue–Sun 9–5, Apr & Oct; closed Nov–Mar
💰 Moderate

Kostlice (Ossuary), Sedlec
➕ 201 off C3 ☎ 03 275 611 43 🕐 Daily
8–6, Apr–Sep; 9–noon, 1–5, Oct; 9–noon, 1–4,
Nov–Mar 💰 Inexpensive

KUTNÁ HORA: INSIDE INFO

Getting there Kutná Hora is 70km (44 miles) from Prague. From behind
Národní muzeum (➤ 153), take Vinohradská Street east, continuing as
Černokostelecká. This becomes Highway 2, signposted Kutná Hora via Kostelec
nad Černými lesy, and takes you right into town.

Top tips Parking is best at the junction of Highway 2 (Kouřímská) with Na
Valech and Husova Street on the west side of the city centre.
● **Time** Give yourself a day, including 75 minutes' journey time to Kutná Hora and
75 minutes back to Prague.

Mělník

This historic town, 33km (21 miles) from Prague, offers a rare opportunity to taste home-grown Czech wines in the romantic surroundings of a nicely restored Renaissance castle. Add to this the magnificent view over the vineyards to the confluence of the Vltava and Labe (Elbe) rivers and you have all the makings of a delightful half-day trip.

The town traces its history back to the 9th century when Ludmila, the grandmother of Good King Wenceslas (Václav, ► 100, 141) presented it to Bohemia as part of her dowry for Prince Bořivoj. Wine-growing was introduced in the 14th century by Emperor Charles IV, who brought vines to Mělník from his home in Burgundy.

1–2

Check with the **tourist information office** on the pleasantly arcaded náměstí Míru for up-to-date details of the town's museums and monuments. Then cross the square to Svatováclavská and turn right at the end to Zámek Mělník (Mělník Castle).

The largely 16th- and 17th-century **Zámek Mělník** is now back in the hands of the Lobkowicz family, who acquired it in 1753. Visits to this Renaissance and baroque castle are by guided tour only. The tour takes 30 minutes, and you can see some of the tastefully decorated rooms, including the Wenceslas Hall and the chapel. Notice, too, the handsome *sgraffiti* on façades in the courtyard. There is a separate

The town of Mělník has Emperor Charles IV to thank for founding its wine-growing industry in the 14th century

tour of the 13th-century **wine cellars**, including a wine-tasting. You can do both tours and then explore further around town to work up an appetite before returning for lunch.

You have a choice between the **Vinarna** wine-bar in the vaulted cellars and the less expensive **Zámecká restaurace** on the ground floor. Both have good views.

2–3

Next to the castle is the **Chrám sv Petra a Pavla** (Church of SSPeter and Paul). Stand at the foot of its onion-domed tower for the splendid view south over the terraced vineyards to where **three waterways** flow together. Over to the left is the Labe (Elbe) River on its way to Germany and the North Sea, joined here by the Vltava River flowing in from Prague, and the Plavební Canal immediately opposite. Inside the church is a **Kostnice** (Ossuary) of around 10,000 bones, skeletal remains of medieval plague victims decoratively rearranged by a local professor in the early 20th century.

Behind the church is the **Stára škola**. Commanding a great view, it is a good alternative to the other castle restaurants.

From Burgundy to Bohemia

Mělník's wines are much better than this beer-drinking country might lead you to expect. The Lobkowicz vineyards exploit local patriotism to put Princess Ludmila on their label, even though that good Christian lady lived 500 years before Charles IV brought the first vines here from Burgundy. Ludmila White blends two German grapes, Müller Thurgau and Riesling, to produce a fruity wine, light yellow in colour, easy on the palate. Ludmila Red blends three grapes – Blue Portuguese, St Laurent and Zweigeltrebe – to produce a deep ruby colour and a bouquet of strawberries. They make a rosé and a champagne-style bubbly: Château Mělník (www.lobkowicz-melnik.cz).

3–4

Continuing your pre-lunch stroll, walk back down Svatováclavská and turn right at the bottom to the **Pražská brána** (Prague Tower), last remnant of the town's medieval bastions, rebuilt in 1500. It now houses a gallery of contemporary art.

4–5

Walk back across náměstí Míru to the **Okresní muzeum Mělník** (Mělník Museum) for its interesting display devoted to wine-growing. Leave náměstí Míru north on Legionářů, right on U Tanku and right again on Tyřsova which merges into Pražská, the Prague road leading to Highway 9.

Mělník Castle stands proudly above its terraced vineyards and the Labe (Elbe) River

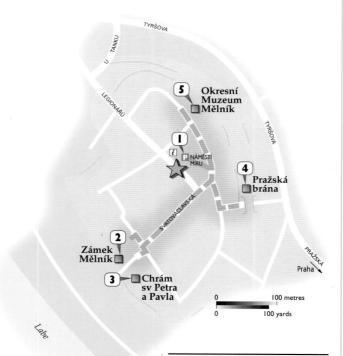

Tourist Information Office
➕ 201 off C5 ✉ Náměstí Míru 30 ☎ 02 066
275 03 ⏰ 9–5, May–Sep; 9–5, Oct–Apr

Zámek Mělník (Mělník Castle)
➕ 201 off C5 ☎ 02 315 622 121 ⏰ Wine
cellar 10–6 (last tour 5) 💰 Castle tour:
moderate; wine tour with tasting: moderate

**Okresní muzeum Mělník
(Mělník District Museum)**
➕ 201 off C5 ✉ Náměstí Míru 54 ☎ 02 315
630 922 ⏰ Tue–Sun 9–12, 1–5; closed Mon
💰 Inexpensive

TAKING A BREAK

The **Vinarna** wine-bar in the vaulted
cellars of Mělník Castle, and **Zámecká
restaurace** on the ground floor of
Mělník Castle, are both good places
to take a break. To make an advance
booking, tel: 02 315 622 108.

MĚLNÍK: INSIDE INFO

Getting there From Prague, behind Národní muzeum, drive north on the
Wilsonova freeway through the Holešovice district onto the E55 expressway
and take the Mělník exit onto Highway 9. This leads straight into town on
Pražská. At the city centre, Pražská merges into Tyršova from which you take
a left on U Tanku and left again on Legionářů, which brings you to the main
square's car-park on náměstí Míru.

Terezín
(Theresienstadt)

An hour's drive from Prague, Terezín was the "showcase" – the one concentration camp the Germans were prepared to show to the outside world. After nearly 50 years of deliberate neglect by the Communist regime, the town presents painful but vital testimony to the Jewish ghetto that became a transit camp for Auschwitz. For anyone interested in a harsher reality of Prague's hinterland, it has to be seen.

The Facts

Habsburg Emperor Joseph II founded Theresienstadt, 60km (37 miles) from Prague, in 1782 as a fortified garrison town, named after his mother, Maria Theresa. In October 1941, Reinhard Heydrich, Reich Protector of the German-occupied Czech lands, turned the town into a Jewish ghetto – of a special kind. It was to receive, among others, Germany's Jewish war veterans decorated in World War I and the families of prominent Jews – artists, musicians, writers – whose internment elsewhere

Náměstí Československe armády, or Marktplatz, is the main square of Terezín

might arouse international questions. Life was to be as "normal" as possible, with theatre, opera, jazz, puppet shows and painting lessons for the children – even soccer teams of electricians, butchers, gardeners and cooks. This was a cover for its main function as a transit for deportation to the extermination camps.

Of the 140,000 Jews who passed through Theresienstadt – Czechs, Slovaks, Danes, Dutch, Austrians, Germans – over 88,000 were deported and 34,000 died in the camp. While this went on, a "beautification" programme (Verschönerungsaktion) prepared the camp for an inspector

the end of the park, turn left on Komenského (Hauptstrasse) to the town's central square, Náměstí Čsekoslovenské armády (Marktplatz).

2–3

At the corner of Komenského and B. Němcové (Rathausgasse), the **Muzeum Ghetta** (Ghetto Museum) tells Theresienstadt's wartime story in graphic detail, but without pathos. The building was a home for 10- to 15-year-old boys who for two years turned out a clandestine newspaper, *Vedem* (*We Are Leading*), up in the attic.

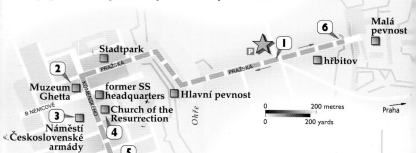

from the International Red Cross Committee in 1944. The shows he saw convinced him all was well. The Soviet Army found 18,000 survivors in May 1945. Terezín is still laid out to the 18th-century's strict grid plan. It iš little more than a ghost town, but each place you pass has a memory of another living reality.

1–2

Beyond the main gate in the massive redbrick fortifications, go straight along Pražská (Berggasse to the Germans). You pass the *Stadtpark*, the park where a children's pavilion and playground were set up for the Red Cross inspection of 1944. At

The museum's 20-minute **documentary** is well worth watching.

3–4

Across from the Muzeum Ghetta, the corner building opposite the park was a **headquarters for SS officers**. Walk south along the east side of the square. Beyond the church was the home where children painted the pictures now displayed in Prague's Pinkasova synagoga (► 116–117). On the southeast corner of the square, a clothes shop re-sold clothes confiscated from the inmates' own suitcases.

4–5

Continue along Komenského, now Tyršova, to **Magdeburská kasárna** (Magdeburg Barracks) on your left, which is the second of the ghetto's two museums. The exhibits here are devoted to the inmates' artistic activities, the theatre sets they built, musical scores they composed,

paintings, poems and underground magazines. There is a reconstructed women's dormitory with three-tier wooden bunks.

5–6

Double back on Tyršova to Pražská to exit through the main gate. The road passes to the left of the **cemetery**, its 2,300 graves dominated by a huge cross and smaller Star of David. Beyond the cemetery is the old garrison's **Malá pevnost** (Small Fortress) which the SS used as a concentration camp for political prisoners, mainly Communists, 32,000 in all.

The Stadtkirche is located in the very centre of Terezín

TAKING A BREAK

Apart from **U hojtašů** on Komenského, the town has little to offer. It's better to pack a picnic and plan a hearty meal back in Prague.

➕ 201 off C5 ✉ Památnik Terezín (Theresienstadt Memorial), Principova alej 304, Terezín ☎ 416 782 225; www.pamatnik-terezin.cz 🌐 Small Fortress, Ghetto Museum, Crematorium and Ceremonial Halls open all year daily. Hours vary between 8 am and 6 pm 🎟 Expensive

---

TEREZÍN: INSIDE INFO

Getting there From Prague, behind Národní muzeum, drive north on the Wilsonova freeway through the Holešovice district onto the E55 expressway and take the exit signposted Roudnice onto Highway 8. Past Roudnice, follow signposts to Terezín. The Prague road leads past the cemetery to a car-park in front of the entrance east of the old garrison town's Hlavná pevnost (Main fortress).

Walks

1 ON AND OFF THE ROYAL ROUTE

Walk

Start out where the kings paraded through Staré Město (Old Town), but then, unlike the monarchs of old (and most tourists), slip away from the main streets down the back lanes and along their covered passages. Without missing at least a glimpse of the monuments, you'll explore the heart of Staré Město along its medieval byways. Interesting enough by day, this walk is even more fun at night.

DISTANCE 1.6km (1 mile) **TIME** 2 hours
START POINT Metro náměstí Republiky ✚ 201 E4
END POINT Novotného lávka, corner Smetanovo nábřeží (Smetana Embankment) ✚ 199 D3

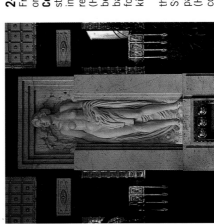

1–2

From Náměstí Republiky Metro station, cross the square to the grand **Obecní dům** (Municipal House, ➤ 138) and walk around it to the left to the medieval **Prašná brána** (Powder Gate Tower, ➤ 152). This is the last of 13 gates that used to guard the entrance to the Old Town. The ornately carved 19th-century façade pretties up what was for centuries a store for black gunpowder.

2–3

From the west side of the gate tower, start out on the Royal Route (*královska cesta*) along **Celetná Street** (➤ 68). This modern shopping street is also one of the town's most ancient – in English it would be Baker Street, Celetná referring to makers of medieval *calty* bread. (However, beware that the arcaded passages between and through the old Gothic-turned-baroque buildings here made great getaways for pickpockets working the crowds at the king's parade.)

On the right, at No 27, if it's open, duck through the arcade to peek into old Templova Street and duck back again to cross Celetná, passing the cubist **Dům U černé Matky Boží** (House of the Black Madonna) on the west corner, south into Ovocný trh (the Fruit Market, no longer there).

Preceding page: Malá Strana and Charles Bridge
Left: An art nouveau statue inside Obecní dům

counter service at **Praha Tamura**, Havelská 6 (opens 11 am). Return past the Church of sv Havel (not an ancestor of the President, but St Gall, a 6th-century Irish monk) to the red-brick **Karolinum** (▶ 69). The university's illustrious rebels include Jan Hus

3–4

At the far end of Ovocný trh is the rear entrance of the **Stavovské divadlo** (Estates Theatre, ▶ 63), where opera singers are seen wandering around in 18th-century tunics over a pair of jeans. Round the front of the theatre, cut over to the right past the Church of sv Havel to stroll through **Havelská street market** (▶ 45) and back. If you've made a late start, you may like some genuine Japanese sushi from

Pick up the ingredients for a picnic at Havelská street market

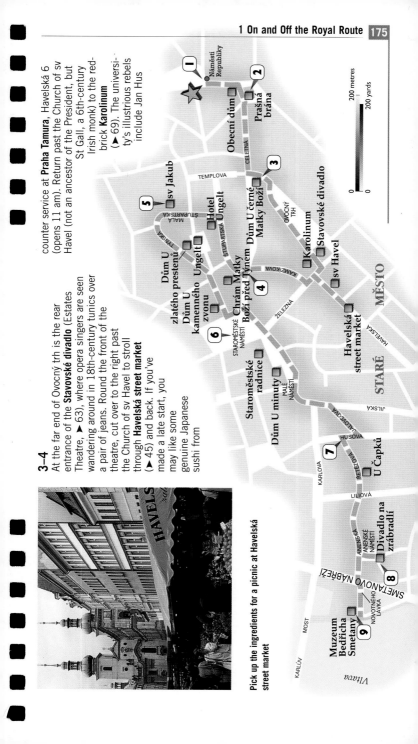

and Franz Kafka. Turn left on narrow Kamzíkova through either of the two covered passages back into Celetná.

4–5

Cross Celetná and turn right, past the south side of **Týn Church** (▶ 60), onto Štupartská, passing on the left the charming little Hotel Ungelt. Turn left on Malá Štupartská, leading to an archway into **Ungelt Court** (▶ 61) on the left and, on the right, the handsome baroque portal of the Gothic **Church of sv Jakub** (▶ 67).

5–6

Back on Malá Štupartská, turn left at the bend into Týnská Street with two fine remodelled Gothic houses: on the right, Renaissance at No 6, **Dům U zlatého prstenů** (House of the Golden Ring, ▶ 67) and baroque across the street at No 7. At the Týn Church, the street narrows into Týnská ulička, lined by souvenir vendors, which leads between the House of the Stone Bell and the old Týn School to **Staroměstské náměstí** (Old Town Square, ▶ 56).

6–7

Walk left through the Týn School's Gothic arcade. On the south side of Old Town Square, the ornate step-gabled Storch

publishing house has a *sgraffito* painting by Mikuláš Aleš of St Wenceslas on a white horse beside the neo-Gothic oriel window. Next door, **U bílého jednorožce** (At the White Unicorn, though the stone sign beside the second-floor

Crowds gather on Old Town Square

balcony is in fact a ram with one horn missing) was renowned as Berta Fanta's literary salon. Besides rounding up the town's usual literary suspects, Franz Werfel, Max Brod and Franz Kafka, Berta also hosted those masters of science and parascience Albert Einstein and Rudolf Steiner.

Now for a sharp manoeuvre to escape the crowds on Old Town Square. Hurry on past the south side of Old Town Hall, pausing only to admire the *sgraffito* façade on **Dům U minuty** (The Minute House) in the far southwest corner of the square. Then cross Malé náměstí and, shunning the souvenir-hunters milling on Karlova, take a diagonal left on

Taking a Break

If you feel like breaking the walk in two with an elegant meal, step into Ungelt Court where **Rybí trh** serves fine seafood (▶ 72).

The **Muzeum Bedřicha Smetany** (Smetana Museum, ▶ 64) has a café with a beautiful view over the Vltava to the Charles Bridge. At **Café Slavia** (▶ 74), it's the same view as from the Smetana Museum, with the best of Czech cuisine on the embankment.

Beautiful *sgraffiti* decoration adorns the front of the **Dům U minuty (The Minute House)**

Jalovcová. Cross Husova and turn left into Řetězová.

7–8

This is the cobblestoned heart of Old Town's medieval maze, but don't worry, we'll get you out of it. The house at Řetězová 3, **U Čapků** (At the Stork, ▶ 68), is one of the oldest in the city. The museum of its most illustrious resident, King George of Poděbrady, may be of only marginal interest, but it's worth going inside for a peek at the Romanesque vaults down in the basement. This was once the ground floor of what may have been a small town-palace which may date back at least to 1200.

Continue west on Řetězová and its prolongation, Anenská. Just before the river, turn left into Anenské náměstí, home of the **Divadlo na zábradlí** (Balustrade Theatre), where the future President Václav Havel worked first as a stage-hand, then resident playwright in the 1960s (▶ 13).

Converted from an old warehouse, this hub of Prague's absurdist satirical theatre is now making a comeback.

8–9

Back on Anenská and turn left to the embankment road, Smetanovo nábřeží. Cross over to Novotného lávka, a bridge that leads to the old waterworks that is now the **Muzeum Bedřicha Smetany** (Smetana Museum, ▶ 64).

2 CASTLE HILL

Walk

DISTANCE 3km (2 miles) **TIME** 3 hours
START POINT Belvedere (Královský Letohrádek tram stop) ⊞ 194 B5
END POINT Malá Strana Bridge Towers on Charles Bridge ⊞ 194 C4

Imagine you are the King or Queen of Bohemia. This visit to your royal domain gets away from Prague Castle to stroll through gardens, around the aristocrats' palaces on Castle Square and over to Hradčany's remaining medieval houses on Nový Svět. From there amble down – the great thing about this hill walk is that it is almost all downhill – past a couple of splendid embassies to Malá Strana's main square. Stop for lunch or continue down to the Charles Bridge. A majestic ramble.

1–2

The Belvedere entrance to the **Královská zahrada** (Royal Gardens, ▶ 93) is on the south side of the busy Mariánské hradby highway. Cross carefully if getting off at the westbound tram stop. Walk around the lovely west façade of the 16th-century **Belvedere**. Queen Anna, for whom

Ferdinand I built this summer palace (Královský Letohrádek), died before it was completed. If it's playing, listen to the "music" of the Singing Fountain on the Italian-style *giardinetto* (garden-terrace). Take in the **view** of the castle, especially the north side of St Vitus Cathedral (▶ 89–91), which you don't get to see up close.

2–3

From the Belvedere's *giardinetto*, walk west past the long Orangery to the **Míčovna** (Jeu de Paume), where the Habsburgs played real

(royal) tennis originally using the palm of the hand (*paume*) rather than a racket. Stroll among the almond trees and,

Above: It is hard to resist the temptation to spend the whole day in the Royal Gardens

MARIÁNSKÉ HRADBY

Belvedere (Královský Letohrádek)

Královská zahrada

Míčovna

Lví dvůr

Jelení

Příkop

PRAŠNÉHO MOSTU

Taking a Break

The chic **U Zlaté hrušky** (At the Golden Pearl) is on Nový Svět 3 (➤ 106). Check out the stylish restaurant **Square** (➤ 96) on Malostranské náměstí, which has a good view on to the square and serves an international menu.

in season, the azaleas and tulips, before leaving the gardens beside the **Lví dvůr** (Lion's Court) restaurant (➤ 94). Turn left onto **Prašný most** (Powder Bridge) over the wooded Jelení příkop (Stag Moat).

3–4

Prašný most leads to the north gate of the Second Courtyard in the castle precincts (free access). Cross the courtyard to the second exit, Matyášova brána (Matthias Gate) leading out of the castle through the first courtyard.

If you have timed it to be here at noon, brave the crowds to see the main parade of the **Changing of the Guard** (➤ 82), the whole works.

4–5

Otherwise, escape through the castle gates into **Hradčanské náměstí** (Castle Square). Walk left to the ramparts for the view south over

Malá Strana and across the Vltava River to Staré Město (Old Town).

Continue west along the south side of the square. The first of two palaces owned by the powerful Schwarzenberg family is now the Swiss Embassy. The adjoining step-gabled **Schwarzenberský palác** (No 2), notable for its ornate *sgraffiti*, houses the Military History Museum, which all but war buffs will prefer to visit another day. Next door, the hotel in the converted Barnabite convent at No 3 is usually reserved for guests of the President. In the middle of the square, the baroque Plague Column was the work of Ferdinand Brokof, commemorating the victims of 1679.

5–6

Turn right at the west end of the square past the **Thun-Hohenštejnský palác**, with its austere version of an Italian Renaissance façade. Exit the square in the northwest corner along Kanovnická, to the left of the **Martinický palác**,

a more decorative Renaissance restyling of three Gothic houses.

6–7

Kanovnická curves round to the fine baroque Church of sv Jan Nepomucký (St John of Nepomuk, ▶ 32), one of Kilián Ignác Dienzenhofer's first Prague buildings. The lavish interior merits a quick peek.

Continue north past the church and turn left into **Nový Svět** (New World Street). Nothing American about it, but its charming, brightly painted cottages are a last vestige of Hradčany's medieval quarter – castle-workers' homes that have now been refurbished as smart wine bars and restaurants.

7–8

Turn left on Černínská for one of the few uphill stretches on this walk to Loretánské náměstí (Loreta Square). On the right is the monstrous **Černínský palác**, the Foreign Ministry building from which Jan Masaryk fell to his death from an upper window in 1948 (▶ 19). Ideological or psychological causes apart, the architecture might be cause enough to jump.

Cannons at rest in the Military History Museum

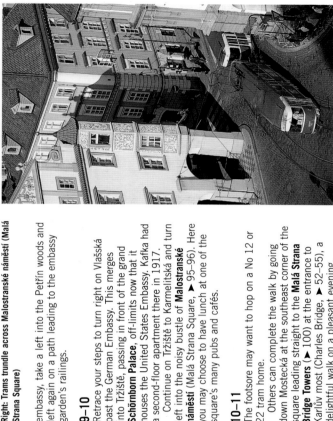

Right: Trams trundle across Malostranské náměstí (Malá Strana Square)

Directly opposite is the more peaceful **Loreta** pilgrimage sanctuary (➤ 103).

8–9

At the southern end of Loretánské náměstí, turn left to walk east along Loretánská street just past the south side of Thun-Hohenšteinsky palác on Castle Square and turn right down the Radnické schody stairway.

At the bottom of the stairs, leave cobbled Ke Hradu on your left and take the right fork down Nerudova. Past the old Dittrich pharmacy (1821) at No 32, turn right again down the Jánský vršek stairs.

Take another right on Šporkova which bends right to come out in front of the baroque **Lobkovický palác**, housing the German Embassy.

To see the palace's splendid rear façade and historic garden (➤ 102), at the west end of the

An old-fashioned gas lamp graces a corner of Castle Square

embassy, take a left into the Petřín woods and left again on a path leading to the embassy garden's railings.

9–10

Retrace your steps to turn right on Vlašská past the German Embassy. This merges into Tržiště, passing in front of the grand **Schönborn Palace**, off-limits now that it houses the United States Embassy. Kafka had a second-floor apartment there in 1917.

Continue on Tržiště to Karmelitská and turn left into the noisy bustle of **Malostranské náměstí** (Malá Strana Square, ➤ 95–96). Here you may choose to have lunch at one of the square's many pubs and cafés.

10–11

The footsore may want to hop on a No 12 or 22 tram home.

Others can complete the walk by going down Mostecká at the southeast corner of the square leading straight to the **Malá Strana Bridge Towers** (➤ 100) at the entrance to Karlův most (Charles Bridge, ➤ 52–55), a delightful walk on a pleasant evening.

3 MALÁ STRANA
Walk

This Left Bank walk mixes town and country. South of the Strahovský klášter (Strahov Monastery), head through the refreshing greenery of Petřín Hill, and then make your way down by the funicular railway to Malá Strana's riverside mansions and the different world of peaceful Kampa Island. End the walk with the bonus of Malá Strana's lovely terraced gardens, Kolovratská, Ledeburská and Pálffyovská.

DISTANCE 3km (2 miles) **TIME** 2–3 hours (including funicular railway)
START POINT Strahov (Pohořelec tram-stop) [+] 196 B1
END POINT Malostranská Metro [+] 194 C4

Petřín's mini Eiffel Tower peeks above the Hladová zed ("Hunger Wall")

1–2

From the tram-stop, cross through the gated entrance to **Strahovský klášter** (Strahov Monastery, ▶97–98), with its magnificent libraries. If you do not want to see the libraries at this particular time, however, keep to the right and leave the monastery again by a doorway in the east wall leading to the orchards and gardens.

The Strahov Monastery's gardens stand at the northern end of **Petřín Hill** (▶104). The views over the city are a joy and the park's attractions also make it worth a visit. Make your way along the park's eastern perimeter wall, the so-called "Hunger Wall" (Hladová zed) that leads south to the unmissable mini-Eiffel Tower, **Rozhledna** (literally "look-out tower") built 60m (197 feet) high as a tribute in 1891, just two years after the original in Paris.

Taking a Break

Have a snack or lunch (good venison and other wild game in season) on the terrace at **Restaurace Nebozízek** (▶105, tel: 257 315 329), on Újezd Street at the end of the funicular railway ride.

Romanesque but given its present baroque form in 1770. The church gives the hill its German name, Laurenziberg. Behind the Hunger Wall is the **Růžový sad** (rose garden, ➤ 104).

3–4

Walk past the funicular railway station to **Štefániko-va hvězdárna** (astronomical observatory). This is worth a look inside only at night. Otherwise make your way back to the funicular railway and head downhill. The funicular terminus is at Újezd Street, but you can make a stop at the halfway stage to take in the view.

4–5

Take the stairs from the funicular terminus and turn left on Újezd. After about 400m (437 yards), where Újezd merges into Karmelitská, is the astonishing Church of

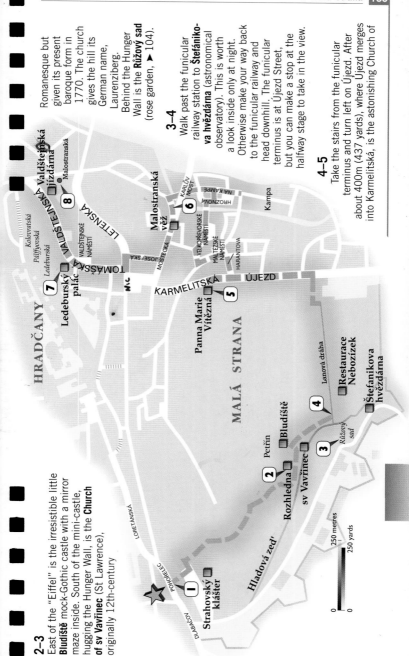

2–3

East of the "Eiffel" is the irresistible little **Bludiště** mock-Gothic castle with a mirror maze inside. South of the mini-castle, hugging the Hunger Wall, is the **Church of sv Vavřinec** (St Lawrence), originally 12th-century

at Valdštejnské náměstí 3, is the entrance, through Ledebur Palace, to the three adjacent **Kolovratská, Ledeburská** and **Pálffyovská** gardens (▶ 84).

7–8

Exit the gardens onto Valdštejnské náměstí and walk east down Valdštejnská road into the courtyard of Malostranská Metro. Inside the Metro courtyard is the thoroughly renovated **Valdštejnská jízdárna** (Wallenstein Palace riding school), now a modern art gallery.

Charming houses on Na Kampé Square, which takes you away from it all on Kampa Island

Panna Marie Vítězná (Our Lady of Victory, ▶ 101) on the left. Pilgrims and poets will want to stop in to see the costumed statue of Pražské Jezulátko (Infant Jesus of Prague).

5–6

Cross Karmelitská and double back to turn west on Harantova, leading to **Maltézské náměstí** (Maltese Square, ▶ 100). Turn right into Velkopřevorské náměstí, which crosses a bridge onto **Kampa Island** (▶ 101). Turn right on Hroznová, left and right again on Na Kampé to stroll south through the island's riverside park and back north again to climb the stairs from Na Kampé up onto Karlův most (Charles Bridge, ▶ 52).

6–7

Decisions. At this point the tired can head home from Charles Bridge. The valiant can carry on to Malá Strana's terraced gardens. Continue west through Malá Strana Bridge Gate to Mostecká. Turn right on Josefská, left on Letenská and right on Tomášská to the monumental square of **Valdštejnské náměstí**. On the north side of the square,

A statue guards an embassy on Maltézské náměstí (Maltese Square)

Practicalities

GETTING ADVANCE INFORMATION

Websites
- Prague Information Service: www.pis.cz
- Prague TV: www.prague.tv

In Prague
Prague Information Service
Staroměstská radnice (Old Town Hall)
Staré Město
☎ 12 444

In the UK
Czech Tourism Great Britain
13 Harley Street
London W1G 9QG
☎ 0906 3640641;
www.czechtourism.com

BEFORE YOU GO

WHAT YOU NEED

		UK	Germany	USA	Canada	Australia	Ireland	Netherlands	Spain
● Required	Some countries require a passport to remain valid for at least six months beyond the date of entry – contact their consulate or embassy or your travel agent for details.								
○ Suggested									
▲ Not required									
△ Not applicable									
Passport/National Identity Card		●	●	●	●	●	●	●	●
Visa (regulations can change – check before your journey)		▲	▲	▲	▲	▲	▲	▲	▲
Onward or Return Ticket		▲	▲	▲	▲	▲	▲	▲	▲
Health Inoculations (tetanus and polio)		▲	▲	▲	▲	▲	▲	▲	▲
Health Documentation		●	●	○	○	▲	○	●	●
Travel Insurance		○	○	○	○	○	○	○	○
Driver's Licence (national)		●	●	●	●	●	●	●	●
Car Insurance Certificate		●	●	●	●	●	●	●	○
Car Registration Document		●	●	●	●	●	●	●	○

WHEN TO GO

Prague

High season   Low season

JAN	FEB	MAR	APR	MAY	JUN	JUL	AUG	SEP	OCT	NOV	DEC
0°C	1°C	7°C	12°C	18°C	21°C	23°C	22°C	18°C	12°C	5°C	1°C
32°F	34°F	45°F	54°F	64°F	70°F	73°F	72°F	64°F	54°F	41°F	34°F
Cloud	Cloud	Cloud	Sun	Sun	Sun/Showers	Sun/Showers	Sun/Showers	Sun	Wet	Wet	Wet

☀ Sun   ☁ Cloud   🌧 Wet   🌦 Sun/Showers

Temperatures are the **average daily maximum** for each month.

Its Continental climate makes Prague's summers really hot and winters bitterly cold.

If **good weather** is the decisive factor, May and June and then September and October are the best times to go – but on the principle that there is no such thing as bad weather, just bad clothing.

If you go prepared, Prague's winter snow can be great, with the concert and opera seasons at their height.

If you want to **avoid the crowds** that can make life in the city centre really uncomfortable, mid-March to mid-April and October are the best times to go.

In the USA
Czech Tourism USA
1109–1111 Madison
Avenue
New York, NY 10028
☎ (212) 288 0830
www.czechtourism.com

In Canada
Czech Tourist Authority
(Czech Airlines Office)
401 Bay Street, Suite
1510, Simpson Tower
Toronto, Ontario M5H 2YA
☎ 416 363 9928

In Australia
Czech Embassy
8 Culgoa Circuit
O'Malley
ACT 2606
Canberra
☎ 02 6290 1386

GETTING THERE

s**By Air** From London Heathrow, both **Czech Airlines** (tel: 239 007 007;
www.csa.cz/en/) and **British Airways** (tel: 0870 8509850; www.britishairways.com)
operate two daily scheduled flights non-stop to Prague. There are no direct flights
from the Republic of Ireland, making the cheapest way via London.
From North America, only **Czech Airlines** operates non-stop flights to Prague from
New York (tel: 1-800 223 2365) and in Canada from Montreal and Toronto (tel: 800
641 0641).
From Australia the most direct flight to Prague is via Vienna from Sydney, with **Lauda
Air**, a subsidiary of Austria Airlines, 11th floor, 143 MacQuarie Street, Sydney, NSW
2000, Australia. To reserve call 1-800 642 438.
Discount Flights Many other airlines are starting to fly to Prague as its popularity as a
tourist destination increases. Competition has resulted in a drop in prices, so it is
worth checking the ads in travel sections of papers for discounted fares.

By Train From London Waterloo, take a noon train through the Channel Tunnel on
Eurostar (tel: 08705 186186; www.eurostar.com) via Brussels, then on to Cologne
for the overnight train, arriving in Prague around 8 am.

By Bus Daily from London Victoria, **Eurolines** (tel: 08705 808080 – reservation fee
applies; www.eurolines.co.uk – no reservation fee) takes 24 hours to Prague's Florenc
bus station.

TIME

The Czech Republic is on Central European Time, one hour ahead of GMT,
six hours ahead of New York and nine hours ahead of Los Angeles, with
summertime operating generally (but variably) from May to September.

CURRENCY AND FOREIGN EXCHANGE

Currency is the Czech *crown*, koruna Česká (Kč), divided into 100 *hellers*, haléř,
which have practically gone out of use. Coins come in denominations of 1, 2, 5, 10,
20 and 50Kč, notes 20, 50, 100, 200, 500, 1,000 and very rarely 2,000 and
5,000Kč.

Travellers' cheques are still the safest way to carry your money. You can exchange
them for cash at American Express, Václavské náměstí 56 (tel: 222 800 111) and at
most banks. Try the Czech National Bank (Česky Narodni Banka) Na Příkopě 28, tel:
224 411 411).

Credit cards are accepted at practically all hotels and most restaurants and shops in
the main tourist areas.

Exchange You'll find that ATM (cash-dispenser) machines are increasingly common in
the city centre.

Practicalities 187

TIME DIFFERENCES

GMT 12 noon	Prague 1 pm	USA New York 7 am	USA Los Angeles 4 am	Germany 1 pm	Australia Sydney 10 pm

WHEN YOU ARE THERE

CLOTHING SIZES

UK	Rest of Europe	USA	
36	46	36	
38	48	38	
40	50	40	Suits
42	52	42	
44	54	44	
46	56	46	
7	41	8	
7.5	42	8.5	
8.5	43	9.5	Shoes
9.5	44	10.5	
10.5	45	11.5	
11	46	12	
14.5	37	14.5	
15	38	15	
15.5	39/40	15.5	Shirts
16	41	16	
16.5	42	16.5	
17	43	17	
8	34	6	
10	36	8	
12	38	10	Dresses
14	40	12	
16	42	14	
18	44	16	
4.5	38	6	
5	38	6.5	
5.5	39	7	Shoes
6	39	7.5	
6.5	40	8	
7	41	8.5	

NATIONAL HOLIDAYS

1 Jan	New Year's Day
Mar/Apr	Easter Monday
1 May	May Day
8 May	National Liberation Day
5 Jul	Saints Cyril and Methodius
6 Jul	Jan Hus Day
28 Oct	Foundation of Czechoslovak Republic (1918)
24 Dec	Christmas Eve
25 Dec	Christmas Day
26 Dec	St Stephen's Day

OPENING HOURS

○ Shops   ● Post Offices
● Offices   ● Museums/Monuments
● Banks   ● Pharmacies

8 am 9 am 10 am noon 1 pm 2 pm 4 pm 5 pm 7 pm

☐ Day   ☐ Midday   ☐ Evening

Shops Most open Mon–Fri 9–5, supermarkets and tourist shops open later. The supermarket Tesco, at Narodni and Spalena, opens earlier and closes later than most.
Offices Mon–Fri 9–5 **Banks** Mon–Fri 8–5.
Post Offices Times vary considerably. With the advent of hotel faxes, email, Internet cafés, phone cards and postage stamps being available at tobacconists and many hotel reception desks, most people don't use traditional post offices in the same way as they used to.
Museums and Galleries Tue–Sun 9–5 or 10–6.
Pharmacies Usually open Mon–Fri 8 am–6 pm; not all are open at weekends.

EMERGENCY 112

POLICE 112

FIRE 112

AMBULANCE 112

PERSONAL SAFETY

Crime has risen in Prague since the fall of Communism, but mostly involves theft rather than physical aggression. It is worth taking the following precautions:

- Leave valuables and important papers in the hotel safe. Carry a photocopy of your passport with you.
- When parking a car, don't leave anything visible.
- If you do have something stolen, report it to the police.
- Be aware of pickpockets, especially in tourist areas.

Police assistance:
 112 from any phone

TELEPHONES

Almost all public phone boxes in the city centre take phone cards only – available from tobacconists, post offices and some newspaper kiosks. For calls to Prague from elsewhere in the Czech Republic, the city code is 02. Cheap rate is 7 am–7 pm, but this changes, so check on 1151. For the international operator (charge), dial 00420 004401 for UK; 00420 00101 for USA; 00420 00151 for Canada; 00420 006101 for Australia.

International Dialling Codes	
Dial 00 followed by	
UK:	**44**
USA/Canada:	**1**
Republic of Ireland:	**353**
Australia:	**61**
Germany:	**49**

POST

The main post office is at Jindřišská 14, tel: 221 131 445. Open 24 hours. Prague Castle's post office is open Mon–Fri 8–7, Sat and Sun 10–7. Mail boxes are orange.

ELECTRICITY

Power supply is 220 volts. Plugs are two round-pin Continental types. UK and North American visitors require an adaptor. North American visitors should bring a voltage transformer for their 110/120-volt AC appliances.

TIPS/GRATUITIES

Tipping is generally expected for all services. As a general guide:

Restaurants (service not included)	Round up to nearest whole number
Bar service	Round up to nearest whole number
Tour guides	Discretion
Taxis	Round up to nearest 100Kč
Porters	Round up to nearest 100Kč
Chambermaids	Round up to nearest 100Kč

CONSULATES and EMBASSIES

UK
☎ 257 402 111

USA
☎ 257 530 663

Ireland
☎ 257 530 061

Canada
☎ 272 101 800

Australia
☎ 251 018 350

HEALTH

Insurance Citizens of EU countries receive reciprocal emergency health care with relevant documentation (European Health Insurance Card), but private medical insurance is still advised and essential for all other visitors

Dental Services Make sure your health insurance covers dental treatment. Emergency care is at Palackého 5, tel: 224 946 981.

Weather Prague is hottest from April to August, although the temperature rarely goes above 23°C (73°F). However, it is worth taking the precaution of applying a good sunscreen if you are out sightseeing, covering up and drinking plenty of fluids.

Drugs Take a supply of your own prescription medicines, as you may not be able to find exactly the same in Prague. For general requirements, there are 24-hour pharmacies at Palackého 5, tel: 224 946 982, and at Belgická 37, tel: 224 237 207.

Safe Water Drinking unboiled tap water is safe. Mineral water is cheap and readily available.

CONCESSIONS

Students Holders of an International Student Identification Card (ISIC) are entitled to discounts for public transport, museums, galleries and theatres.
Senior Citizens Senior citizens must produce identity cards proving they are over 70 to obtain discounts on public transport and other facilities.
Prague Card This is a three-day **tourist pass**. One version allows entry to Prague Castle and the city's major museums and historic buildings (adults: 590Kč; children/students 410Kč). Another version covers entry fees plus unlimited travel on the Metro, trams and buses (adults: 810Kč; children/students: 630Kč). For information on where to buy the cards ➤ 36.

TRAVELLING WITH A DISABILITY

Only the newest trams, a few Metro stations and two main railway stations (Hlavní nádraží and Nádraží Holešovice) are equipped for wheelchairs. Only since 1994 has there been a law improving access for those with disabilities to all new buildings. Restaurants, hotels, stations and other institutions with wheelchair access are listed in the guidebook *Accessible Prague* (*Přístupná Praha*), available from the Prague Wheelchair Association, Benediktská 6, Nové Město, Prague, tel: 224 827 810.

CHILDREN

Hotels and restaurants often don't have baby-changing facilities, but some hotels may have a baby-sitting service. Children are generally welcome in restaurants.

TOILETS

The cleanest ones are in the major hotels and big cafés. Some places may charge.

CUSTOMS

The import of wildlife souvenirs from rare or endangered species may be illegal or require a special permit. Before buying, check your home country's regulations.

PRONOUNCING "ANTONÍN DVOŘÁK"

The Czech language seems to have more accents, especially on consonants, than you may be used to. While you may not get around to learning the language, you may want to know how to pronounce the place names you'll see on signposts and maps.

a as in **cat**
á as in **bar**
c as **ts** in **its**
č as **ch** in **cheap**
ch as **ch** in **loch**
ď as in **duration**
e as in **elf**
é as **ea** in **wear**
ě as **ye** in **yell**
i as in **kit**
í as **ie** in **belief**
j as **y** in **yellow**
ň as **ni** in **opinion**
q is pronounced **kv**
r is rolled
ř (as in Dvořák) combines **rolled r** and **zh sound** in **measure**
š as **ss** in **mission**
ť as **t** in **overture**
u as **ou** in **could**
ú and **ů** as **oo** in **soon**
w is pronounced **v**
y as **i** in **kit**
ý as **ie** in **belief**
ž as **zh sound** in **measure**

SURVIVAL WORDS AND PHRASES

yes/no **ano/ne**
please **prosím**
thank you **děkuji**
sorry **pardon**
hello **ahoj** (formal: **dobrý den**)
goodbye **na shledanou**
good morning **dobré ráno**
goodnight **dobrou noc**
good evening **dobrý večer**
excuse me **promiňte**
help! **pomoc!**
open **otevřeno**
closed **zavřeno**
today **dnes**
tomorrow **zítra**
yesterday **včera**
day **den**
week **týden**
month **měsíc**
year **rok**

Monday **pondělí**
Tuesday **úterý**
Wednesday **středa**
Thursday **čtvrtek**
Friday **pátek**
Saturday **sobota**
Sunday **neděle**
small **malý**
large **velký**
quickly **rychle**
slowly **pomalu**
cold **studený**
hot **horký**
left **nalevo**
right **napravo**
straight ahead **přímo**
entrance **vchod**
exit **východ**
where? **kde?**
when? **kdy?**
why? **proč?**
here **tady**
there **tam**
near **blízko**
far **daleko**
bank **banka**
post office **pošta**
art gallery **galerie**
church **kostel**
garden **zahrada**
library **knihovna**
museum **muzeum**
tourist information
   turistické informace
foreign exchange **směnárna**
credit card **kreditní karta**
how much? **kolik?**
cheap **levný**
expensive **drahý**
free (no charge) **zdarma**
more **více**
less **méně**
Do you speak English?
   Mluvíte anglicky?

GETTING AROUND

aeroplane **letadlo**
airport **letiště**
train **vlak**
train station **nádraží**
Metro station **stanice**
bus **autobus**
bus station **autobusové nádraží**
tram **tramvaj**
bus/tram stop **zastávka**
pleasure steamer **parník**
small boat **lodička**

ticket **lístek**
  single/return **jednosměrná/zpáteční**
  first/second class **první/druhá třída**
ticket office **pokladna**
seat reservation **místenka**

ACCOMMODATION

hotel **hotel**
room **pokoj**
I would like a room **potřebuji pokoj**
  single/double **jednolůžkový/**
          dvoulůžkový
  for one night **na jednu noc**
How much per night?
  kolik stojí jedna noc?
reservation **rezervace**
breakfast **snídaně**
toilet **záchod/WC**
bath **koupelna**
shower **sprcha**
cold/hot water **studená/teplá voda**
towel **ručník**
soap **mýdlo**
room number **číslo pokoje**
key **klíč**

SHOPPING

bakery **pekárna**
bookstore **knihkupectví**
butcher **řeznictví**
pharmacy **lékárna**
grocery **potraviny**
supermarket **samoobsluha**

EATING OUT

restaurant **restaurace**
coffee house **kavárna**
pub **hospoda**
wine bar **vinárna**
table **stůl**
menu **jídelní lístek**
fixed-price menu **standardní menu**
the bill **účet**

wine list **nápojový lístek**
lunch **oběd**
dinner **večeře**
starter **předkrm**
main course **hlavní jídlo**
dish of the day **nabídka dne**
dessert **moučník/dezert**
waiter/waitress **číšník/servírka**
bon appetit **dobrou chuť**

MENU READER

bílé víno
  white wine
bamborové
  knedlíky
  potato
  dumplings
brambory
  potatoes
chléb bread
cibule onion
cukr sugar
čaj tea
červené víno
  red wine
dort cake
grilované grilled
houby
  mushrooms
houskové
  knedlíky
  bread
  dumplings
hovězí beef
hranolky chips/
  French fries
jablko apple
jahody
  strawberries
jehněčí lamb
kachna duck
káva coffee
kuře chicken
maso meat
máslo butter

minerálka
  mineral water
šumivá fizzy
nešumivá still
mléko milk
okurka
  cucumber
párek sausage/
  frankfurter
pečené baked/
  roasted
pepř pepper
polévka soup
pomeranč orange
pomerančový džús
  orange juice
pivo beer
rajské tomato
ryba fish
rýže rice
salát salad
sůl salt
sýr cheese
šunka ham
  vařená cooked
  uzená smoked
vajíčko egg
vepřové pork
voda water
zelí cabbage
zelenina
  vegetables
zmrzlina
  ice-cream

NUMBERS

1	**jeden**	11	**jedenáct**	21	**dvacet jedna**	80	**osmdesát**
2	**dva**	12	**dvanáct**	22	**dvacet dva**	90	**devadesát**
3	**tří**	13	**třináct**	23	**dvacet tři**	100	**sto**
4	**čtyři**	14	**čtrnáct**	24	**dvacet čtyři**		
5	**pět**	15	**patnáct**	25	**dvacet pět**	1,000	**tisíc**
6	**šest**	16	**šestnáct**	30	**třicet**	2,000	**dva tisíce**
7	**sedm**	17	**sedmnáct**	40	**čtyřicet**	5,000	**pět tisíc**
8	**osm**	18	**osmnáct**	50	**padesát**		
9	**devět**	19	**devatenáct**	60	**šedesát**		
10	**deset**	20	**dvacet**	70	**sedmdesát**	1,000,000	**milión**

Streetplan

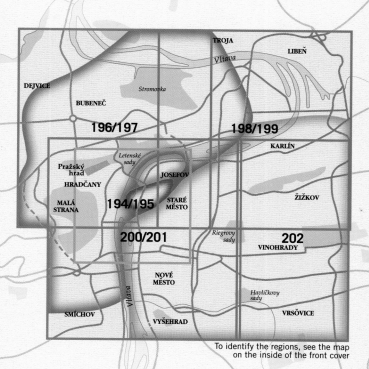

DEJVICE

TROJA

LIBEŇ

Vltava

Stromovka

BUBENEČ

196/197

198/199

KARLÍN

Letenské sady

Pražský hrad

HRADČANY

JOSEFOV

ŽIŽKOV

MALÁ STRANA

194/195

STARÉ MĚSTO

200/201

Riegrovy sady

202
VINOHRADY

NOVÉ MĚSTO

Vltava

Havlíčkovy sady

SMÍCHOV

VYŠEHRAD

VRŠOVICE

To identify the regions, see the map
on the inside of the front cover

Key to Streetplan

Motorway/dual carriageway	Funicular railway
Main road	City/castle wall
Other road	Park
Tunnel	Important building
Footpath	Featured place of interest
Steps	Metro station

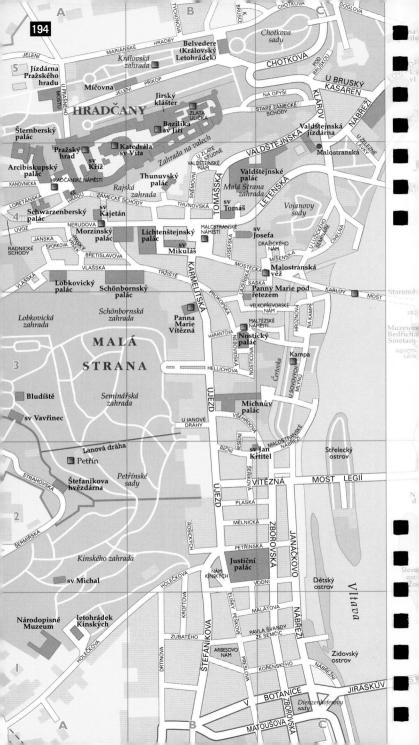

A

5 Jízdárna Pražského hradu

Jeleni

B

Marianské Hradby

Tychonova

Belvedere (Královský Letohrádek)

Královská zahrada

Míčovna

Příkop

Jeleni

Jirský klášter

HRADČANY

Bazilika sv Jiří

Zlatá ulička

Staré zámecké schody

Na Opyši

CHOTKOVA

Chotkova sady

C

Goglova

Pod Bruskou

U BRUSKÝ KASÁREN

Klárov

Nábřeží

Valdštejnská jízdárna

Šternberský palác

Pražský hrad

sv Kříž

Katedrála sv Víta

Arcibiskupský palác

Hradčanské náměstí

Kanovnická

U hradu

Zámecké schody

Zahrada na valech

U Zlaté studně

Valdštejnské nám

Snemovní

Thunovská

Rajská zahrada

Valdštejnská

Malostranská

Malostranská

Valdštejnské palác

Malá Strana zahrada

Vojanovy sady

U lužického semináře

Cihelna

Loretánská

Schwarzenberský palác

Nerudova

sv Kajetán

Morzinský palác

Lichtenštejnský palác

sv Mikuláš

Malostranské náměstí

Tomáššká

sv Tomáš

Letenská

Josefská

sv Josefa

Dražického nám

Mišenská

Malostranská věž

Karlův most

Staroměst

Uvoz

Janská

Spořkova

Vlašský

Břetislavova

Vlašská

Lobkovický palác

Schönbornský palác

Tržiště

Vlašská

Prokopská

Mostecká

Saská

Panny Marie pod řetězem

Velkopřevorské nám

Na Kampě

Muzeum Bedřicha Smetany

Novotná Lávka

Lobkovická zahrada

Schönbornská zahrada

MALÁ STRANA

Panna Marie Vítězná

Harantova

Nebovidská

Maltézské náměstí

Nostický palác

Hroznová

Na Kampě

Čertovka

Kampa

Bludiště

Seminářská zahrada

sv Vavřinec

Lanová dráha

Petřín

Hellichova

Úlezd

U Šovových mlýnů

Michnův palác

Všehrdová

U Ianové dráhy

Říční

sv Jan Křtitel

Šeříkova

Malostranské nábřeží

Střelecký ostrov

Štefánikova hvězdárna

Petřínské sady

Úlezd

Vítězná

MOST LEGII

N

Plaská

Mělnická

Zborovská

Janáčkovo

Strahovská

Šermířská

Kinského zahrada

Rošických

Petřínská

Nám Kinských

Justiční palác

Vodní

Dětský ostrov

Vltava

Slova ost

sv Michal

Holečkova

Kroftova

Eliščky Peškové

Malátova

Pavla Švandy ze Semčíc

Nábřeží

Národopisné Muzeum

letohrádek Kinských

Holečkova

Drtinova

Zubatého

Arbesovo nám

Presslova

Kořenského

Nábřežní

Židovský ostrov

I

Štefánikova

V Botanice

Zborovská

Matousova

Botanice

Dienzenhoferovy sady

JIRÁSKŮV

A

B

C

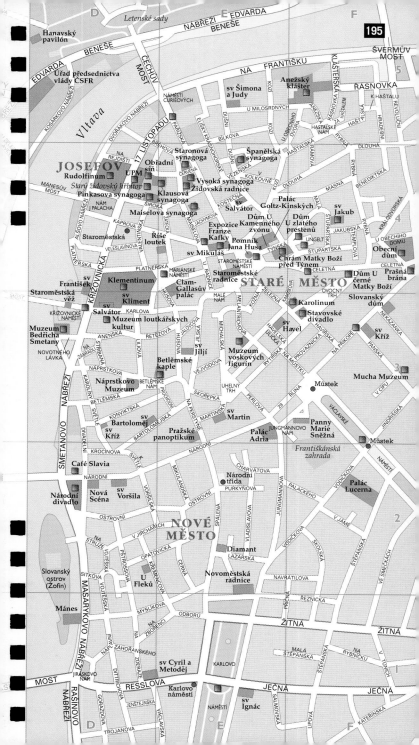

Letenské sady

NÁBŘEŽÍ EDVARDA

NÁBŘEŽÍ EDVARDA BENEŠE

ŠVERMŮV MOST

Hanavský pavilón

BENEŠE

EDVARDA

Úřad předsednictva vlády ČSFR

NA FRANTIŠKU

Anežský klášter

ŘÁSNOVKA

ČECHŮV MOST

sv Šimon a Judy

K HAŠTALU

NÁMĚSTÍ CURIEOVÝCH

U MILOSRDNÝCH

HAŠTALSKÉ NÁM

Vltava

17 LISTOPADU

Staronová synagoga

Španělská synagoga

DLOUHÁ

JOSEFOV

Obřadní síň

Vysoká synagoga
Židovská radnice

Palác Goltz-Kinských

sv Jakub

Rudolfinum

Starý židovský hřbitov

Klausová synagoga

Salvátor

Dům U Kamenného zvonu

Dům U zlatého prestenů

OBECNÍ DŮM

Pinkasova synagoga

Maiselova synagoga

Expozice Franze Kafky

Pomník Jana Husa

UNGELT

Obecní dům

Staroměstská

Říše loutek

sv Mikuláš

Chrám Matky Boží před Týnem

Prašná brána

sv Jakub

Dům U černé Matky Boží

Františkek

Klementinum

STAROMĚSTSKÉ NÁMĚSTÍ

STARÉ MĚSTO

Slovanský dům

Staroměstská věž

Staroměstská radnice

Clam-Gallasův palác

Karolinum

sv Kliment

sv Havel

Stavovské divadlo

sv Kříž

Salvátor

Muzeum loutkářských kultur

Muzeum Bedřicha Smetany

sv Jiljí

Muzeum voskových figurín

Mucha Muzeum

Betlémská kaple

Můstek

Náprstkovo Muzeum

sv Bartoloměj

sv Martin

sv Kříž

Pražské panoptikum

Panny Marie Sněžná

Palác Adria

Můstek

Café Slavia

Františkánská zahrada

Národní třída

Palác Lucerna

Národní divadlo

Nová Scéna

sv Voršila

NOVÉ MĚSTO

Slovanský ostrov (Žofin)

Diamant

U Fleků

Novoměstská radnice

Mánes

ŽITNÁ

ŽITNÁ

sv Cyril a Metoděj

Karlovo náměstí

sv Ignác

JEČNÁ

JEČNÁ

RESSLOVA

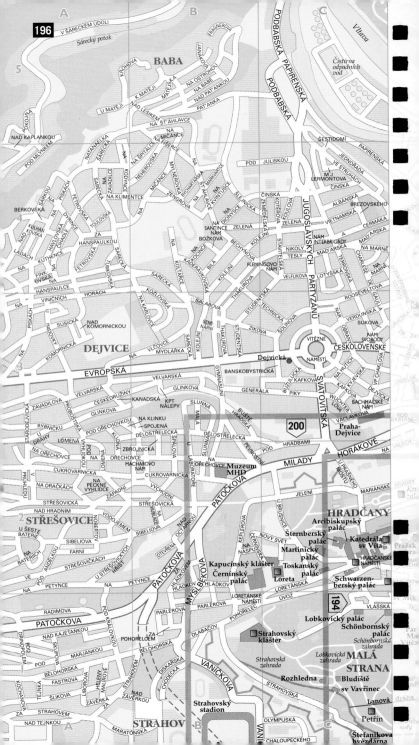

V ŠÁRECKÉM ÚDOLÍ
Šárecký potok

BABA

Vltava
Čistírna
odpadních
vod

PODBABSKÁ
PAPÍRENSKÁ
PODBABSKÁ

KRÓHOVA
JANKOVCA
NA OSTROHU
NA BABĚ
NAD PATANKOU
PATANKA
POD JULISKOU

U MATEJE II
NAD LESÍKEM
NA STŘÁHLAVCE
NA MIČÁNCE
NA FIŠERCE

NAD KAPLANKOU
POD MLÝNKEM

ŠESTIDOMÍ
JEDNOŘADÁ
PAPÍRENSKÁ
VE STRUHÁCH
M J LERMONTOVA

BERKOVSKÁ
NATANAELKA
ŠÁRKOU
NA PÍSKÁCH
FETROVSKÁ
KODYMCE
NA VOZOVCE
NA KLIMENTCE
NA MIČÁNCE
NEHEROVSKÁ
MYLNEROVA
RYCHTÁŘSKÁ
NA ŠTÁHLAVCE
NA MARKVARTCE
ČÍNSKÁ
KOTĚROVA
ZEMĚDĚLSKÁ
ČÍNSKÁ
ALBÁNSKÁ
BŘEZOVSKÉHO

KULHÁN
KOVSKÁ
HAVLOVSKÁ
DRINCE
TOULOVSKÁ
ZA
ZENGROVA
SANTINCE
NÁM
ŽELEZNIČÁŘŮ
DIONÝSE
ZELENÁ
KVINTLCE
ŠŤÁHLAVCE
STAVITELSKÁ
ZELENÁ
VÍTĚZNÁ
NÁM
INTERBRIGÁDY
MADARSKÁ
VIETNAMSKÁ
ČERMÁKA

NAD
LADACH
FINK
OVSKÁ
NA
KUTHENCE
PETROVSKÁ
HANSPAULKOU
ŠÁRECKÁ
TURKOVSKÁ
NA
KOČÍNCE
BOŽKOVA
BÍLÁ
KADEŘÁVKOVSKÁ
KOLEJNÍ
BECHYŇOVA
KOLEJNÍ
FLEMINGOVO
NÁM
NIKOLY
TESLY
MADARSKÁ
TERRONSKÁ
CHARLESE
DE GALLA
NA MARNE
NA MARNE

HANSPAULCE
VINIČNÍCH
HORÁCH
KOZLOVSKÁ
ŠÁRECKÁ
NA KARLOVCE
ŠÁRECKÁ
ŠALAMOVA
THÁKUROVA
STUDENTSKÁ
VELFLÍKOVA
LOTYŠSKÁ
ROOSEVELTOVA

NA
PÍSKÁCH
SUSICKÁ
NAD
KOMORNICKOU
SEMI
NÁRNÍ
THÁKUROVA
STUDENTSKÁ
ŽIKOVA
TECHNICKÁ
SOLÍNOVA
NÁR
VERDUNSKÁ
SUKOVA
NÁM
SVOBODY

KOMORNICKÁ
DEJVICE
NA
VLČOVCE
MYDLÁŘKA
ŠÁRECKÁ
KOLEJNÍ
BANSKOBYSTRICKÁ
Dejvická
VÍTĚZNÉ
NÁMĚSTÍ
ČESKOSLOVENSKÉ
NA
HUTICH
KYJEVSKÁ
DEJVICKÁ

EVROPSKÁ
VELVARSKÁ
GYMNASIJNÍ
BUZULUCKÁ
KAFKOVA
SVATOVÍTSKÁ
KAFKOVA
WUCHTER
LOVA
BACHMAČSKÉ

VELVARSKÁ
ČESKÉDRUŽINY
GLINKOVA
GENERÁLA
PIKY
VÁCLAVKOVA

ZAVADILOVA
PROBOŠTSKÁ
GLINKOVA
KANADSKÁ
KPT
NÁLEPY
SLUNNÁ
MALÁ
BUŠTĚ
HRADSKÁ
200
**Praha-
Dejvice**

STARODEJVICKÁ
RYBNÍČKU
U
DRAHY
POD OŘECHOVKOU
SPOJENÁ
NA KLINKU
UNITŘNÍ
DĚLOSTŘELECKÁ
PEVNOSTNÍ
POD
HRADBAMI
HORÁKOVÉ
NA

LOMENÁ
KLÍNA
ŠPALOVA
DĚLOSTŘELECKÁ
MILADY
U PRAŠNÉHO
MOSTU
MARIÁNSKÉ

NA OŘECHOVCE
POD
VLÍDKOU
ZBROJNICKÁ
NA
OŘECHOVCE
**Muzeum
MHD**
LABORATOŘE
JELENÍ

CUKROVARNICKÁ
MACHAROVO
NÁM
CUKROVARNICKÁ
VÝCHODNÍ
NA
OŘECHOVCE
U BRUSNICE
U
BRUSNICE
KEPLEROVA
NOVÝ SVĚT
HRADČANY
Arcibiskupský
palác

NA DRAČKÁCH
NA
PECKNÉ
VYHLÍDCE
ZÁPADNÍ
PATOČKOVA
NA
PÚSTKÁCH
Šternberský
palác
**Katedrála
sv Víta**

STŘEŠOVICKÁ
NAD HRADNÍM
STŘEŠOVICKÁ
VODOJEMEM
NAD
OCTÁRNOU
ČERNÍNSKÁ
NÁM
NA
NAD
NAD
HRADČANSKÉ
NÁMĚSTÍ
Martinický
palác
Toskánský
palác

STŘEŠOVICE
U ŠESTÉ
BATERIE
ROBERTOVA
SIBELIOVA
MYSLBEKOVA
HLÁDKOVEM
Kapucínský klášter
Černínský
palác
Loreta
LORETÁNSKÁ
Schwarzen-
berský palác

SIBELIOVA
FARNÍ
NAD
Loreta
LORETÁNSKÉ
NÁMĚSTÍ

U BATERIÍ
VE
POD ANDĚLKOU
U STŘEŠOVICKÝCH
HŘBIT
OTEVŘENÁ
PARLÉŘOVA
PARLÉŘOVA
POHOŘELEC
ÚVOZ
194
VLAŠSKÁ

PETYNCE
PETYNCE
PATOČKOVA
ZA
HLÁDKOVEM
HLÁDKOV
DLABAČOV
Lobkovický palác
Schönbornský
palác

RADIMOVA
POD KRÁLOVKOU
PARLÉŘOVA
**Strahovský
klášter**
MALÁ
Schönbornská
zahrada

PATOČKOVA
NAD KAJETÁNKOU
ZA
POHOŘELCEM
BĚLOHORSKÁ
Strahovská
zahrada
Lobkovická
zahrada
STRANA

DŘINOPOLEM
POD
SKALKOU
MARJÁNKOU
VANÍČKOVA
Rozhledna
Bludiště

BĚLOHORSKÁ
HELENY
MALÍŘOVÉ
DISKAŘSKÁ
CHODECKÁ
sv Vavřinec

KOCHANOVA
TEJNKA
FASTROVA
LIBOCKÁ
ŠLIKOVA
ZÁVĚRKA
NAD
STRAHOVEM
NAD
ZÁVĚRKOU
STRAHOVSKÁ
Lanová
dráha

ZA
STRAHOVEM
NAD TEJNKOU
MARATÓNSKÁ
STRAHOV
**Strahovský
stadion**
OLYMPIJSKÁ
CHALOUPECKÉHO
VANÍ
Petřín
**Štefánikova
hvězdárna**

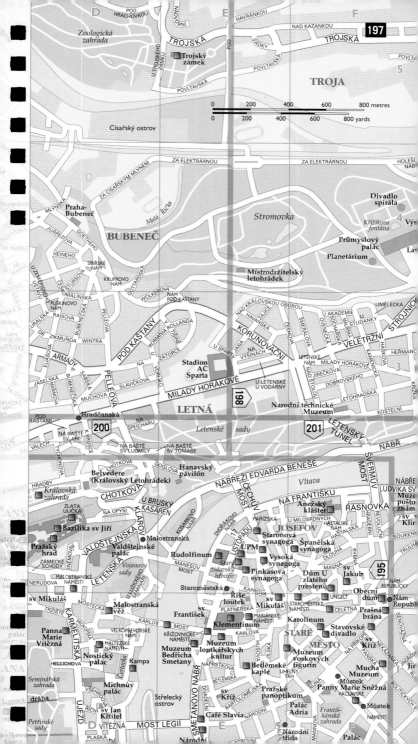

D **E** **F**

POD HRACHOVKOU

NADÝ URNÍ

HAVRÁNKOU

NAD KAZANKOU

Zoologická zahrada

TROJSKÁ

TROJSKÁ

POD SÁDKY

POVLT

5

U TROJSKÉHO ZÁMKU

Trojský zámek

POD

TROJA

POVLTAVSKÁ

POVLTAVSKÁ

0   200   400   600   800 metres

0   200   400   600   800 yards

Císařský ostrov

ZA ELEKTRÁRNOU

ZA ELEKTRÁRNOU

HOLEŠO NÁB

ZA CÍSAŘSKÝM MLÝNEM

Divadlo spirála

MLÝNSKÁ

Praha-Bubeneč

Malá Řítka

Stromovka

Křížikova fontána

4 Výs

GOETHEHO

JUÁREZOVA

BUBENEČ

Průmyslový palác

La

HEINEHO

SIBIŘSKÉ NÁM

Planetárium

U ZEMĚDĚL MUSEA

TURSOVA

KRUPKOVO NÁM.

WOLKEROVA

NÁM POD KAŠTANY

Místodržitelský letohrádek

ČESKOMALÍNSKÁ

UMĚLECKÁ

URALSKÁ

PUŠKINOVO NÁM.

RAISOVA

PELLÉOVA

NAD KRÁLOVSKOU OBOROU

NAD HRADNÍ

U AKADEMIE

STROJNIC

DR ZIKMUNDA

WINTRA

ROMÁINA ROLLANDA

ZÁTORCE

HAVÁNSKÁ

ŠMERALOVA

OVENECKÁ

ČECHOVA

U STUDÁNKY

ŠIMÁČKOVA

TASKOVA

VELETRŽNÍ

ELIÁŠOVA

BUBENEČSKÁ

NA

VORTKU

U SPARTY

NA VÝŠINÁCH

LETENSKÉ NÁM

MILADY HORÁKOVÉ

KAMENICKÁ

HERMAN

ARMÁDY

JASELSKÁ

MÁCHAROVA

SAARSKÁ

MUCHOVA

SLAVÍČKOVA

KORUNOVAČNÍ

Stadion AC Sparta

198

NAD ŠTOLOU

NAD JIŘEČKOVÉ

DOBROVSKÉHO

LETOHRADSKÁ

KŘIŽÍ

3

MILADY HORÁKOVÉ

U LETENSKÉ U VODÁRNY

LETNÁ

Národní technické Muzeum

KOSTELNÍ

POD BAŠTAMI

● Hradčanská

NA ŠPEJCHARU

200

Letenské sady

201

LETENSKÝ TUNEL

NÁBŘ

VALECH

NA BAŠTĚ SV JIŘÍ

NA BAŠTĚ SV LUDMILY

NA BAŠTĚ SV TOMÁŠE

TYCHONOVA

CHOTKOVA

GOGLIOVA

Hanavský pavilón

NÁBŘEZÍ EDVARDA BENEŠE

Vltava

ŠVERMŮV MOST

NÁBŘE LUDVÍKA SV

HRADBY

Belvedere (Královský Letohrádek)

NA FRANTIŠKU

Muze pošto znám

Královská zahrada

CHOTKOVA

U BRUSKÝ KASÁREN

ČECHŮV MOST

Anežský klášter

U MILOSRDNÝCH

RÁSNOVKA

sv Klír

ZLATÁ ULIČKA

NA OPYŠI

KLÁROV

PAŘÍŽSKÁ

JOSEFOV

HAŠTALSKÁ

HAŠTALSKÉ NÁM

SOUKEN

dráha

● Bazilika sv Jiří

VALDŠTEJNSKÁ

● Malostranská

DVOŘÁKOVO NÁBŘ

17 LISTOPADU

Staronová synagoga

Španělská synagoga

DLOUHÁ

TRUHL

Pražský hrad

ZÁMECKÉ SCHODY

LETENSKÁ

Valdštejnské palác

Vojanovy sady

U LUŽICKÉHO SEMINÁŘE

KOSÁRKOVO NÁBŘ

UPM

Vysoká synagoga

MASNÁ

sv Jakub

RYBNÁ

195

NERUDOVA

SNĚMOVNÍ

MÁNESŮV MOST

Rudolfinum

Starý židovský hřbitov

Pinkasova synagoga

Dům U zlatého prestenů

UNGELT

NÁM REPUBLIKY

MALOSTRANSKÉ NÁMĚSTÍ

Staroměstská

Obecní dům

Nám Republ

sv Mikuláš

Malostranská věž

MOSTECKÁ

Říše loutek

PLATNÉŘSKÁ

sv Mikuláš

STAROMĚSTSKÉ NÁMĚSTÍ

CELETNÁ

Prašná brána

SENOVÁŽNA

TRŽIŠTĚ

KARMELITSKÁ

PROKOPSKÁ

sv František

MARIÁNSKÉ NÁMĚSTÍ

Karolinum

Stavovské divadlo

sv Kříž

NA PŘÍKOPĚ

HAVÍŘSKÁ

PANSKÁ

Panna Marie Vítězná

VELKOPŘEVORSKÉ NÁM

KARLŮV MOST

Klementinum

KARLOVA

STARÉ

MĚSTO

JINDŘI

Jir

KŘÍŽOVNICKÉ NÁMĚSTÍ

MALTÉZSKÉ NÁMĚSTÍ

Muzeum Bedřicha Smetany

Muzeum loutkářských kultur

JILSKÁ

Muzeum voskových figurín

Mucha Muzeum

Nostický palác

HELLICHOVA

Čertovka

Kampa

NAPRŠTKOVA

Betlémské kaple

UHELNÝ TRH

Pražské panoptikum

VODIČKOVA

Panny Marie Sněžná

● Můstek

Seminářská zahrada

Michnův palác

BETLÉMSKÁ

BARTOLOMĚJSKÁ

RÝINA

Palác Adria

● Můstek

VŠEHRDOVA

VÍTĚZNÁ

sv Jan Křtitel

Střelecký ostrov

DIVADELNÍ

sv Kříž

Café Slavia

SMETANOVO NÁBŘ

NÁRODNÍ

Františkánská zahrada

NÁMĚSTÍ

Petřínské sady

UJEZD

dráha

MOST LEGIÍ

Národní

SPÁLENÁ

MARTINSKÁ

Národní třída

Palác

PLASKÁ

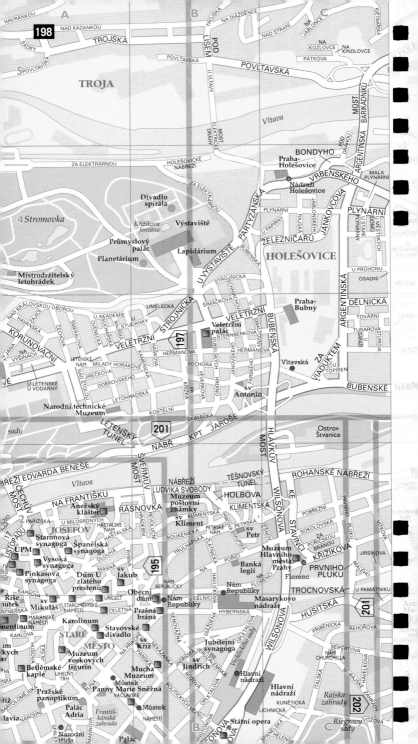

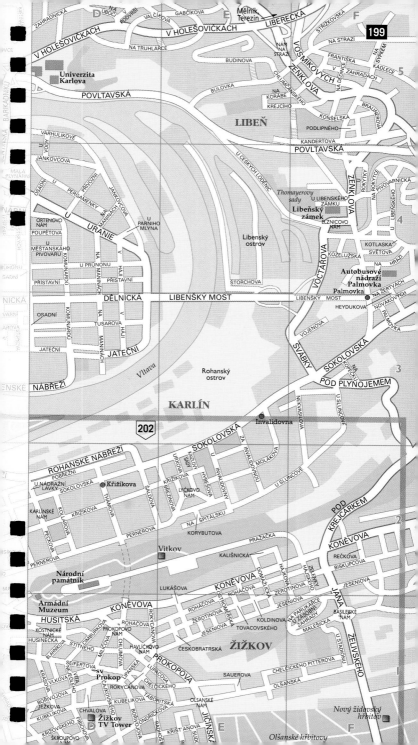

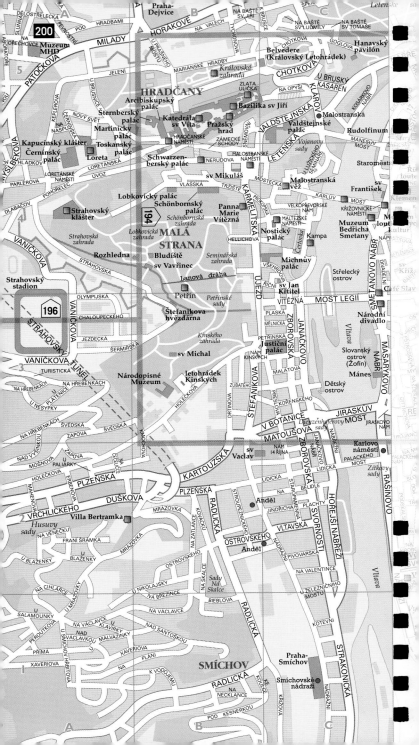

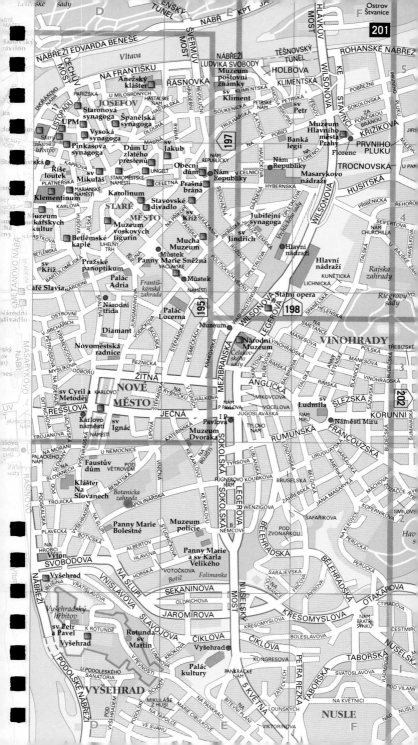

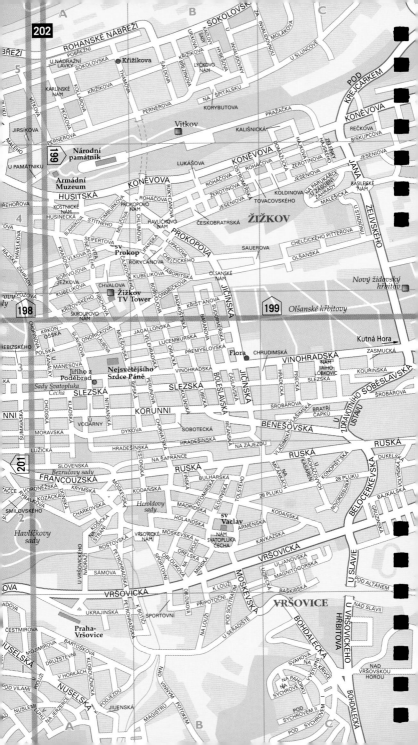

STREET INDEX

nám námestí
nábř nábřeží

Picture credits

Abbreviations for terms appearing above (t) top; (b) bottom; (l) left; (r) right; (c) centre

Front and Back Covers (t) AA Photo Library/Clive Sawyer, (ct) AA Photo Library/Jon Wyand, (cb) AA Photo Library/Jon Wyand, (b) AA Photo Library/Clive Sawyer; Spine AA Photo Library/Clive Sawyer

The Automobile Association wishes to thank all the photographers, libraries and associations for their assistance with the preparation of this book;

© ADAGP, Paris and DACS, London 2001 136c, 140; AKG LONDON 19t, 20/1, 22/3, 140 © ADAGP, Paris and DACS, London 2001; JACK ALTMAN 15; JAMES DAVIS WORLDWIDE 2iii, 47, 96; MARY EVANS PICTURE LIBRARY 8t, 8c, 17t, 32, 32 inset; HULTON ARCHIVE 17b, 19b, 20, 26, 28, 28/9, 29, 143; OLDRICH KARASEK 144, 147, 166, 168, 170, 172; THE LEBRECHT MUSIC COLLECTION 24tl, 24tr, 24b; MAGNUM PICTURES 13; PICTOR INTERNATIONAL, LONDON 24t; REX FEATURES LTD; 12/13, 14t; THE ROLAND GRANT ARCHIVE 9b; GORDON SINGER 24b, 30b 31t, 31b, 117, 119, 120, 189t, 189l, 189r

The remaining photographs are held in the Association's own photo library (AA PHOTO LIBRARY) and were taken by SIMON McBRIDE with the exception of the following:2i, 2ii, 3iv, 5, 6/7, 11b, 33, 54, 57, 61, 63, 69, 81b, 83, 102, 118/9, 123, 136b, 151, 155, 156, 173, 177, 184l, 184r, which were taken by CLIVE SAWYER, 128, which was taken by ANTONY SOUTER, and 3iii, 9t, 23, 25, 27c, 27b, 58b, 65, 68, 87t, 99, 101, 103, 104, 112, 121, 122, 126, 139, 148, 161, 164, 165, 181l, 182, which were taken by JON WYAND

Questionnaire

Dear Traveler

Your comments, opinions and recommendations are very important to us. So please help us to improve our travel guides by taking a few minutes to complete this simple questionnaire.

Send to: Spiral Guides, MailStop 66, 1000 AAA Drive, Heathrow, FL 32746–5063

Your recommendations...
We always encourage readers' recommendations for restaurants, nightlife or shopping – if your recommendation is added to the next edition of the guide, we will send you a FREE AAA Spiral Guide of your choice. Please state below the establishment name, location and your reasons for recommending it.

_____

_____

_____

_____

_____

Please send me AAA Spiral_____
(see list of titles inside the back cover)

About this guide...
Which title did you buy?

_____ **AAA Spiral**

Where did you buy it? _____

When? m m/ y y

Why did you choose a AAA Spiral Guide? _____

_____

_____

_____

Did this guide meet your expectations?

Exceeded ☐   Met all ☐   Met most ☐   Fell below ☐

Please give your reasons _____

_____

_____

_____

continued on next page...

Were there any aspects of this guide that you particularly liked?

Is there anything we could have done better?

About you...

Name (Mr/Mrs/Ms) ______

Address ______

______ Zip ______

Daytime tel nos. ______

Which age group are you in?

Under 25 ☐ 25–34 ☐ 35–44 ☐ 45–54 ☐ 55–64 ☐ 65+ ☐

How many trips do you make a year?

Less than one ☐ One ☐ Two ☐ Three or more ☐

Are you a AAA member? Yes ☐ No ☐

Name of AAA club ______

About your trip...

When did you book? m m/ y y When did you travel? m m/ y y

How long did you stay? ______

Was it for business or leisure? ______

Did you buy any other travel guides for your trip? ☐ Yes ☐ No

If yes, which ones? ______

Thank you for taking the time to complete this questionnaire.

All information is for AAA internal use only and will NOT be distributed outside the organization to any third parties.